2nd Workshop on Deep Learning on Graphs for Natural Language Processing (DLG4NLP 2022)

AA001694

Online
15 July 2022

ISBN: 978-1-7138-5630-6

Printed from e-media with permission by:

Curran Associates, Inc.
57 Morehouse Lane
Red Hook, NY 12571

Some format issues inherent in the e-media version may also appear in this print version.

Copyright© (2022) by the Association for Computational Linguistics
All rights reserved.

Printed with permission by Curran Associates, Inc. (2022)

For permission requests, please contact the Association for Computational Linguistics
at the address below.

Association for Computational Linguistics
209 N. Eighth Street
Stroudsburg, Pennsylvania 18360

Phone: 1-570-476-8006
Fax: 1-570-476-0860

acl@aclweb.org

Additional copies of this publication are available from:

Curran Associates, Inc.
57 Morehouse Lane
Red Hook, NY 12571 USA
Phone: 845-758-0400
Fax: 845-758-2633
Email: curran@proceedings.com
Web: www.proceedings.com

DLG4NLP 2022

The 2nd Workshop on Deep Learning on Graphs for Natural Language Processing

Proceedings of the Workshop

©2022 Association for Computational Linguistics

July 15, 2022

Introduction

We are excited to welcome you to DLG4NLP 2022, the 2nd Workshop on Deep Learning on Graphs for Natural Language Processing, to be held on July 15, 2022 as part of NAACL in Seattle. The DLG4NLP workshop aims to bring together both academic researchers and industrial practitioners from different backgrounds and perspectives to solve challenges in deep learning on graphs for NLP. This workshop intends to share visions of investigating new approaches and methods at the intersection of graph machine learning and NLP. The workshop will consist of contributed talks, invited talks, position talks, and panelists on a wide variety of novel GNN methods and NLP applications.

The NAACL conference is a premier publication venue for research in NLP. This year, the DLG4NLP workshop includes four keynote talks, eight presentation sessions, two position talks, and a panel discussion. We have a big "thank you" to say to the authors and speakers (Prof. Jiawei Han, Prof. Heng Ji, Prof. Meng Jiang, and we are inviting more speakers when writing our preface).

This year, we had 12 Program Committee (PC) members who were responsible for reviewing 2 papers each. Every submission received at least three reviews. The members of the Program Committee did an excellent job in reviewing the submitted papers, and we thank them (Zhong Zhang, Sijie Cheng, Suyuchen Wang, Sifan Wu, Haochen Shi, Qianggang Ding, Yu Chen, Qingkai Zeng, Yile Wang, Yulong Chen, Meng Qu, Yuyan Chen) for their essential role in reviewing the papers and helping produce a high quality program for the conference.

In addition, we thank Ryan Cotterell, the Publications Chair, and Ashish Sabharwal, Yunyao Li, Dan Goldwasser, the Workshop Chairs for NAACL 2022, for their dedicated work in assisting workshop organizers to produce high quality proceedings.

Finally, we thank all the conference organizers and participants for making DLG4NLP workshop at NAACL 2022 a success and for growing the research areas of NLP with their fine work.

Lingfei Wu, Bang Liu, Rada Mihalcea, Jian Pei, Yue Zhang, Yunyao Li, workshop co-organizers.

Organizing Committee

Program Chairs

Lingfei Wu, JD.COM Silicon Valley Research Center
Bang Liu, University of Montreal
Rada Mihalcea, University of Michigan
Jian Pei, Simon Fraser University
Yue Zhang, Westlake University
Yunyao Li, Apple

Program Committee

Program Chairs

Lingfei Wu, JD.COM Silicon Valley Research Center
Bang Liu, University of Montreal
Rada Mihalcea, University of Michigan
Jian Pei, Simon Fraser University
Yue Zhang, Westlake University
Yunyao Li, Apple

Table of Contents

Program

Friday, July 15, 2022

09:00 - 09:15 *Welcome + Opening Remarks*

09:15 - 10:00 *Keynote Talk 1*

10:00 - 10:45 *Keynote Talk 2*

10:45 - 11:00 *Coffe Break/Social Networking*

11:00 - 11:45 *Panel Discussion*

11:45 - 12:45 *Paper Presentations Session A*

Diversifying Content Generation for Commonsense Reasoning with Mixture of Knowledge Graph Experts
Wenhao Yu, Chenguang Zhu, Lianhui Qin, Zhihan Zhang, Tong Zhao and Meng Jiang

Continuous Temporal Graph Networks for Event-Based Graph Data
Jin Guo, Zhen Han, su Zhou, Jiliang Li, Volker Tresp and Yuyi Wang

Scene Graph Parsing via Abstract Meaning Representation in Pre-trained Language Models
Woo Suk Choi, Yu-Jung Heo, Dharani Punithan and Byoung-Tak Zhang

Explicit Graph Reasoning Fusing Knowledge and Contextual Information for Multi-hop Question Answering
Zhenyun Deng, Yonghua Zhu, Qianqian Qi, Michael Witbrock and Patricia J. Riddle

14:00 - 14:45 *Keynote Talk 3*

14:45 - 15:30 *Keynote Talk 4*

15:30 - 15:45 *Coffe Break/Social Networking*

15:45 - 16:15 *Two Position Talks*

Friday, July 15, 2022 (continued)

16:15 - 17:15 *Paper Presentations Session B*

Improving Neural Machine Translation with the Abstract Meaning Representation by Combining Graph and Sequence Transformers
Changmao Li and Jeffrey Flanigan

Graph Neural Networks for Adapting Off-the-shelf General Domain Language Models to Low-Resource Specialised Domains
Merieme Bouhandi, Emmanuel Morin and Thierry Hamon

GraDA: Graph Generative Data Augmentation for Commonsense Reasoning
Adyasha Maharana and Mohit Bansal

LiGCN: Label-interpretable Graph Convolutional Networks for Multi-label Text Classification
Irene Li, Aosong Feng, Hao Wu, Tianxiao Li, Toyotaro Suzumura and Ruihai Dong

17:15 - 17:30 *Closing Remarks*

Diversifying Content Generation for Commonsense Reasoning with Mixture of Knowledge Graph Experts

Wenhao Yu[♣], Chenguang Zhu[♠], Lianhui Qin[♡], Zhihan Zhang[♣], Tong Zhao[♣], Meng Jiang[♣]

[♣]University of Notre Dame [♡]University of Washington

[♠]Microsoft Cognitive Services Research

[♣]{wyu1, zzhang23, tzhao2, mjiang2}@nd.edu

[♠]chezhu@microsoft.com [♡]lianhuiq@cs.washington.edu

Abstract

Generative commonsense reasoning (GCR) in natural language is to reason about the commonsense while generating coherent text. Recent years have seen a surge of interest in improving the generation quality of commonsense reasoning tasks. Nevertheless, these approaches have seldom investigated diversity in the GCR tasks, which aims to generate alternative explanations for a real-world situation or predict all possible outcomes. Diversifying GCR is challenging as it expects to generate multiple outputs that are not only semantically different but also grounded in commonsense knowledge. In this paper, we propose MoKGE, a novel method that diversifies the generative reasoning by a mixture of expert (MoE) strategy on commonsense knowledge graphs (KG). A set of knowledge experts seek diverse reasoning on KG to encourage various generation outputs. Empirical experiments demonstrated that MoKGE can significantly improve the diversity while achieving on par performance on accuracy on two GCR benchmarks, based on both automatic and human evaluations.

1 Introduction

An important desideratum of natural language generation (NLG) is to produce outputs that are not only correct but also diverse (Tevet and Berant, 2021). The term "diversity" in NLG is defined as the ability of a generative model to create a set of possible outputs that are each valid given the input and vary as widely as possible in terms of *content, language style, and word variability* (Gupta et al., 2018). This research problem is also referred as *one-to-many generation* (Shen et al., 2019; Cho et al., 2019; Yu et al., 2021; Shen et al., 2022).

Diversity in NLG has been extensively studied for various tasks in the past few years, such as machine translation (Shen et al., 2019) and paraphrase generation (Gupta et al., 2018). In these tasks, output spaces are constrained by input context, i.e., the contents of multiple outputs should be similar, and globally, under the same topic. However, many NLG tasks, e.g., generative commonsense reasoning, pose unique challenges for generating multiple reasonable outputs that are *semantically different*.

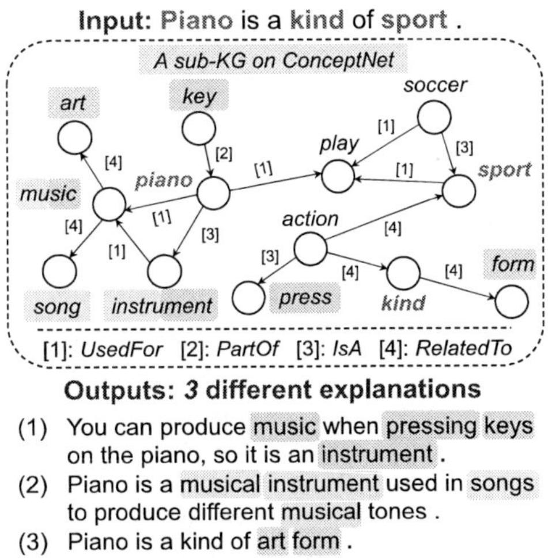

Figure 1: An example of diverse commonsense explanation generation. It aims at generating multiple reasonable explanations given a counterfactual statement. Relevant concepts on the commonsense KG (in shade) can help to perform diverse knowledge reasoning.

Figure 1 shows an example in the commonsense explanation generation (ComVE) task. The dataset has collected explanations to counterfactual statements for sense-making from three annotators (Wang et al., 2020). From the annotations, we observed that different annotators gave explanations to the unreasonable statement from different perspectives to make them diverse in terms of content, e.g., wrong effect and inappropriate usage.

In order to create diversity, existing methods attempted to produce *uncertainty* by introducing random noise into a latent variable (Gupta et al., 2018) or sampling next token widely from the vo-

§ Codes of our model and baselines are available at `https://github.com/DM2-ND/MoKGE.`

Proceedings of the 2nd Workshop on Deep Learning on Graphs for Natural Language Processing (DLG4NLP 2022), pages 1 - 11
July 15, 2022 ©2022 Association for Computational Linguistics

Table 1: Under human evaluation, the performance of existing diversity promoting methods is still far from that of humans. Our method MoKGE can exceed the human performance on the ComVE task.

	ComVE	α-NLG
Avg. # human references	3.00	4.20
Avg. # meanings ($\Uparrow$)		
Human references	2.60	**3.79**
Nucleus sampling	2.15	3.35
MoKGE (our method)	**2.63**	3.72

cabulary (Holtzman et al., 2020). However, these methods were not able to explicitly control varying semantics units and produce outputs of diverse content. Meanwhile, the input text alone contains too limited knowledge to support diverse reasoning and produce multiple reasonable outputs (Yu et al., 2022c). As an example, Table 1 shows the human evaluation results on two GCR tasks. While human annotators were able to produce 2.60 different yet reasonable explanations on the ComVE dataset, one SoTA diversity-promoting method (i.e., nucleus sampling (Holtzman et al., 2020)) could produce only 2.15 reasonable explanations.

To improve the diversity in outputs for GCR tasks, we investigated the ComVE task and found that 75% of the concepts (nouns and verbs) in human annotations were among 2-hop neighbors of the concepts contained in the input sequence on the commonsense KG ConceptNet[1]. Therefore, to produce diverse GCR, our idea is enabling NLG models to reason from different perspectives of knowledge on commonsense KG and use them to generate diverse outputs like the human annotators.

Thus, we present a novel Mixture of Knowledge Graph Expert (MoKGE) method for diverse generative commonsense reasoning on KG. MoKGE contains two major components: (i) a knowledge graph (KG) enhanced generative reasoning module to reasonably associate relevant concepts into the generation process, and (ii) a mixture of expert (MoE) module to produce diverse reasonable outputs. Specifically, the generative reasoning module performs compositional operations on KG to obtain structure-aware representations of concepts and relations. Then, each expert uses these representations to seek different yet relevant sets of concepts and sends them into a standard Transformer model to generate the corresponding output. To encourage different experts to specialize in different reasoning abilities, we employ the stochastic hard-EM algorithm by assigning full responsibility of the largest joint probability to each expert.

We conducted experiments on two GCR benchmarks, i.e., commonsense explanation generation and abductive commonsense reasoning. Empirical experiments demonstrated that our proposed MoKGE can outperform existing diversity-promoting generation methods in diversity, while achieving on par performance in quality.

To the best of our knowledge, this is the first work to boost diversity in NLG by diversifying knowledge reasoning on commonsense KG.

2 Related Work

2.1 Diversity Promoting Text Generation

Generating multiple valid outputs given a source sequence has a wide range of applications, such as machine translation (Shen et al., 2019), paraphrase generation (Gupta et al., 2018), question generation (Cho et al., 2019), dialogue system (Dou et al., 2021), and story generation (Yu et al., 2021). For example, in machine translation, there are often many plausible and semantically equivalent translations due to information asymmetry between different languages (Lachaux et al., 2020).

Methods of improving diversity in NLG have been explored from various perspectives. Sampling-based decoding is one of the most effective solutions to improve diversity. For example, nucleus sampling (Holtzman et al., 2020) samples next tokens from the dynamic nucleus of tokens containing the vast majority of the probability mass, instead of decoding text by maximizing the likelihood. Another line of work focused on introducing random noise (Gupta et al., 2018) or changing latent variables (Lachaux et al., 2020) to produce uncertainty. In addition, Shen et al. (2019) adopted a mixture of experts to diversify machine translation, where a minimum-loss predictor is assigned to each source input. Shi et al. (2018) employed an inverse reinforcement learning approach for unconditional diverse text generation.

However, no existing work considered performing diverse knowledge reasoning to generate multiple reasonable outputs of different contents.

2.2 Knowledge Graph for Text Generation

Incorporating external knowledge is essential for many NLG tasks to augment the limited textual

[1]ConceptNet: `https://conceptnet.io/`

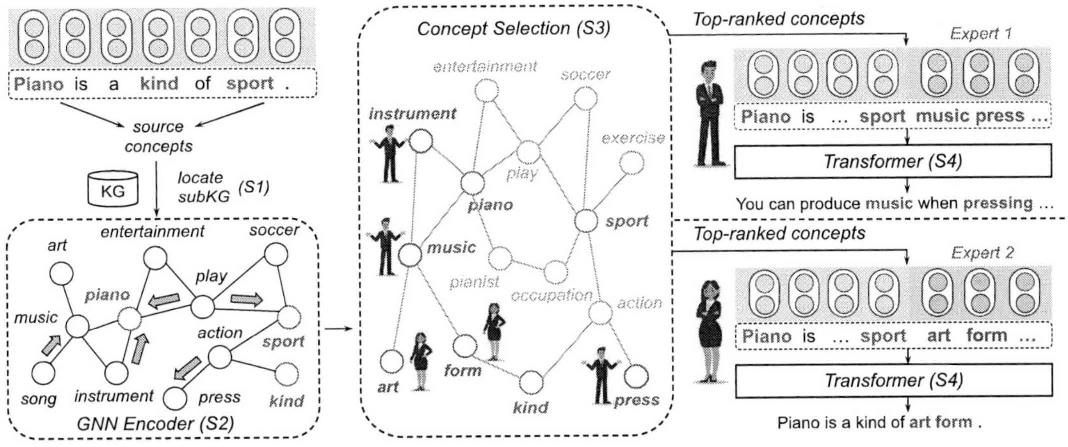

Figure 2: The overall architecture of MoKGE. The MoKGE consists of four steps: (S1) the model constructs a sequence-associated subgraph from the commonsense KG; (S2) a relational-GCN iteratively updates the representation of a concept node by aggregating information from its neighboring nodes and edges; (S3) each knowledge expert selects different salient concepts that should be considered during generation; (S4) the model generates the outputs by integrating the token embeddings of the input sequence and the top-ranked entities.

information (Yu et al., 2022c; Dong et al., 2021; Yu et al., 2022b). Some recent work explored using graph neural networks (GNN) to reason over multi-hop relational knowledge graph (KG) paths (Zhou et al., 2018; Jiang et al., 2019; Zhang et al., 2020a; Wu et al., 2020; Yu et al., 2022a; Zeng et al., 2021). For example, Zhou et al. (2018) enriched the context representations of the input sequence with neighbouring concepts on ConceptNet using graph attention. Ji et al. (2020) performed dynamic multi-hop reasoning on multi-relational paths extracted from the external commonsense KG. Recently, some work attempted to integrate external commonsense knowledge into generative pretrained language models (Guan et al., 2020; Bhagavatula et al., 2020; Liu et al., 2021). For example, Guan et al. (2020) conducted post-training on sythetic data constructed from commonsense KG by translating triplets into natural language texts using templates. Yu et al. (2022c) wrote a comprehensive survey for more detailed comparisons of different knowledge graph enhanced NLG methods.

3 Proposed Method

Problem formulation. In this paper, we focus on diversifying the outputs of generative commonsense reasoning (GCR) tasks, e.g. commonsense explanation generation and abductive commonsense reasoning. These tasks require *one-to-many* generation, i.e., creating a set of reasonable outputs that vary as widely as possible in terms of contents, language style and word variability. Formally, given a source input x, our goal is to model a conditional distribution for the target outputs $p(y|x)$ that assigns high values to $\{p(y_1|x), \cdots, p(y_K|x)\}$ for K mappings, i.e., $\{x \rightarrow y_1, \cdots, x \rightarrow y_K\}$. Meanwhile, the outputs $\{y_1, \cdots, y_K\}$ are expected to be diverse with each other in terms of *contents*.

Existing diversity-promoting methods only varied the language styles and failed to perform different knowledge reasoning to generate diverse contents (Cho et al., 2019; Shen et al., 2019; Holtzman et al., 2020). Here, incorporating commonsense KG is essential for the generative reasoning (GR) tasks because the KG cannot only augment the limited information in the input text, but also provide a rich searching space for knowledge reasoning. Therefore, we propose to employ commonsense KG to play the central role of performing diverse knowledge reasoning, then use different sets of selected concepts to produce diverse outputs.

Model Outline. Our model has two major components: (i) a knowledge graph (KG) enhanced generative reasoning module to reasonably associate relevant concepts and background into the generation process, and (ii) a mixture of expert (MoE) module to diversify the generation process and produce multiple reasonable outputs.

3.1 KG-enhanced Generative Reasoning

The KG-enhanced generative reasoning module is illustrated in Figure 2. It consists of four steps.

First, a sequence-associated subgraph is retrieved from the KG given the input sequence (§3.1.1). Then, a multi-relational graph encoder iteratively updates the representation of each node by aggregating information from its neighboring nodes and edges (§3.1.2). Next, the model selects salient concepts that should be considered during generation (§3.1.3). Finally, the model generates outputs by integrating the token embeddings of both the input sequence and the top-ranked concepts (§3.1.4).

3.1.1 Sequence-aware subgraph construction

To facilitate the reasoning process, we resort to an external commonsense knowledge graph $\mathcal{G} = \{\mathcal{V}, \mathcal{E}\}$, where $\mathcal{V}$ denotes the concept set and $\mathcal{E}$ denotes the edges with relations. Since direct reasoning on the entire graph is intractable, we extract a sequence-associated subgraph $\mathcal{G}_x = \{\mathcal{V}_x, \mathcal{E}_x\}$, where $\mathcal{V}_x$ consists of the concepts extracted from the input sequence (denoted as C_x) and their inter-connected concepts within two hops, i.e., $\mathcal{V}_x = \{C_x \cup \mathcal{N}(C_x) \cup \mathcal{N}(\mathcal{N}(C_x))\}$. For example, in Figure 2, $C_x = \{\text{piano}, \text{sport}, \text{kind}\}$ and $\mathcal{V}_x = \{\text{piano}, \text{sport}, \text{kind}, \text{art}, \text{music}, \text{press}, ...\}$. Next, the generation task is to maximize the conditional probability $p(y|x, \mathcal{G}_x)$.

3.1.2 Multi-relational graph encoding

To model the relational information in the commonsen KG, we employ the relational graph convolutional network (R-GCN) (Schlichtkrull et al., 2018) which generalizes GCN with relation specific weight matrices. We follow Vashishth et al. (2020) and Ji et al. (2020) to use a non-parametric compositional operation $\phi(\cdot)$ to combine the concept node embedding and the relation embedding. Specifically, given the input subgraph $\mathcal{G}_x = \{\mathcal{V}_x, \mathcal{E}_x\}$ and an R-GCN with L layers, we update the embedding of each node $v \in \mathcal{V}_x$ at the $(l+1)$-th layer by aggregating information from the embeddings of its neighbours in $\mathcal{N}(v)$ at the l-th layer:

$$\mathbf{o}_v^l = \frac{1}{|\mathcal{N}(v)|} \sum_{(u,v,r)\in\mathcal{E}} \mathbf{W}_N^l \phi(\mathbf{h}_u^l, \mathbf{h}_r^l), \quad (1)$$

$$\mathbf{h}_v^{l+1} = \text{ReLU}(\mathbf{o}_v^l + \mathbf{W}_S^l \mathbf{h}_v^l), \quad (2)$$

where $\mathbf{h}_v$ and $\mathbf{h}_r$ are node embedding and relation embedding. We define the compositional operation as $\phi(\mathbf{h}_u, \mathbf{h}_r) = \mathbf{h}_u - \mathbf{h}_r$ inspired by the TransE (Bordes et al., 2013). The relation embedding is also updated via another linear transformation:

$$\mathbf{h}_r^{l+1} = \mathbf{W}_R^l \mathbf{h}_r^l. \quad (3)$$

Finally, we obtain concept embedding $\mathbf{h}_v^L$ that encodes the sequence-associated subgraph context.

3.1.3 Concept selection on knowledge graph

Not all concepts in $\mathcal{G}$ appear in the outputs. Thus, we design a concept selection module to choose salient concepts that should be considered during generation. For each concept $v \in \mathcal{V}_x$, we calculate its probability of being selected by taking a multi-layer perception (MLP) on the top of graph encoder: $p_v = Pr[v \text{ is selected}|x] = \text{MLP}(\mathbf{h}_v^L)$.

To supervise the concept selection process, we use the overlapping concepts between concepts appearing in the output sequence C_y and concepts in input sequence associated subgraph $\mathcal{G}_x$, i.e., $\mathcal{V}_x \cap C_y$, as a simple proxy for the ground-truth supervision. So, the concept selection loss (here only for one expert, see MoE loss in Eq.(8)) is:

$$\mathcal{L}_{\text{concept}} = -\Big(\sum_{v\in\mathcal{V}_x\cap C_y} v \log p_v \quad (4)$$
$$+ \sum_{v\in\mathcal{V}_x - C_y} (1-v)\log(1-p_v)\Big).$$

Finally, the top-N ranked concepts on the subgraph G_x (denoted as $v_1, ..., v_N$) are selected as the additional input to the generation process.

3.1.4 Concept-aware sequence generation

We utilize a standard Transformer (Vaswani et al., 2017) as our generation model. It takes the concatenation of the sequence x and all the selected concepts $v_1, ..., v_N$ as input and auto-regressively generates the outputs y. We adopt the cross-entropy loss, which can be written as:

$$\mathcal{L}_{\text{generation}} = -\log p(y|x, v_1, \cdots, v_N) \quad (5)$$
$$= -\sum_{t=1}^{|y|} \log p(y_t|x, v_1, \cdots, v_N, y_{<t}).$$

Note that since the selected concepts do not have a rigorous order, we only apply positional encodings (used in Transformer) to the input sequence x.

3.1.5 Overall objective

We jointly optimizes the following loss:

$$\mathcal{L} = \mathcal{L}_{\text{generation}} + \lambda \cdot \mathcal{L}_{\text{concept}}. \quad (6)$$

where λ is a hyperparameter to control the importance of different tasks[2].

[2]We performed a hyperparameter search and found when λ was around 0.3, the model performed the best. Therefore, we set $\lambda = 0.3$ in the following experiments.

3.2 MoE-Promoted Diverse Generation

To empower the generation model to produce multiple reasonable outputs, we employ a mixture of expert (MoE) module to model uncertainty and generate diverse outputs. While the MoE models have primarily been explored as a means of increasing model capacity, they are also being used to boost diverse generation process (Shen et al., 2019; Cho et al., 2019). Formally, the MoE module introduces a multinomial latent variable $z \in \{1, \cdots, K\}$, and decomposes the marginal likelihood as follows:

$$p(y|x, \mathcal{G}_x) = \sum_{z=1}^{K} p(z|x, \mathcal{G}_x)p(y|z, x, \mathcal{G}_x). \quad (7)$$

Training. We minimize the loss function (in Eq.(6)) using the MoE decomposition,

$$\nabla \log p(y|x, \mathcal{G}_x) \quad (8)$$
$$= \sum_{z=1}^{K} p(z|x, y, \mathcal{G}_x) \cdot \nabla \log p(y, z|x, \mathcal{G}_x),$$

and train the model with the EM algorithm (Dempster et al., 1977). Ideally, we would like different experts to specialize in different reasoning abilities so that they can generate diverse outputs. The specialization of experts means that given the input, only one element in $\{p(y, z|x, \mathcal{G}_x)\}_{z=1}^{K}$ should dominate in value (Shen et al., 2019). To encourage this, we employ a hard mixture model to maximize $\max_z p(y, z|x, \mathcal{G}_x)$ by assigning full responsibility to the expert with the largest joint probability. Training proceeds via hard-EM can be written as:

- E-step: estimate the responsibilities of each expert $r_z \leftarrow \mathbb{1}[z = \arg\max_z p(y, z|x, \mathcal{G}_x)]$ using the current parameters θ;
- M-step: update the parameters with gradients of the chosen expert ($r_z = \mathbb{1}$) from E-step.

Expert parameterization. Independently parameterizing each expert may exacerbate overfitting since the number of parameters increases linearly with the number of experts (Shen et al., 2019). We follow the parameter sharing schema in Cho et al. (2019); Shen et al. (2019) to avoid this issue. This only requires a negligible increase in parameters over the baseline model that does not uses MoE. In our experiments, we compared adding a unique expert embedding to each input token with adding an expert prefix token before the input text sequence, where they achieved very similar performance.

Producing K outputs during inference. In order to generate K different outputs on test set, we follow Shen et al. (2019) to enumerate all latent variables z and then greedily decoding each token by $\hat{y}_t = \arg\max p(y|\hat{y}_{1:t-1}, z, x)$. In other words, we ask each expert to seek different sets of concepts on the knowledge graph, and use the selected concepts to generate K different outputs. Notably, this decoding procedure is efficient and easily parallelizable. Furthermore, to make fair comparisons with sampling-based methods, we use greedy decoding without any sampling strategy.

4 Experiments

4.1 Tasks and Datasets

Commonsense explanation generation. It aims to generate an explanation given a counterfactual statement for sense-making (Wang et al., 2019). We use the benchmark dataset ComVE from SemEval-2020 Task 4 (Wang et al., 2020). The dataset contains 10,000 / 997 / 1,000 examples for training / development / test sets, respectively. The average input/output length is 7.7 / 9.0 words. All examples in the dataset have 3 references.

Abductive commonsense reasoning. It is also referred as α-NLG. It is the task of generating a valid hypothesis about the likely explanations to partially observable past and future. We use the $\mathcal{ART}$ benchmark dataset (Bhagavatula et al., 2020) that consists of 50,481 / 1,779 / 3,560 examples for training / development / test sets. The average input/output length is 17.4 / 10.8 words. Each example in the $\mathcal{ART}$ dataset has 1 to 5 references.

4.2 Baseline Methods

We note that as we targeted at the *one-to-many* generation problem, we excluded those baseline methods mentioned in the related work that cannot produce multiple outputs, e.g., Zhang et al. (2020a); Ji et al. (2020); Liu et al. (2021). Different from aforementioned methods, our MoKGE can seek diverse reasoning on KG to encourage various generation outputs *without any additional conditions*.

To the best of our knowledge, we are the first work to explore diverse knowledge reasoning on commonsense KG to generate multiple diverse output sequences. Therefore, we only compared our MoKGE with existing diversity-promoting baselines without using knowledge graph.

VAE-based method. The variational auto-encoder (VAE) (Kingma and Welling, 2014) is a deep generative latent variable model. VAE-based methods produce diverse outputs by sampling different latent variables from an approximate posterior distribution. CVAE-SVG (SVG is short for sentence variant generation) (Gupta et al., 2018) is a conditional VAE model that can produce multiple outputs based an original sentence as input.

MoE-based method. Mixture models provide an alternative approach to generate diverse outputs by sampling different mixture components. We compare against two mixture of experts (MoE) implementations by Shen et al. (2019) and Cho et al. (2019). We refer them as MoE-prompt (Shen et al., 2019) and MoE-embed (Cho et al., 2019).

Sampling-based method. Sampling methods create diverse outputs by sampling next token widely from the vocabulary. We compare against two sampling algorithms for decoding, including truncated sampling (Fan et al., 2018) and nucleus sampling (Holtzman et al., 2020). Truncated sampling (Fan et al., 2018) randomly samples words from top-k probability candidates of the predicted distribution at each decoding step. Nucleus sampling (Holtzman et al., 2020) avoids text degeneration by truncating the unreliable tails and sampling from the dynamic nucleus of tokens containing the vast majority of the probability mass.

4.3 Implementation Details

All baseline methods were built on the Transformer architecture with 6-layer encoder and decoder, and initialized with pre-trained parameters from BART-base (Lewis et al., 2020), which is one of the state-of-the-art pre-trained Transformer models for natural language generation (Gehrmann et al., 2021). In our MoKGE, the Transformer parameters were also initialized by BART-base, in order to make fair comparison with all baseline methods. The R-GCN parameters were random initialized.

For model training, we used Adam with batch size of 60, learning rate of 3e-5, L2 weight decay of 0.01, learning rate warm up over the first 10,000 steps, and linear decay of learning rate. Our models were trained by one Tesla V100 GPU card with 32GB memory, and implemented on PyTorch with the Huggingface's Transformer (Wolf et al., 2020). All Transformer-based methods were trained with 30 epochs, taken about 4-5 hours on the ComVE dataset and 7-9 hours on the α-NLG dataset.

In addition to our MoKGE implementation, we also provide the baseline implementation code on GitHub `https://github.com/DM2-ND/MoKGE`.

4.4 Automatic Evaluation

We evaluated the performance of different generation models from two aspects: *quality* (or say *accuracy*) and *diversity*. *Quality* tests the appropriateness of the generated response with respect to the context, and *diversity* tests the lexical and semantic diversity of the appropriate sequences generated by the model. These evaluation metrics have been widely used in existing work (Ott et al., 2018; Vijayakumar et al., 2018; Zhu et al., 2018; Cho et al., 2019; Yu et al., 2021).

Quality metrics ($\Uparrow$). The quality is measured by standard N-gram based metrics, including the BLEU score (Papineni et al., 2002) and the ROUGE score (Lin, 2004). This measures the highest accuracy comparing the best hypothesis among the top-K with the target (Vijayakumar et al., 2018). Concretely, we generate hypotheses $\{\hat{Y}^{(1)}, \cdots \hat{Y}^{(K)}\}$ from each source X and keep the hypothesis $\hat{Y}^{\text{best}}$ that achieves the best sentence-level metric with the target Y. Then we calculate a corpus-level metric with the greedily-selected hypotheses $\{Y^{(i),\text{best}}\}_{i=1}^{N}$ and references $\{Y^{(i)}\}_{i=1}^{N}$.

The diversity of evaluated by three aspects: concept, pairwise and corpus diversity.

Concept diversity. The number of unique concepts (short as Uni.C) measures how many unique concepts on the commonsense KG are covered in the generated outputs. A higher value indicates the higher concept diversity. Besides, we also measure the pairwise concept diversity by using Jaccard similarity. It is defined as the size of the intersection divided by the size of the union of two sets. Lower value indicates the higher concept diversity.

Pairwise diversity ($\Downarrow$). Referred as "self-" (e.g., self-BLEU) (Zhu et al., 2018), it measures the within-distribution similarity. This metric computes the average of sentence-level metrics between all pairwise combinations of hypotheses $\{Y^{(1)}, \cdots, Y^{(K)}\}$ generated from each source sequence X. Lower pairwise metric indicates high diversity between generated hypotheses.

Corpus diversity ($\Uparrow$). Distinct-k (Li et al., 2016) measures the total number of unique k-grams normalized by the total number of generated k-gram tokens to avoid favoring long sentences. Entropy-k (Zhang et al., 2018) reflects how evenly the empirical k-gram distribution is for a given sentence when word frequency is considered.

Table 2: Diversity and quality evaluation on the **ComVE** (upper part) and α-**NLG** (lower part) datasets. Each model is required to generate three outputs. All experiments are run three times with different random seeds, and the average results on the test set is calculated as the final performance, with standard deviations as subscripts.

Methods	Model Variant	Concept diversity		Pairwise diversity		Corpus diversity		Quality	
		#Uni.C(⇑)	Jaccard (⇓)	SB-3 (⇓)	SB-4 (⇓)	D-2(⇑)	E-4(⇑)	B-4 (⇑)	R-L (⇑)
CVAE	z = 16	4.56$_{0.1}$	64.74$_{0.3}$	66.66$_{0.4}$	62.83$_{0.5}$	33.75$_{0.5}$	9.13$_{0.1}$	16.67$_{0.3}$	41.52$_{0.3}$
	z = 32	5.03$_{0.3}$	47.27$_{0.8}$	59.20$_{1.3}$	54.30$_{1.5}$	32.86$_{1.1}$	9.07$_{0.5}$	17.04$_{0.2}$	42.17$_{0.5}$
	z = 64	4.67$_{0.0}$	54.69$_{0.8}$	55.02$_{0.8}$	49.58$_{1.0}$	32.55$_{0.5}$	9.07$_{0.2}$	15.54$_{0.4}$	41.03$_{0.3}$
Truncated sampling	k = 5	4.37$_{0.0}$	71.38$_{0.7}$	74.20$_{0.2}$	71.38$_{0.2}$	31.32$_{0.4}$	9.18$_{0.1}$	16.44$_{0.2}$	40.99$_{0.2}$
	k = 20	4.60$_{0.0}$	63.42$_{1.2}$	64.47$_{2.1}$	60.33$_{2.4}$	33.69$_{0.6}$	9.26$_{0.1}$	17.70$_{0.2}$	42.58$_{0.5}$
	k = 50	4.68$_{0.1}$	60.98$_{1.8}$	61.39$_{2.4}$	56.93$_{2.8}$	34.80$_{0.3}$	9.29$_{0.1}$	17.48$_{0.4}$	42.44$_{0.5}$
Nucleus sampling	p = .5	4.19$_{0.1}$	72.78$_{1.0}$	77.66$_{0.8}$	75.14$_{0.9}$	28.36$_{0.6}$	9.05$_{0.3}$	16.09$_{0.6}$	40.95$_{0.5}$
	p = .75	4.41$_{0.1}$	67.01$_{1.7}$	71.41$_{2.5}$	68.22$_{2.9}$	31.21$_{0.3}$	9.16$_{0.1}$	17.07$_{0.5}$	41.88$_{0.7}$
	p = .95	4.70$_{0.1}$	61.92$_{2.6}$	63.43$_{3.4}$	59.23$_{3.8}$	34.17$_{0.3}$	9.27$_{0.2}$	17.68$_{0.4}$	42.60$_{0.8}$
MoE	embed	5.41$_{0.0}$	47.55$_{0.5}$	33.64$_{0.2}$	28.21$_{0.1}$	46.57$_{0.2}$	9.61$_{0.1}$	18.66$_{0.5}$	43.72$_{0.2}$
	prompt	5.45$_{0.2}$	47.54$_{0.4}$	33.42$_{0.3}$	28.40$_{0.3}$	46.93$_{0.2}$	9.60$_{0.2}$	18.91$_{0.4}$	43.71$_{0.5}$
MoKGE (ours)	embed	5.35$_{0.2}$	48.18$_{0.5}$	35.36$_{1.1}$	29.71$_{1.2}$	47.51$_{0.4}$	9.63$_{0.1}$	**19.13**$_{0.1}$	43.70$_{0.1}$
	prompt	**5.48**$_{0.2}$	**44.37**$_{0.4}$	**30.93**$_{0.9}$	**25.30**$_{1.1}$	**48.44**$_{0.2}$	**9.67**$_{0.2}$	19.01$_{0.1}$	**43.83**$_{0.3}$
Human		6.27$_{0.0}$	26.49$_{0.0}$	12.36$_{0.0}$	8.01$_{0.0}$	63.02$_{0.0}$	9.55$_{0.0}$	100.0$_{0.0}$	100.0$_{0.0}$
		#Uni.C(⇑)	Jaccard (⇓)	SB-3 (⇓)	SB-4 (⇓)	D-2(⇑)	E-4(⇑)	B-4 (⇑)	R-L (⇑)
CVAE	z = 16	4.80$_{0.0}$	56.88$_{0.1}$	67.89$_{0.4}$	64.72$_{0.5}$	26.27$_{0.2}$	10.34$_{0.0}$	13.64$_{0.1}$	37.96$_{0.1}$
	z = 32	5.05$_{0.0}$	50.92$_{0.4}$	62.08$_{0.2}$	58.25$_{0.3}$	26.67$_{0.1}$	10.36$_{0.0}$	13.35$_{0.1}$	37.73$_{0.1}$
	z = 64	5.14$_{0.0}$	47.04$_{0.7}$	57.87$_{0.4}$	53.61$_{0.4}$	24.91$_{0.1}$	10.21$_{0.1}$	11.77$_{0.1}$	36.35$_{0.2}$
Truncated sampling	k= 5	4.86$_{0.1}$	72.78$_{1.1}$	67.09$_{1.0}$	63.82$_{1.1}$	25.47$_{0.3}$	10.44$_{0.1}$	13.33$_{0.2}$	38.07$_{0.2}$
	k= 20	5.48$_{0.1}$	45.65$_{1.8}$	54.65$_{2.1}$	50.36$_{2.4}$	29.30$_{0.5}$	10.62$_{0.2}$	14.12$_{0.7}$	38.76$_{0.6}$
	k= 50	5.53$_{0.0}$	45.84$_{0.5}$	52.11$_{3.7}$	47.75$_{4.2}$	30.08$_{0.3}$	10.64$_{0.1}$	14.01$_{0.8}$	**38.98**$_{0.6}$
Nucleus sampling	p= .5	4.19$_{0.1}$	62.54$_{1.8}$	73.34$_{0.3}$	71.01$_{0.3}$	25.49$_{0.0}$	10.46$_{0.0}$	11.71$_{0.1}$	36.53$_{0.2}$
	p= .75	5.13$_{0.0}$	54.25$_{0.6}$	64.49$_{0.4}$	61.45$_{0.5}$	27.72$_{0.1}$	10.54$_{0.1}$	12.63$_{0.0}$	37.48$_{0.1}$
	p= .95	5.49$_{0.0}$	46.76$_{0.5}$	56.32$_{0.5}$	52.44$_{0.6}$	29.92$_{0.1}$	10.63$_{0.0}$	13.53$_{0.2}$	38.42$_{0.3}$
MoE	embed	6.22$_{0.1}$	29.18$_{0.4}$	29.02$_{1.0}$	24.19$_{1.0}$	36.22$_{0.3}$	10.84$_{0.0}$	**14.31**$_{0.2}$	38.91$_{0.2}$
	prompt	6.05$_{0.1}$	29.34$_{1.2}$	28.05$_{2.0}$	23.18$_{1.9}$	36.71$_{0.1}$	10.85$_{0.0}$	14.26$_{0.3}$	38.78$_{0.4}$
MoKGE (ours)	embed	6.27$_{0.2}$	30.46$_{0.8}$	29.17$_{1.5}$	24.04$_{1.6}$	**38.15**$_{0.3}$	**10.90**$_{0.1}$	13.74$_{0.2}$	38.06$_{0.2}$
	prompt	**6.35**$_{0.1}$	**28.06**$_{0.6}$	**27.40**$_{2.0}$	**22.43**$_{2.4}$	38.01$_{0.6}$	10.88$_{0.2}$	14.17$_{0.2}$	38.82$_{0.7}$
Human		6.62$_{0.0}$	12.43$_{0.0}$	10.36$_{0.0}$	6.04$_{0.0}$	53.57$_{0.0}$	10.84$_{0.0}$	100.0$_{0.0}$	100.0$_{0.0}$

* Metrics: SB-3/4: Self-BLEU-3/4 (⇓), D-2: Distinct-2 (⇑), E-4: Entropy-4 (⇑), B-4: BLEU-4 (⇑), R-L: ROUGE-L (⇑)

4.4.1 Experimental results

Comparison with baseline methods. We evaluated our proposed MoKGE and baseline methods based on both *quality* and *diversity*. As shown in Table 2, MoE-based methods achieved the best performance among all baseline methods. MoKGE can further boost diversity by at least 1.57% and 1.83% on Self-BLEU-3 and Self-BLEU-4, compared with the vanilla MoE methods. At the same time, MoKGE achieved on par performance with other baseline methods based on the quality evaluation. Specifically, on the ComVE dataset, MoKGE achieved the best performance on BLEU-4 and ROUGE-L, and on the α-NLG dataset, the performance gap between MoKGE and the best baseline method was always *less than 0.5%* on BLEU-4.

Ablation study. We conducted an ablation study to analyze the two major components in the MoKGE. The experimental results are shown in Table 3. First, we note that when not using MoE (line –w/o MoE), we used the most basic decoding strategy – beam search – to generate multiple outputs. We observed that the outputs generated by beam search differed only on punctuation and minor morphological variations, and typically only the last few words were different from others. Besides, integrating commonsense knowledge graph into the MoE-based generation model brought both quality and

Table 3: Ablation studies. When not suing MoE (line –w/o MoE), we set beam as three to generate three outputs.

Methods	ComVE (left part: diversity; right part: quality)					α-NLG (left part: diversity; right part: quality)				
	SB-4 (⇓)	D-2 (⇑)	E-4 (⇑)	B-4 (⇑)	R-L (⇑)	SB-4 (⇓)	D-2 (⇑)	E-4 (⇑)	B-4 (⇑)	R-L (⇑)
MoKGE	**25.30** $_{1.1}$	**48.44** $_{0.2}$	**9.67** $_{0.2}$	**19.01** $_{0.1}$	**43.83** $_{0.3}$	**22.43** $_{2.4}$	**38.01** $_{0.6}$	**10.88** $_{0.2}$	14.17 $_{0.2}$	**38.82** $_{0.7}$
⊢ w/o KG	28.40 $_{0.3}$	46.93 $_{0.2}$	9.60 $_{0.2}$	18.91 $_{0.4}$	43.71 $_{0.5}$	23.18 $_{1.9}$	36.71 $_{0.1}$	10.85 $_{0.0}$	**14.26** $_{0.3}$	38.78 $_{0.4}$
⊢ w/o MoE	74.15 $_{0.2}$	31.92 $_{0.1}$	9.14 $_{0.0}$	15.87 $_{0.1}$	40.24 $_{0.2}$	77.34 $_{0.2}$	19.19 $_{0.1}$	10.10 $_{0.0}$	12.84 $_{0.1}$	37.52 $_{0.2}$

Table 4: Human evaluations by independent scoring based on *diveristy*, *quality*, *flency* and *grammar*. In addition, * indicates p-value < 0.05 under paired t-test between MoKGE and baseline methods.

Methods	ComVE			α-NLG		
	Diversity	Quality	Flu. & Gra.	Diversity	Quality	Flu. & Gra.
Truncated samp.	2.15±0.76	2.22±1.01	3.47±0.75	2.31±0.76	2.63±0.77	3.89±0.36
Nucleus samp.	2.03±0.73	**2.29**±1.03	**3.52**±0.70	2.39±0.73	**2.67**±0.72	**3.91**±0.28
MoKGE (ours)	**2.63**±0.51*	2.10±0.99	3.46±0.81	**2.66**±0.51*	2.57±0.71	3.87±0.34
Human Ref.	2.60±0.59	3.00	4.00	2.71±0.57	3.00	4.00

Table 5: Human evaluations by pairwise comparison: MoKGE v.s. two baseline methods based on *diversity*.

Against methods	ComVE			α-NLG		
	Win (%)	Tie (%)	Lose (%)	Win (%)	Tie (%)	Lose (%)
v.s. Truncated samp.	**47.85**±5.94	37.09±4.56	15.06±3.31	**45.35**±5.06	43.19±2.78	11.46±2.31
v.s. Nucleus samp.	**54.30**±4.62	36.02±2.74	9.68±3.48	41.53±1.55	**46.99**±2.04	11.48±2.36

diversity improvement on the ComVE, but might sacrifice a little quality (less than 0.5% on BLEU-4) on the α-NLG dataset. Overall, our MoKGE benefited from KG and MoE modules, and achieved great performance on both diversity and quality.

4.5 Human Evaluation

Automatic diversity evaluation (e.g., Self-BLEU, Distinct-k) cannot reflect the *content-level diversity*. Therefore, we conducted extensive human evaluations to assess both the quality and diversity of outputs generated from different models.

The human evaluation was divided into two parts: *independent scoring* and *pairwise comparisons*. All evaluations were conducted on Amazon Mechanical Turk (AMT), and each evaluation form was answered by at least three AMT workers.

Independent scoring. In this part, human annotators were asked to evaluate the generated outputs from a single model. We first presented top-3 generated outputs from a certain model to human annotators. The annotators would first evaluate the *diversity* by answering "How many different meanings do three outputs express?" Then we presented human-written outputs to the annotators. The annotator would evaluate the quality by comparing machine generated outputs and human-written outputs, and answering "How many machine generated outputs are correct?" The diversity and quality scores are normalized to the range from 0 to 3. Besides, the annotators need to give a fluency and grammar score from 1 to 4 for each generated output.

Pairwise comparisons. In this part, the annotators were given two sets of top-3 generated explanations from two different methods each time and instructed to pick the more diverse set. The choices are "win," "lose," or "tie."

As shown in Table 4-5, our MoKGE can significantly outperform the state-of-the-art sampling-based methods in *diversity* evaluation (p-value < 0.05 under paired t-test), even slightly better than human performance on the ComVE task. At the same time, we can observe MoKGE is able to obtain on par performance with other methods based on *quality* evaluation. The p-value is not smaller than 0.05 (i.e., not significant difference) under paired t-test between MoKGE and baseline methods based on the quality evaluation.

4.6 Case Study

Figure 3 demonstrates human-written explanations and generated explanations from different diversity-promoting methods, including nucleus sampling, mixture of experts (MoE) and our MoKGE. Overall, we observed that the nucleus sampling and MoE methods typically expressed very similar

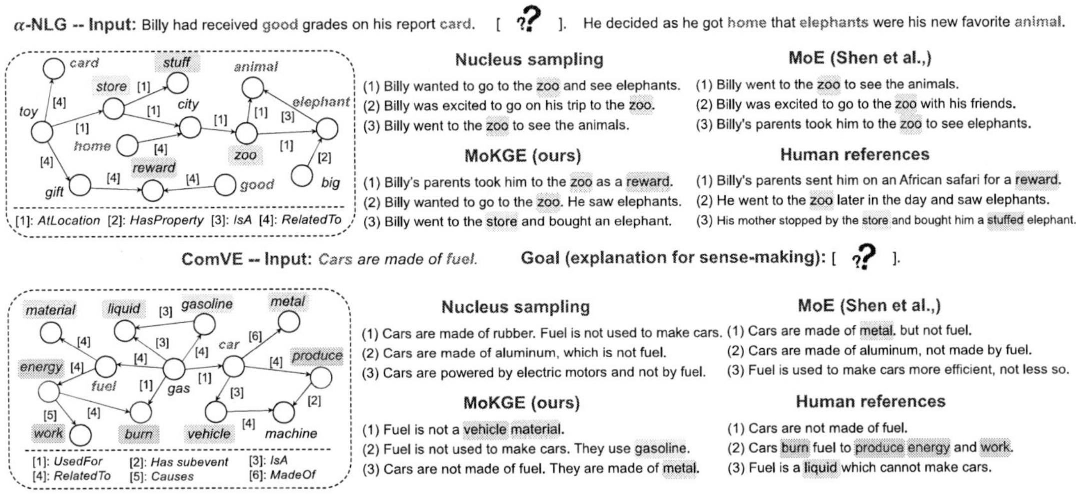

Figure 3: Case studies. MoKGE can produce diverse knowledge reasoning on commonsense KG, select different relevant concepts (in shades of different colors), then generate diverse outputs. The outputs diversity of MoKGE is significantly better than that of beam search and nucleus sampling, and close to human performance.

meanings, e.g., "go to the zoo and see elephants" and "took him to the zoo and see elephants" in the α-NLG case. On the contrary, MoKGE can generate semantically richer and more diverse contents than the other two methods by incorporating more commonsense concepts on the knowledge graph.

5 Future Directions

Improving content diversity in NLG. Most of the existing diversity-promoting work has focused on improving syntactic and lexical diversity, such as different language style in machine translation (Shen et al., 2019) and word variability in paraphrase generation (Gupta et al., 2018). Nevertheless, methods for improving content diversity in NLG systems have been rarely studied in the existing literature. We believe that generating diverse content is one of the most promising aspects of machine intelligence, which can be applied to a wide range of real-world applications, not only limited to commonsense reasoning.

Besides, leveraging knowledge graph is not the only way to promote content diversity as it is a highly knowledge-intensive task. Many existing knowledge-enhanced methods (Yu et al., 2022c) can be used to acquire different external knowledge for producing diverse outputs, e.g., taking different retrieved documents as conditions for generator.

Designing neural diversity metrics. In spite of growing interest in NLG models that produce diverse outputs, there is currently no principled neural method for evaluating the diversity of an NLG system. As described in Tevet and Berant (2021), existing automatic diversity metrics (e.g. Self-BLEU) perform worse than humans on the task of estimating content diversity, indicating a low correlation between metrics and human judgments.

Therefore, neural-based diversity metrics are highly demanded. Intuitively, the metrics should include computational comparisons of multiple references and hypotheses by projecting them into the same semantic space, unlike metrics for evaluating the generation quality, e.g., BERTScore (Zhang et al., 2020b) and BLEURT (Sellam et al., 2020), which only measures the correlation between a pair of reference and hypothesis.

6 Conclusions

In this paper, we proposed a novel method that diversified the generative reasoning by a mixture of expert strategy on commonsense knowledge graph. To the best of our knowledge, this is the first work to boost diversity in NLG by diversifying knowledge reasoning on commonsense knowledge graph. Experiments on two generative commonsense reasoning benchmarks demonstrated that MoKGE outperformed state-of-the-art methods on diversity, while achieving on par performance on quality.

Acknowledgements

The work is supported by NSF IIS-1849816, CCF-1901059, IIS-2119531 and IIS-2142827.

References

Chandra Bhagavatula, Ronan Le Bras, Chaitanya Malaviya, Keisuke Sakaguchi, Ari Holtzman, Hannah Rashkin, Doug Downey, Scott Wen-tau Yih, and Yejin Choi. 2020. Abductive commonsense reasoning. In *International Conference for Learning Representation (ICLR)*.

Antoine Bordes, Nicolas Usunier, Alberto Garcia-Duran, Jason Weston, and Oksana Yakhnenko. 2013. Translating embeddings for modeling multi-relational data. In *Advances in Neural Information Processing Systems (NeurIPS)*.

Jaemin Cho, Minjoon Seo, and Hannaneh Hajishirzi. 2019. Mixture content selection for diverse sequence generation. In *Proceedings of the 2019 Conference on Empirical Methods in Natural Language Processing (EMNLP)*.

Arthur P Dempster, Nan M Laird, and Donald B Rubin. 1977. Maximum likelihood from incomplete data via the em algorithm. In *Journal of the Royal Statistical Society (Methodological)*. Wiley Online Library.

Xiangyu Dong, Wenhao Yu, Chenguang Zhu, and Meng Jiang. 2021. Injecting entity types into entity-guided text generation. In *Conference on Empirical Methods in Natural Language Processing (EMNLP)*.

Yao Dou, Maxwell Forbes, Ari Holtzman, and Yejin Choi. 2021. Multitalk: A highly-branching dialog testbed for diverse conversations. In *AAAI Conference on Artificial Intelligence (AAAI)*.

Angela Fan, Mike Lewis, and Yann Dauphin. 2018. Hierarchical neural story generation. In *Proceedings of the 56th Annual Meeting of the Association for Computational Linguistics (ACL)*.

Sebastian Gehrmann, Tosin Adewumi, Karmanya Aggarwal, Pawan Sasanka Ammanamanchi, Anuoluwapo Aremu, Antoine Bosselut, Khyathi Raghavi Chandu, Miruna-Adriana Clinciu, Dipanjan Das, Kaustubh Dhole, et al. 2021. The gem benchmark: Natural language generation, its evaluation and metrics. In *Proceedings of the 1st Workshop on Natural Language Generation, Evaluation, and Metrics (GEM 2021)*.

Jian Guan, Fei Huang, Zhihao Zhao, Xiaoyan Zhu, and Minlie Huang. 2020. A knowledge-enhanced pretraining model for commonsense story generation. In *Transactions of the Association for Computational Linguistics (TACL)*.

Ankush Gupta, Arvind Agarwal, Prawaan Singh, and Piyush Rai. 2018. A deep generative framework for paraphrase generation. In *AAAI Conference on Artificial Intelligence (AAAI)*.

Ari Holtzman, Jan Buys, Li Du, Maxwell Forbes, and Yejin Choi. 2020. The curious case of neural text degeneration. In *International Conference for Learning Representation (ICLR)*.

Haozhe Ji, Pei Ke, Shaohan Huang, Furu Wei, Xiaoyan Zhu, and Minlie Huang. 2020. Language generation with multi-hop reasoning on commonsense knowledge graph. In *Conference on Empirical Methods in Natural Language Processing (EMNLP)*.

Tianwen Jiang, Tong Zhao, Bing Qin, Ting Liu, Nitesh V Chawla, and Meng Jiang. 2019. The role of" condition" a novel scientific knowledge graph representation and construction model. In *ACM SIGKDD International Conference on Knowledge Discovery & Data Mining (KDD)*.

Diederik P Kingma and Max Welling. 2014. Auto-encoding variational bayes. In *International Conference for Learning Representation (ICLR)*.

Marie-Anne Lachaux, Armand Joulin, and Guillaume Lample. 2020. Target conditioning for one-to-many generation. In *Conference on Empirical Methods in Natural Language Processing (EMNLP-Findings)*.

Mike Lewis, Yinhan Liu, Naman Goyal, Marjan Ghazvininejad, Abdelrahman Mohamed, Omer Levy, Veselin Stoyanov, and Luke Zettlemoyer. 2020. Bart: Denoising sequence-to-sequence pre-training for natural language generation, translation, and comprehension. In *Annual Meeting of the Association for Computational Linguistics (ACL)*.

Jiwei Li, Michel Galley, Chris Brockett, Jianfeng Gao, and Bill Dolan. 2016. A diversity-promoting objective function for neural conversation models. In *Conference of the North American Chapter of the Association for Computational Linguistics (NAACL-HLT)*.

Chin-Yew Lin. 2004. Rouge: A package for automatic evaluation of summaries. In *Text summarization branches out*.

Ye Liu, Yao Wan, Lifang He, Hao Peng, and Philip S Yu. 2021. Kg-bart: Knowledge graph-augmented bart for generative commonsense reasoning. In *AAAI Conference on Artificial Intelligence (AAAI)*.

Myle Ott, Michael Auli, David Grangier, and Marc'Aurelio Ranzato. 2018. Analyzing uncertainty in neural machine translation. In *International Conference on Machine Learning (ICML)*.

Kishore Papineni, Salim Roukos, Todd Ward, and Wei-Jing Zhu. 2002. Bleu: a method for automatic evaluation of machine translation. In *Proceedings of the 40th annual meeting of the Association for Computational Linguistics (ACL)*.

Michael Schlichtkrull, Thomas N Kipf, Peter Bloem, Rianne Van Den Berg, Ivan Titov, and Max Welling. 2018. Modeling relational data with graph convolutional networks. In *European Semantic Web Conference (ESWC)*.

Thibault Sellam, Dipanjan Das, and Ankur Parikh. 2020. Bleurt: Learning robust metrics for text generation. In *Annual Meeting of the Association for Computational Linguistics (ACL)*.

Tianxiao Shen, Myle Ott, Michael Auli, and Marc'Aurelio Ranzato. 2019. Mixture models for diverse machine translation: Tricks of the trade. In *International Conference on Machine Learning (ICML)*.

Xinyao Shen, Jiangjie Chen, Jiaze Chen, Chun Zeng, and Yanghua Xiao. 2022. Diversified query generation guided by knowledge graph. In *ACM Conference on Web Search and Data Mining (WSDM)*.

Zhan Shi, Xinchi Chen, Xipeng Qiu, and Xuanjing Huang. 2018. Toward diverse text generation with inverse reinforcement learning. In *International Joint Conference on Artificial Intelligence (IJCAI)*.

Guy Tevet and Jonathan Berant. 2021. Evaluating the evaluation of diversity in natural language generation. In *Conference of the European Chapter of the Association for Computational Linguistics (EACL)*.

Shikhar Vashishth, Soumya Sanyal, Vikram Nitin, and Partha Talukdar. 2020. Composition-based multi-relational graph convolutional networks. In *International Conference for Learning Representation (ICLR)*.

Ashish Vaswani, Noam Shazeer, Niki Parmar, Jakob Uszkoreit, Llion Jones, Aidan N Gomez, Łukasz Kaiser, and Illia Polosukhin. 2017. Attention is all you need. In *Advances in neural information processing systems (NeurIPS)*.

Ashwin K Vijayakumar, Michael Cogswell, Ramprasaath R Selvaraju, Qing Sun, Stefan Lee, David Crandall, and Dhruv Batra. 2018. Diverse beam search for improved description of complex scenes. In *AAAI Conference on Artificial Intelligence (AAAI)*.

Cunxiang Wang, Shuailong Liang, Yili Jin, Yilong Wang, Xiaodan Zhu, and Yue Zhang. 2020. Semeval-2020 task 4: Commonsense validation and explanation. In *Proceedings of the Fourteenth Workshop on Semantic Evaluation (SemEval-14)*.

Cunxiang Wang, Shuailong Liang, Yue Zhang, Xiaonan Li, and Tian Gao. 2019. Does it make sense? and why? a pilot study for sense making and explanation. In *Annual Meeting of the Association for Computational Linguistics (ACL)*.

Thomas Wolf et al. 2020. Transformers: State-of-the-art natural language processing. In *Conference on Empirical Methods in Natural Language Processing (EMNLP)*.

Sixing Wu, Ying Li, Dawei Zhang, Yang Zhou, and Zhonghai Wu. 2020. Diverse and informative dialogue generation with context-specific commonsense knowledge awareness. In *Annual Meeting of the Association for Computational Linguistics (ACL)*.

Donghan Yu, Chenguang Zhu, Yuwei Fang, Wenhao Yu, Shuohang Wang, Yichong Xu, Xiang Ren, Yiming Yang, and Michael Zeng. 2022a. Kg-fid: Infusing knowledge graph in fusion-in-decoder for open-domain question answering. In *Annual Meeting of the Association for Computational Linguistics (ACL)*.

Wenhao Yu, Chenguang Zhu, Yuwei Fang, Donghan Yu, Shuohang Wang, Yichong Xu, Michael Zeng, and Meng Jiang. 2022b. Dict-bert: Enhancing language model pre-training with dictionary. In *Annual Meeting of the Association for Computational Linguistics (ACL)*.

Wenhao Yu, Chenguang Zhu, Zaitang Li, Zhiting Hu, Qingyun Wang, Heng Ji, and Meng Jiang. 2022c. A survey of knowledge-enhanced text generation. In *ACM Computing Survey (CSUR)*.

Wenhao Yu, Chenguang Zhu, Tong Zhao, Zhichun Guo, and Meng Jiang. 2021. Sentence-permuted paragraph generation. In *Conference on empirical methods in natural language processing (EMNLP)*.

Qingkai Zeng, Jinfeng Lin, Wenhao Yu, Jane Cleland-Huang, and Meng Jiang. 2021. Enhancing taxonomy completion with concept generation via fusing relational representations. In *ACM SIGKDD Conference on Knowledge Discovery & Data Mining (KDD)*.

Houyu Zhang, Zhenghao Liu, Chenyan Xiong, and Zhiyuan Liu. 2020a. Grounded conversation generation as guided traverses in commonsense knowledge graphs. In *Annual Meeting of the Association for Computational Linguistics (ACL)*.

Tianyi Zhang, Varsha Kishore, Felix Wu, Kilian Q Weinberger, and Yoav Artzi. 2020b. Bertscore: Evaluating text generation with bert. In *International Conference for Learning Representation (ICLR)*.

Yizhe Zhang, Michel Galley, Jianfeng Gao, Zhe Gan, Xiujun Li, Chris Brockett, and Bill Dolan. 2018. Generating informative and diverse conversational responses via adversarial information maximization. In *Advances in Neural Information Processing Systems (NeurIPS)*.

Hao Zhou, Tom Young, Minlie Huang, Haizhou Zhao, Jingfang Xu, and Xiaoyan Zhu. 2018. Commonsense knowledge aware conversation generation with graph attention. In *International Joint Conference on Artificial Intelligence (IJCAI)*.

Yaoming Zhu, Sidi Lu, Lei Zheng, Jiaxian Guo, Weinan Zhang, Jun Wang, and Yong Yu. 2018. Texygen: A benchmarking platform for text generation models. In *ACM SIGIR Conference on Research & Development in Information Retrieval (SIGIR)*.

Improving Neural Machine Translation with the Abstract Meaning Representation by Combining Graph and Sequence Transformers

Changmao Li and **Jeffrey Flanigan**
University of California, Santa Cruz
{changmao.li, jmflanig}@ucsc.edu

Abstract

Previous studies have shown that the Abstract Meaning Representation (AMR) can improve Neural Machine Translation (NMT). However, there has been little work investigating incorporating AMR graphs into Transformer models. In this work, we propose a novel encoder-decoder architecture which augments the Transformer model with a Heterogeneous Graph Transformer (Yao et al., 2020) which encodes source sentence AMR graphs. Experimental results demonstrate the proposed model outperforms the Transformer model and previous non-Transformer based models on two different language pairs in both the high resource setting and low resource setting. Our source code, training corpus and released models are available at `https://github.com/jlab-nlp/amr-nmt`.

1 Introduction

Neural Machine Translation (NMT, Bahdanau et al. 2015; Vaswani et al. 2017) has proven to be an effective approach, and is the dominant method for machine translation in recent years. However, state-of-the-art NMT methods sometimes repeat words, leave out important pieces of the translation, and hallucinate information not contained in the source, or in other words, fail to accurately capture the semantics of the source in some cases.

To address this problem, researchers have explored incorporating syntactic and semantic information into NMT systems. While most of previous NMT studies incorporating extra information are focused on syntax-based NMT (Stahlberg et al., 2016; Aharoni and Goldberg, 2017; Li et al., 2017; Chen et al., 2017; Bastings et al., 2017; Wu et al., 2017; Chen et al., 2018; Currey and Heafield, 2019; Zhang et al., 2019; Eriguchi et al., 2019; Sundararaman et al., 2019; Zhang et al., 2021; Ni et al., 2021), there has recently been interest in incorporating semantic information into NMT. Marcheggiani et al.

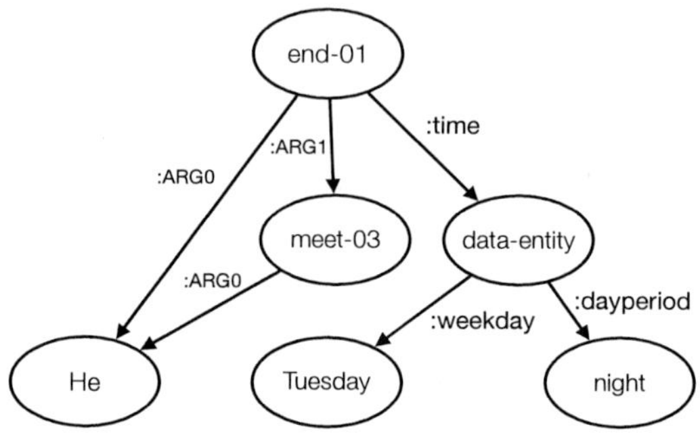

Figure 1: The AMR graph for sentence "He ended his meeting on Tuesday night.".

(2018) shows that incorporating Semantic Role Labeling (SRL) information can alleviating the "argument switching" problem for NMT. Song et al. (2019) shows that Abstract Meaning Representation (AMR, Banarescu et al. 2013) graphs can be helpful for NMT for the Bi-LSTM with attention. AMR (Banarescu et al., 2013) is a semantic formalism that encodes the meaning of a sentence as a rooted, directed graph. Figure 1 shows an AMR graph, in which the nodes (eg. end-01) represent the concepts, and edges (eg. AGR0) represent the relations between concepts they connect.

In prior work, Nguyen et al. (2021) examined the effect of AMRs in different NMT models, proposing a method for incorporating AMR into NMT. However, the method Nguyen et al. (2021) proposed for incorporating AMR into the Transformer showed limited success, as their performance with the Transformer with AMR was less than their Bi-LSTM with AMR.

In this work, we re-examine methods for incorporating AMR graphs into Transformer models. The Transformer (Vaswani et al., 2017) architecture has been the state-of-the-art for NMT for several years. We propose to improve upon the Transformer model by incorporating AMR graphs with a graph Transformer in a novel manner. In partic-

Proceedings of the 2nd Workshop on Deep Learning on Graphs for Natural Language Processing (DLG4NLP 2022), pages 12 - 21
July 15, 2022 ©2022 Association for Computational Linguistics

ular, we observe the best performance gains when integrating the semantic information contained in the AMR graphs into *both* the encoder and decoder modules of the Transformer.

While much research on Transformers is for text, many researchers have also investigated Transformer-like architectures for the encoding of graph structures. Yao et al. (2020) proposed the Heterogeneous Graph Transformer which independently models the different relations in the individual subgraphs of the original graph, including direct relations, indirect relations and other possible relations between nodes.

We improve the performance of the Transformer by employing a vanilla Transformer to encode and decode the source sentence and a Heterogeneous Graph Transformer to encode an AMR graph of the source sentence. We use a novel integration model to combine the graph representations (§3) into the encoder and decoder. We show that our method improves upon the Transformer, and improves upon the best previous method for incorporating AMR graphs into NMT.

Experiments on the WMT16 English to German dataset and IWSLT15 English to Vietnamese show that incorporating AMR into Transformer models with proper encoding representation combination models can robustly improve the vanilla sequence-to-sequence Transformer baseline and outperforms all previous approaches when incorporating AMR in both low data setting and large data setting.

In summary, our contributions are the following:

- We propose a novel integration encoder-decoder model which combines the sentence representations from the vanilla sequence Transformer and graph representations from Heterogeneous Graph Transformer to better incorporate AMR into machine translation purely using Transformers.

- We introduce two encoder integration methods and two decoder integration methods to combine the two Transformers which enforces the model to combine information from both representations independently and coherently.

- We perform several comparison experiments and results show that our proposed models robustly performs better than both vanilla sequence Transformer and previous baselines which shows that including AMR into machine translation can be more effective by only using Transformer-based models.

2 Background

In this section, we review the original Transformer architecture for sequences as well as the Heterogeneous Graph Transformer, and introduce notation we will use in later sections.

2.1 Transformer

The Transformer (Vaswani et al., 2017) contains several layers, which has a multi-head self-attention layer (Bahdanau et al. 2015; Graves et al. 2014; Weston et al. 2015) followed by a feedforward layer, along with residual connections (He et al., 2016) and layer normalization (Ba et al., 2016) .

Let the input sequence be $S = [s_1, ..., s_L] \in \mathbb{R}^{Lxe}$, where L is the sequence length and e is the hidden size of the attention layer. Queries Q, keys K, and values V used in the self-attention computation are obtained by linearly projecting the input, or the output of the previous layer, X:

$$Q = SW^Q, K = SW^K, V = SW^V, \quad (1)$$

While $W^Q, W^K, W^V \in \mathbb{R}^{exe}$ are learnable projection matrices. To perform multi-head self attention, Q, K, and V are split into heads $Q_h, K_h, V_h \in \mathbb{R}^{Lxd}$ for h in $1, ..., H$ where H is the number of heads and $d = e/H$. Then, the context representation $E_h \in \mathbb{R}^{Lxd}$, that corresponds to each attention head h, is obtained by:

$$E_h = \text{softmax}(\frac{Q_h K_h^T}{\sqrt{d}}) V_h, \quad (2)$$

Where d is the hidden size dimension of each K_h and the softmax is performed row-wise. The head context representations are concatenated to obtain the final context representation $E_S \in \mathbb{R}^{Lxe}$:

$$E_S = [E_1, ..., E_H] W^R, \quad (3)$$

where $W^R \in \mathbb{R}^{exe}$ is another projection matrix that aggregates all head's representations.

2.2 Heterogeneous Graph Transformer

A Heterogeneous Graph Transformer (Yao et al., 2020) is a Transformer-based graph encoder and decoder model. Yao et al. (2020) extends the input transformed Levi graph (Beck et al., 2018) into multiple types of subgraphs (i.e.fully-connected, reverse, etc.) according to its heterogeneity then updating the node representation in different subgraphs based on its neighbor nodes in the current subgraph and finally combining all the representations of this node in different subgraphs to get the graph final representation.

Let the input graph nodes be $G = [g_1, ..., g_N] \in \mathbb{R}^{N \times e}$, where N is the number of nodes and e is the hidden size of the attention layer. Then the output representation of node i in each attention head Z_i is obtained by:

$$Z_i = \sum_{j \in N_i} \alpha_{ij}(g_j W^V) \quad (4)$$

$$\alpha_{ij} = \text{softmax}(\frac{(g_i W^Q)(g_j W^K)^T}{\sqrt{d}}) \quad (5)$$

where $W^V, W^Q, W^K \in \mathbb{R}^{e \times e}$ are layer-specific learnable parameter matrices and α_{ij} represents the attention score of node j to i and $d = e/H$ where H is the number of attention heads. Then the output Z in each encoder layer is obtained by:

$$Z = [Z^{G_1^{\text{sub}}}, ..., Z^{G_M^{\text{sub}}}]W^R \quad (6)$$

$$Z_i^{G_m^{\text{sub}}} = \sum_{j \in N_i^{G_m^{\text{sub}}}} \alpha_{ij}(g_j W^V), m \in [1, M] \quad (7)$$

where M is the number of subgraphs, $W^R \in \mathbb{R}^{Me \times e}$, G_m^{sub} is the set of subgraphs including M elements (i.e. $G^{\text{sub}} =$ {*fullyconnected, connected, default, reverse*}) and $N_i^{G_m^{\text{sub}}}$ is the set of neighbors in the m-th subgraph of node i. Finally there is a layer aggregation strategy from Xu et al. (2018) using Jumping Knowledge architecture (Xu et al., 2018), so the final output of the graph representation $E_G \in \mathbb{R}^{N \times e}$ is:

$$E_G = [Z^1, , ..., Z^T]W_{\text{jump}} \quad (8)$$

where $W_{\text{jump}} \in \mathbb{R}^{Le \times e}$ and T is the number of layers including the embedding layer.

3 Our AMR-Transformer Model

Figure 2 shows the overview of our proposed model architecture. To encode and decode both source sentences and source AMR graphs to target sentences, our model consists of two parallel stacked encoder and decoder layers, one for sequence encoding and decoding from the neural sequence to sequence model, and the other for graph encoding and decoding from the neural graph to sequence model. Given the encoded sequence representation from the sequence encoder and the encoded graph representation from the graph encoder, the sequence to sequence decoder only receives the sequence representation while the graph to sequence decoder receives the combination of the sequence representation and the graph representation. The specific combination approaches are discussed in §3.2 and §3.3. Finally, two decoder representations are concatenated and fed into the final linear layer to generate target sequence representation. In this way, the model can combine the advantage of the traditional sequence to sequence model which does translation based on source sentence encodings and the graph to sequence model which incorporates AMR graphs into the translation. The combination of source sentence representation and the graph representation into the graph to sequence decoder can lead the graph to sequence decoder to decoding towards good translation quality since using only AMR graphs representation can lead to poor translation quality compared to the vanilla sequence to sequence model using source sentences.

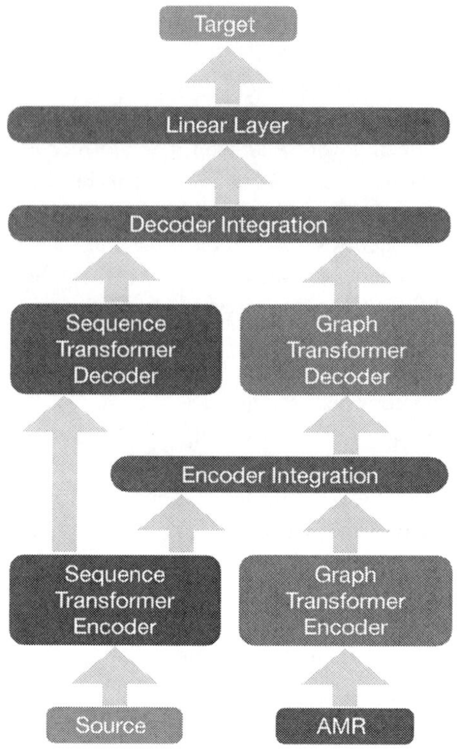

Figure 2: Overview of our AMR-Transformer model.

3.1 Sequence and Graph Encodings

Here we describe our sentence and graph encodings. Let $S = [s_1, ..., s_{L_s}] \in \mathbb{R}^{L_s \times e}$ be the source sentence where s_i is the ith token in S, L_s is the length of the source sentence and e is the hidden size of the encoder. Let $G = [g_1, ...g_N] \in \mathbb{R}^{N \times e}$ be the AMR graph of the source sentence where g_j is the j'th node in G and N is the number of nodes. The source sequence encoding representation E_S is computed by Eq. 3 and the AMR graph encoding representation E_G is computed by Eq. 8.

3.2 Encoder Integration: Multi-head Attention Integration

To integrate the encoder representations for the sequence encode and graph encoder, we employ a multi-head attention mechanism. Figure 3 shows an overview of the multi-head attention (MHA) (Vaswani et al., 2017) integration of the two encoder representations. At a high level, we compute MHA between the source sequence encoding representation E_S and the AMR graph encoding representation E_G, which allows the model to learn correlations between individual tokens and nodes in S and G, s_* and g_*.

Each row in E_S is the representation $E_i^S \in \mathbb{R}^{1 \times e}$ of the corresponding token s_i. Each row in E_G is the representation $E_j^G \in \mathbb{R}^{1 \times e}$ of the corresponding node g_j. These two matrices, E_S and E_G, are fed into two types of multi-head attention (MHA) layers, one finding correlations from S to G (S2G) and the other from G to S (G2S), which generate two attention matrices, $\mathcal{A}^{s2g} \in \mathbb{R}^{L_s \times e}$ and $\mathcal{A}^{g2s} \in \mathbb{R}^{N \times e}$.

$$\mathcal{A}^{s2g} = [h_1^{s2g}, ..., h_H^{s2g}]W^{O_{s2g}} \quad (9)$$

$$h_i^{s2g} = \sigma(\frac{E_S W_i^{Q_{s2g}} (E_G W_i^{K_{s2g}})^T}{\sqrt{d}}) E_G W_i^{V_{s2g}} \quad (10)$$

H is the number of heads and $d = e/H$. $W_i^{Q_{s2g}}, W_i^{K_{s2g}}, W_i^{V_{s2g}} \in \mathbb{R}^{e \times d}$, $W^{O_{s2g}} \in \mathbb{R}^{N \times e}$ are learned parameters and σ represents softmax.

$$\mathcal{A}^{g2s} = [h_1^{g2s}, ..., h_H^{g2s}]W^{O_{g2s}} \quad (11)$$

$$h_i^{g2s} = \sigma(\frac{E_G W_i^{Q_{g2s}} (E_S W_i^{K_{g2s}})^T}{\sqrt{d}}) E_S W_i^{V_{g2s}} \quad (12)$$

$W^{O_{g2s}} \in \mathbb{R}^{e \times e}$ and $W_i^{Q_{g2s}}, W_i^{K_{g2s}}, W_i^{V_{g2s}} \in \mathbb{R}^{e \times d}$ are learned parameters and σ is softmax.

Then the graph to sequence decoder input representation $D_{\text{in}}^g \in \mathbb{R}^{(L_s+N) \times e}$ is computed by:

$$D_{\text{in}}^g = [\mathcal{A}^{s2g}, \mathcal{A}^{g2s}] \quad (13)$$

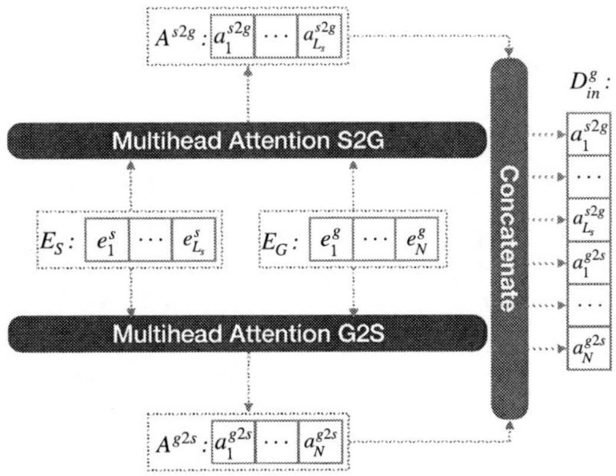

Figure 3: The multi-head attention integration.

3.2.1 Direct Integration

As a baseline, we also experiment with a simpler method of integrating the two encoders, which we call direct integration. Given the previous obtained source sequence encoding representation E_S and AMR graph encoding representation E_G, the graph to sequence decoder input representation $D_{\text{in}}^g \in \mathbb{R}^{(L_s+N) \times e}$ is computed using concatenation:

$$D_{\text{in}}^g = [E_S, E_G] \quad (14)$$

3.3 Decoder Integration

To keep the advantages of the vanilla sequence Transformer, the sequence to sequence decoder input representation D_{in}^s is identical to E_S , then D_{in}^s is fed into the sequence to sequence decoder to obtain the target sentence representation $D_{\text{out}}^s \in \mathbb{R}^{L_t * e}$, where L_t is the length of the target sentence. The previous obtained D_{in}^g which is the graph to sequence decoder input representation is fed into the graph to sequence decoder to obtain the target sentence representation $D_{\text{out}}^g \in \mathbb{R}^{L_t * e}$. Then the final target sentence representation $Z^{target} \in \mathbb{R}^{L_t \times e}$ is obtained by:

$$Z^{target} = (D_{\text{out}}^s + D_{\text{out}}^g)W_e^T + B_e \quad (15)$$

Where $W_e \in \mathbb{R}^{v * e}$ is the embedding weight matrix, $B_e \in \mathbb{R}^{L_t * v}$ is the bias and v is the vocabulary size.

Dataset	Train	Dev	Test	
WMT16 EN-DE NC-V11	238K	3000	2999	
WMT16 EN-DE Full	4.5M			
IWST15 EN-VI	133K	1553	1268	1080

Table 1: The statistics of datasets. EN-DE: English to German; EN-VI: English to Vietnamese. For IWST15 English-Vietnamese, there are two test sets, the left cell in the Test column represents the tst2013 and the right cell in the Test column represents the tst2015.

4 Experiments

4.1 Data and Preprocessing

Following Song et al. (2019), we use the WMT16 English to German dataset[1] in both the news commentary setting (News Commentary v11, NC-V11) and the full data scenario. For all experiments we use newstest2013 and newstest2016 respectively as the development and test sets. To evaluate the model performance on low-resource languages, we also include experiments on IWST15 English to Vietnamese dataset[2]and follow the preprocessing steps described below. For this dataset, we use tst2012 as development set and use tst2013 and tst2015 as test sets following Nguyen et al. (2021). Table 1 shows the number of sentences for training, development and testing splits.

To preprocess the data, we use `Moses`[3] data cleaning and tokenization tools to clean and tokenize all data for both sides. We used Google `sentencepiece`[4] in BPE mode to deal with rare and compound words for both sides and conducted 4000 BPE merges for English-Vietnamese data, 8000 BPE merges for the English-German News Commentary V11 data and 16000 BPE merges for the English-German full data. For the AMR parsing, instead of `JAMR` (Flanigan et al., 2016) used by Song et al. (2019), we employed a recent AMR parser, AMR-gs[5] (Cai and Lam, 2020) to obtain better AMR parsing quality. However we also conducted an AMR parsing ablation experiment using `JAMR` in §5.2 to show comparison of the effect of AMR parsing quality.

4.2 Models

We trained and evaluated the following models on WMT2016 English-German in both subset data setting and full data setting and one real low resource languages and IWST15 English-Vietnamese. Following Nguyen et al. (2021) we also carefully reimplemented and ran their best system which is a non-Transformer based model with our settings to show a fair comparison. We use AMR-Transformer to refer to our proposed model. The models we compare are:

- Vanilla sequence Transformer (Baseline, §2.1)
- AMR-Transformer-DI: Ours with direct integration (§3.2.1)
- AMR-Transformer: Ours with `MHA` integration (§3.2)

We also compared to other Non-Transformer baselines including Dual2seq ((Song et al., 2019)) which leverages the BiLSTM to encode sequences and graph recurrent network (GRN) to encode AMR graphs and an improved version proposed by ((Ni et al., 2021)) which also applies the BiLSTM to encode sequences but employs the graph attention network (GAN) to encode AMR graphs.

4.3 Hyperparameters

We use the Adam optimizer (Kingma and Ba, 2015). The batch size on tokens is set to 4096 with gradient accumulation size 2. Between layers, we apply dropout with a probability of 0.1 for the vanilla sequence Transformer. The best model is selected based on the word accuracy on the development set. BLEU (Papineni et al., 2002), TER (Snover et al., 2006) and Meteor (Denkowski and Lavie, 2014) are used as the metrics on cased and tokenized results. For experiments with WMT16 English-German, both Sequence Transformer and Heterogeneous Graph Transformer word embedding size are 512 and hidden size are 2048, the dropout for the Heterogeneous Graph Transformer part is 0.3 and the models are trained for at most 300000 steps with early stopping and 16000 warm up steps. For experiments with IWST15 English-Vietnamese, the Sequence Transformer word embedding size is 256 and hidden size is 1024, Heterogeneous Graph Transformer embedding size is 256 and hidden size is 512, the dropout for the Heterogeneous Graph Transformer part is 0.8 and the models are trained for at most 120000 steps with early stopping and 2000 warm up steps. All models were trained on either one A40 or A100 GPU.

[1]http://www.statmt.org/wmt16/translation-task.html
[2]https://wit3.fbk.eu/2015-01
[3]http://www.statmt.org/moses/
[4]https://github.com/google/sentencepiece
[5]https://github.com/jcyk/AMR-gs

System on WMT16 English-German	NC-v11					Full				
	BLEU	TER↓	Meteor	PS	GH	BLEU	TER↓	Meteor	PS	GH
Dual2seq (Song et al., 2019)	19.2	63.1	38.4	-	-	25.5	54.8	43.8	-	-
Bi-LSTM -AMR (Nguyen et al. 2021, reimplement)	19.0	66.4	37.5	62M	7h	24.8	58.9	43.1	72M	15h
Vanilla sequence Transformer (§2.1)	20.3	66.3.	39.4	52M	12h	26.0	58.5	45.2	61M	20h
Vanilla sequence Transformer (Double Parameters)	20.9	62.1	40.3	138M	12h	26.2	57.6	45.2	151M	20h
AMR-Transformer-DI (§3.2.1)	21.5	62.7	40.4	117M	16h	26.4	56.7	44.9	132M	28h
AMR-Transformer (§3.2)	**22.1***	**62.0***	**41.1***	117M	16h	**26.5****	**56.4***	**45.2**	133M	28h

Table 2: TEST performance on WMT16 English-German. NC-v11 represents training only with the NC-v11 data, while Full means using the full training data. * represents significant (Koehn, 2004) result ($p < 0.001$) over vanilla sequence Transformer. ** represents significant result ($p < 0.05$) over vanilla sequence Transformer. ↓ indicates lower is better. PS: approximate parameter size. GH: approximate GPU training hours with early stopping.

System on IWST15 English-Vietnamese	PS	GH	tst2013			tst2015		
			BLEU	TER↓	Meteor	BLEU	TER↓	Meteor
Bi-LSTM -AMR (Nguyen et al., 2021)	-	-	29.3	-	-	26.4	-	-
Bi-LSTM -AMR (Nguyen et al. 2021, reimplement)	17M	9h	26.4	56.4	44.1	25.2	60.5	42.1
Vanilla sequence Transformer (§2.1)	13M	5h	30.0	52.1	48.2	27.6	57.6	45.4
Vanilla sequence Transformer (Double parameters)	36M	5h	28.3	54.4	46.4	26.8	59.2	44.2
AMR-Transformer-DI (§3.2.1)	20M	7h	30.2	52.4	48.2	28.2	57.3	45.5
AMR-Transformer (§3.2)	20M	7h	**30.6***	**52.1**	**48.5**	**28.2****	**57.1**	**45.9**

Table 3: TEST performance on IWST15 English-Vietnamese. tst2013 represents the results evaluated on tst2013 and tst2015 represents the results evaluated on tst2015. * represents $p < 0.05$ over vanilla sequence Transformer. ** represents $p < 0.11$ over vanilla sequence Transformer. ↓ indicates lower is better. PS: approximate parameter size. GH: approximate GPU training hours with early stopping.

4.4 Main Results

4.4.1 Results on WMT16 English-German

Table 2 shows the test BLEU, TER and Meteor scores of all systems trained on the small scale News Commentary v11 subset or the large scale full set. The result shows that our Transformer baseline already outperforms all previous non-Transformer based results. Our system using AMR-Transformer whether it is DI or MI are all consistently better than the other systems under all three metrics, showing the effectiveness of the semantic information provided by AMR with Transformers. Particularly, AMR-Transformer is the best performing model for both settings and significantly better than vanilla sequence Transformer baselines under all three metrics. In terms of different settings, our best model shows 1.8 BLEU points improvement over the vanilla sequence Transformer baseline and at least 2.9 BLEU points improvement over the non-Transformer baselines on News Commentary V11 data. For the Full data, the improvement is smaller but our best model is still significantly better than vanilla sequence Transformer baseline in terms of BLEU points and at least 1.0 BLEU points improvement over the non-Transformer baselines. The results show the same conclusion as Song et al. (2019) that AMR graphs helps more on a low resource setting. Our AMR-Transformer model has roughly double the parameters as the baseline Transformer model due to the graph encoder. To show the effectiveness of our approach is not from increasing the parameter size, we conduct experiments on Transformer baselines with doubled parameters. Our approach still shows better performance.

4.4.2 Results on IWST15 English-Vietnamese

Table 3 shows the results of all systems trained on the IWST15 English to Vietnamese data. Our best AMR-Transformer is significantly better than vanilla sequence Transformer on tst2013 and also better than the previous non-Transformer based model. However, the model is not significantly better on tst 2015, which is due to the different data distribution between tst2013 and tst2015. Our experiments also show that adjusting the model dropout rate of Heterogeneous Graph Transformer side when using fixed hyperparameter of the Sequence Transformer side during training can improve the performance since the model dropout rate can control how much AMR information is used to contribute to the final predictions. Our experiments inidcate that a high dropout rate for Heterogeneous Graph Transformer side during low resource settings can enable AMR information help sequence to sequence model better than a low dropout rate.

Ablation on WMT16 English-German	NC-v11			Full		
	BLEU	TER↓	Meteor	BLEU	TER↓	Meteor
AMR-Transformer, No Encoder Integration	20.9	64.1	39.5	26.4	56.5	45.4
AMR-Transformer-DI, Single Decoder	19.9	65.8	36.6	25.5	60.8	42.6
AMR-Transformer, Single Decoder	16.1	72.7	32.3	21.6	65.4	38.7
AMR-Transformer-DI	21.5	62.7	40.4	26.4	56.7	44.9
AMR-Transformer	22.1	62.0	41.1	26.5	56.4	45.2

Table 4: Model ablations TEST performance comparasion on WMT16 English-German. NC-v11 represents training only with the NC-v11 data, while Full means using the full training data.). ↓ indicates lower is better.

The improvement gap between our best model and vanillas Transformer is smaller than the model trained on English to German News commentary V11 data which indicates that the size of the training data in low resource settings takes an effect on how much AMR information can help when incorporating into the sequence to sequence translation models. With more training data when it is in low resource setting, the help of AMR information increases but during high resource setting the help of AMR information decreases. Our AMR-Transformer model has roughly double the parameters as the baseline Transformer model due to the graph encoder. To show the effectiveness of our approach is not because of enlarging the parameter size in this dataset, we also double the parameters of Transformer baselines, and the performance is even lower than the smaller parameters baseline due to the possible over-fitting.

5 Analysis and ablation studies

5.1 Model ablations

To verify the effectiveness of our encoder integration and decoder integration we conduct ablation experiments on WMT16 English-German data. Table 4 shows model ablations test performance. we can see that compared to the best model, the performance drops largely on the both data setting without decoder integration , at least 2.2 BLEU points drop on News Commentary V11 data and at least 2.7 BLEU drop on the full data which indicates the decoder integration have a large contribution to the performance improvement in both data settings. For the encoder integration part, it shows different situations on the two data setttings. On the News Commentary V11 training data, without encoder integration, the BLEU drops 1.2 points while on the full training data, however, the BLEU score does not drop too much which indicates that encoder integration is more helpful in low resource settings.

Generally, the drop gap between the best model and without decoder integration is larger than the drop gap between the best model and without encoder integration which indicates that decoder integration is more helpful for the performance improvement than the encoder integration in both data settings.

5.2 Influence of AMR parsing accuracy

To verify the influence of AMR parsing quality we also conduct an experiment on News Commentary V11 dataset using a previous JAMR paser (Flanigan et al., 2016) with the best model. Table 6 shows the result. We can see that with a lower quality AMR parser the BLEU score drops 0.9 points but it is still better than the vanilla sequence Transformer baseline and previous non-Transformer based models, which indicates that the quality of the AMR parser influences the performance of the model. However, even with lower quality AMR parses, our approach can still improve upon the Transformer baseline.

5.3 Case study

We conduct case studies for a better understanding of the model performance. We compare the outputs of the vanilla Transformer baseline and our AMR-Transformer model with multihead attention integration trained on News commentary V11 data. Tables 5 presents these examples. In the first example, the source sentence is in the syntax of "someone said something" and the vanilla Transformer baseline model completely misses this syntax which causes the incorrect translation while our model perfectly kept the original sentence syntax and meaning. In the second example, the vanilla Transformer baseline model incorrectly translate the verb "hold up" into "verteilt" which means "distributed" in German which causes meaning of the sentence entirely different from the source sentence, while our model perfectly translate it the same as the reference sentence which indicates that our model with AMR graphs is helpful for keeping

AMR: (c0 / say-01 :ARG0 (c2 / we) :ARG1 (c1 / take-01 :ARG0 c2 :ARG1 (c4 / they) :ARG3 (c5 / city :name (c7 / name :op1 "passau")) :manner (c6 / car)) :time (c3 / once))
Src: We said at once that we would take them to Passau by car .
Ref: Wir haben gleich gesagt , wir bringen sie mit dem Auto nach Passau .
Vanilla Transformer: Sobald wir sie zu einem Auto nach Passau nehmen würden .
AMR-Transformer: Wir sagten einmal darauf , dass wir sie mit dem Auto Passau nehmen würden .

AMR: (c0 / and :op2 (c1 / hold-up-11 :ARG1 (c2 / number :mod (c4 / this)) :location (c3 / state :mod (c5 / early))))
Src: And these numbers hold up in early states .
Ref: Und diese Zahlen halten sich in frühen Staaten .
Vanilla Transformer: Und diese Zahlen sind in frühen Bundesstaaten verteilt .
AMR-Transformer: Und diese Zahlen halten an frühe Staaten fest .

AMR: (c0 / note-01 :ARG1 (c1 / it) :ARG1-of (c3 / cause-01 :ARG0 (c4 / reason :ARG1-of (c5 / personal-02))) :mod (c2 / too))
Src: It was noteworthy because of personal reasons , too .
Ref: Sie war auch aus persönlichen Gründen bemerkenswert .
Vanilla Transformer: Auch weil es aus persönlichen Gründen bemerkenswert war , war sie beachtenswert .
AMR-Transformer: Sie war auch aufgrund von persönlichen Gründen bemerkenswert .

AMR: (c0 / contrast-01 :ARG1 (c1 / hard-02 :ARG1 (c3 / find-01 :ARG1 (c7 / keep-01)) :mod (c4 / usual) :polarity -) :ARG2 (c2 / possible-01 :ARG1 (c6 / get-03 :ARG1 (c8 / store) :ARG2 (c9 / busy-01 :ARG1 c8))))
Src: While the store can get busy , parking is usually not hard to find .
Ref: Auch wenn der Laden gut besucht ist , ist es nicht schwer , einen Parkplatz zu finden .
Vanilla Transformer: Während sich der Laden mit dem Glücksfall beschäftigt , ist es normalerweise nicht schwer, einen Parking zu finden .
AMR-Transformer: Während der Stur Busy bekommen kann , ist Parking normalerweise nicht schwer zu finden .

Table 5: Sample system outputs

Ablation with JAMR	NC-v11		
	BLEU	TER↓	Meteor
AMR-Transformer w/ JAMR	21.2	64.4	40.3
AMR-Transformer w/ AMR-gs	22.1	62.0	41.1

Table 6: TEST performance on WMT16 English to German NC-v11 using two different AMR pasers with the best model. ↓ indicates lower is better.

the meaning of the verbs. In the third example, the vanilla sequence Transformer repeatedly translates the same meaning twice while our model correctly translate it only once which indicates our model can avoid the repetition of tokens in the same meaning. However, there are situations that our model performs badly. In the forth example, our model incorrectly translates the noun word "store" while the vanilla Transformer baseline translate it correctly which indicates that AMRs may not be helpful when translating nouns.

Generally from our observations, with the AMR incorporated with our proposed model, although there may be a problem for translation of nouns, our system can more correctly translate the key verbs, more easily keep the same sentence syntax with the source sentence and avoid repetitions which are enable the NMT system more easily to keep the source sentence meaning and generate a better translation quality.

6 Related Work

Several recent studies have investigated on how to incorporate semantic information into neural machine translation (NMT) models. Marcheggiani et al. (2018) studied the semantic role labeling (SRL) information for NMT, which used graph convolutional network (GCN) layers to encode the predicate-argument structure from SRL to improve the translation performance of the NMT model. In line with their work, Song et al. (2019) was the first to exploit the AMR information on NMT, which used a graph recurrent network to encode the AMR graph and found that AMR information can improve attention-based sequence to sequence neural translation model and they only evaluated their model on WMT16 English to German dataset. Nguyen et al. (2021) then examine the effect of AMR in different sequence to sequence machine translation models, however, they found that their proposed single decoder Transformer model to incorporate the AMR information performs worse than the Bi-LSTM model with simple graph attention network. In this paper, we focus on improving the performance of incorporating AMR information purely with Transformers. Our proposed method of integrating vanilla sequence Transformer and Heterogeneous Graph Transformer model with encoder integration and decoder integration provides a better way to incorporate the AMR information into NMT.

7 Conclusion

We combine the Transformer and the Heterogeneous Graph Transformer to incorporate semantics captured in AMR graphs into neural machine translation. Experimental results show that our proposed AMR-Transformer model robustly outperforms the vanilla sequence Transformer baseline and previous non-Transformer based models across two different language pairs in both high resource setting and low resource setting.

Acknowledgements

J.F. was supported in part by the NSF National AI Institute for Student-AI Teaming (iSAT) under grant DRL 2019805. The opinions expressed are those of the authors and do not represent views of the NSF. We are thankful for the computing resources provided by the Pacific Research Platform's Nautilus cluster, supported by the NSF under Award Numbers CNS-1730158, ACI-1540112, ACI1541349, OAC-1826967, the University of California Office of the President, and the University of California San Diego's California Institute for Telecommunications and Information Technology/Qualcomm Institute.

References

Roee Aharoni and Yoav Goldberg. 2017. Towards string-to-tree neural machine translation. In *Proceedings of the 55th Annual Meeting of the Association for Computational Linguistics (Volume 2: Short Papers)*, pages 132–140, Vancouver, Canada. Association for Computational Linguistics.

Jimmy Lei Ba, Jamie Ryan Kiros, and Geoffrey E. Hinton. 2016. Layer normalization.

Dzmitry Bahdanau, Kyunghyun Cho, and Yoshua Bengio. 2015. Neural machine translation by jointly learning to align and translate. In *3rd International Conference on Learning Representations, ICLR 2015, San Diego, CA, USA, May 7-9, 2015, Conference Track Proceedings*.

Laura Banarescu, Claire Bonial, Shu Cai, Madalina Georgescu, Kira Griffitt, Ulf Hermjakob, Kevin Knight, Philipp Koehn, Martha Palmer, and Nathan Schneider. 2013. Abstract Meaning Representation for sembanking. In *Proceedings of the 7th Linguistic Annotation Workshop and Interoperability with Discourse*, pages 178–186, Sofia, Bulgaria. Association for Computational Linguistics.

Jasmijn Bastings, Ivan Titov, Wilker Aziz, Diego Marcheggiani, and Khalil Sima'an. 2017. Graph convolutional encoders for syntax-aware neural machine translation. In *Proceedings of the 2017 Conference on Empirical Methods in Natural Language Processing*, pages 1957–1967, Copenhagen, Denmark. Association for Computational Linguistics.

Daniel Beck, Gholamreza Haffari, and Trevor Cohn. 2018. Graph-to-sequence learning using gated graph neural networks. In *Proceedings of the 56th Annual Meeting of the Association for Computational Linguistics (Volume 1: Long Papers)*, pages 273–283, Melbourne, Australia. Association for Computational Linguistics.

Deng Cai and Wai Lam. 2020. AMR parsing via graph-sequence iterative inference. In *Proceedings of the 58th Annual Meeting of the Association for Computational Linguistics*, pages 1290–1301, Online. Association for Computational Linguistics.

Huadong Chen, Shujian Huang, David Chiang, and Jiajun Chen. 2017. Improved neural machine translation with a syntax-aware encoder and decoder. In *Proceedings of the 55th Annual Meeting of the Association for Computational Linguistics (Volume 1: Long Papers)*, pages 1936–1945, Vancouver, Canada. Association for Computational Linguistics.

Kehai Chen, Rui Wang, Masao Utiyama, Eiichiro Sumita, and Tiejun Zhao. 2018. Syntax-directed attention for neural machine translation. In *AAAI*.

Anna Currey and Kenneth Heafield. 2019. Incorporating source syntax into transformer-based neural machine translation. In *Proceedings of the Fourth Conference on Machine Translation (Volume 1: Research Papers)*, pages 24–33, Florence, Italy. Association for Computational Linguistics.

Michael Denkowski and Alon Lavie. 2014. Meteor universal: Language specific translation evaluation for any target language. In *Proceedings of the Ninth Workshop on Statistical Machine Translation*, pages 376–380, Baltimore, Maryland, USA. Association for Computational Linguistics.

Akiko Eriguchi, Kazuma Hashimoto, and Yoshimasa Tsuruoka. 2019. Incorporating Source-Side Phrase Structures into Neural Machine Translation. *Computational Linguistics*, 45(2):267–292.

Jeffrey Flanigan, Chris Dyer, Noah A. Smith, and Jaime Carbonell. 2016. CMU at SemEval-2016 task 8: Graph-based AMR parsing with infinite ramp loss. In *Proceedings of the 10th International Workshop on Semantic Evaluation (SemEval-2016)*, pages 1202–1206, San Diego, California. Association for Computational Linguistics.

Alex Graves, Greg Wayne, and Ivo Danihelka. 2014. Neural turing machines. *CoRR*, abs/1410.5401.

Kaiming He, Xiangyu Zhang, Shaoqing Ren, and Jian Sun. 2016. Deep residual learning for image recognition. In *Proceedings of the IEEE Conference on Computer Vision and Pattern Recognition (CVPR)*.

Diederik P. Kingma and Jimmy Ba. 2015. Adam: A method for stochastic optimization. In *3rd International Conference on Learning Representations, ICLR 2015, San Diego, CA, USA, May 7-9, 2015, Conference Track Proceedings*.

Junhui Li, Deyi Xiong, Zhaopeng Tu, Muhua Zhu, Min Zhang, and Guodong Zhou. 2017. Modeling source syntax for neural machine translation. In *Proceedings of the 55th Annual Meeting of the Association for Computational Linguistics (Volume 1: Long Papers)*, pages 688–697, Vancouver, Canada. Association for Computational Linguistics.

Diego Marcheggiani, Jasmijn Bastings, and Ivan Titov. 2018. Exploiting semantics in neural machine translation with graph convolutional networks. In *Proceedings of the 2018 Conference of the North American Chapter of the Association for Computational Linguistics: Human Language Technologies, Volume 2 (Short Papers)*, pages 486–492, New Orleans, Louisiana. Association for Computational Linguistics.

Long H. B. Nguyen, Viet H. Pham, and Dien Dinh. 2021. Improving neural machine translation with amr semantic graphs. *Mathematical Problems in Engineering*, 2021:1–12.

Bin Ni, Xiaolei Lu, and Yiqi Tong. 2021. Synxlm-r: Syntax-enhanced xlm-r in translation quality estimation. In *Natural Language Processing and Chinese Computing*, pages 27–40, Cham. Springer International Publishing.

Kishore Papineni, Salim Roukos, Todd Ward, and Wei-Jing Zhu. 2002. Bleu: a method for automatic evaluation of machine translation. In *Proceedings of the 40th Annual Meeting of the Association for Computational Linguistics*, pages 311–318, Philadelphia, Pennsylvania, USA. Association for Computational Linguistics.

Matthew Snover, Bonnie Dorr, Rich Schwartz, Linnea Micciulla, and John Makhoul. 2006. A study of translation edit rate with targeted human annotation. In *Proceedings of the 7th Conference of the Association for Machine Translation in the Americas: Technical Papers*, pages 223–231, Cambridge, Massachusetts, USA. Association for Machine Translation in the Americas.

Linfeng Song, Daniel Gildea, Yue Zhang, Zhiguo Wang, and Jinsong Su. 2019. Semantic neural machine translation using AMR. *Transactions of the Association for Computational Linguistics*, 7:19–31.

Felix Stahlberg, Eva Hasler, Aurelien Waite, and Bill Byrne. 2016. Syntactically guided neural machine translation. In *Proceedings of the 54th Annual Meeting of the Association for Computational Linguistics (Volume 2: Short Papers)*, pages 299–305, Berlin, Germany. Association for Computational Linguistics.

Dhanasekar Sundararaman, Vivek Subramanian, Guoyin Wang, Shijing Si, Dinghan Shen, Dong Wang, and Lawrence Carin. 2019. Syntax-infused transformer and BERT models for machine translation and natural language understanding. *CoRR*, abs/1911.06156.

Ashish Vaswani, Noam Shazeer, Niki Parmar, Jakob Uszkoreit, Llion Jones, Aidan N Gomez, Ł ukasz Kaiser, and Illia Polosukhin. 2017. Attention is all you need. In *Advances in Neural Information Processing Systems*, volume 30. Curran Associates, Inc.

Jason Weston, Sumit Chopra, and Antoine Bordes. 2015. Memory networks. In *3rd International Conference on Learning Representations, ICLR 2015, San Diego, CA, USA, May 7-9, 2015, Conference Track Proceedings*.

Shuangzhi Wu, Ming Zhou, and Dongdong Zhang. 2017. Improved neural machine translation with source syntax. In *Proceedings of the Twenty-Sixth International Joint Conference on Artificial Intelligence, IJCAI-17*, pages 4179–4185.

Keyulu Xu, Chengtao Li, Yonglong Tian, Tomohiro Sonobe, Ken ichi Kawarabayashi, and Stefanie Jegelka. 2018. Representation learning on graphs with jumping knowledge networks. In *ICML*.

Shaowei Yao, Tianming Wang, and Xiaojun Wan. 2020. Heterogeneous graph transformer for graph-to-sequence learning. In *Proceedings of the 58th Annual Meeting of the Association for Computational Linguistics*, pages 7145–7154, Online. Association for Computational Linguistics.

Meishan Zhang, Zhenghua Li, Guohong Fu, and Min Zhang. 2019. Syntax-enhanced neural machine translation with syntax-aware word representations. In *Proceedings of the 2019 Conference of the North American Chapter of the Association for Computational Linguistics: Human Language Technologies, Volume 1 (Long and Short Papers)*, pages 1151–1161, Minneapolis, Minnesota. Association for Computational Linguistics.

Tianfu Zhang, Heyan Huang, Chong Feng, and Longbing Cao. 2021. Self-supervised bilingual syntactic alignment for neural machine translation. *Proceedings of the AAAI Conference on Artificial Intelligence*, 35(16):14454–14462.

Continuous Temporal Graph Networks for Event-Based Graph Data

Jin Guo[1]*, **Zhen Han**[2,3]*, **Zhou Su**[1], **Jiliang Li**[1], **Volker Tresp**[2,3], **Yuyi Wang**[1,4]
[1]School of Cyber and Engineering, Xi'an Jiaotong University
[2]Institute of Informatics, LMU Munich [3]Corporate Technology, Siemens AG
[4]CRRC Zhuzhou Institute Co., Ltd.
guojin0080@163.com, hanzhen02111@163.com

Abstract

There has been an increasing interest in modeling continuous-time dynamics of temporal graph data. Previous methods encode time-evolving relational information into a low-dimensional representation by specifying discrete layers of neural networks, while real-world dynamic graphs often vary continuously over time. Hence, we propose Continuous Temporal Graph Networks (CTGNs) to capture continuous dynamics of temporal graph data. We use both the link starting timestamps and link duration as evolving information to model continuous dynamics of nodes. The key idea is to use neural ordinary differential equations (ODE) to characterize the continuous dynamics of node representations over dynamic graphs. We parameterize ordinary differential equations using a novel graph neural network. The existing dynamic graph networks can be considered as a specific discretization of CTGNs. Experiment results on both transductive and inductive tasks demonstrate the effectiveness of our proposed approach over competitive baselines.

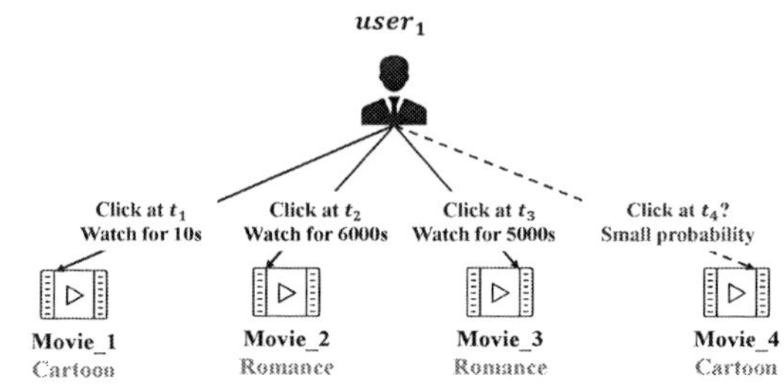

Figure 1: The importance of link duration. Consider the behavior of a user watching movies. There are two types of nodes in the graph: $user$ nodes and $item$ nodes. Given the user's historical behavior, the predicted target is ($user_1$, *don't_click*, *Movie_4*). If we ignore the link duration information, $user_1$ seems interested in cartoon movies because he clicked on it at timestamp t_1. But $user_1$ only watched the *Movie_ 1* for 10s. The link duration indicated that although the user clicked, he was not interested.

1 Introduction

Graph neural networks (GNNs) have attracted growing interest in the past few years due to their universal applicability in various fields, *e.g.*, social networks (Fan et al., 2019) and natural language processing (Liu et al., 2021a). Graph neural networks (GNNs) learn a lower-dimensional representation for a node in a vector space by aggregating the information from its neighbors using discrete hidden layers. Then the embedding can be used for downstream tasks such as node classification (Atwood and Towsley, 2015), link prediction (Zhang and Chen, 2018; Li et al., 2020), and knowledge completion (Liu et al., 2021b).

Most graph neural networks only accept static graphs as input, although real-life graphs of interactions, such as user-item interactions, often change over time. Learning the node representation on dynamic graphs is a very challenging task. Dynamic graph methods can be divided into discrete-time dynamic graph (DTDG) models and continuous-time dynamic graph (CTDG) models. More recently, an increasing interest in CTDG-based graph representation learning algorithms can be observed (Xu et al., 2020; Trivedi et al., 2018; Kumar et al., 2019; Rossi et al., 2020; Wang et al., 2020b; Ding et al., 2021).

Although the above continuous-time dynamic methods have achieved impressive results, they still have limitations. The majority of research (Rossi et al., 2020; Wang et al., 2020b; Xu et al., 2020; Trivedi et al., 2018; Kumar et al., 2019) pays attention to the contact sequence dynamic graphs, in which the links are permanent, and no link duration is provided (*e.g.*, email networks and citation networks). However, most real-life networks are event-based dynamic graphs in which the interactions between source nodes and destination nodes are not permanent (*e.g.*, employment networks and

*Equal Contribution.

Proceedings of the 2nd Workshop on Deep Learning on Graphs for Natural Language Processing (DLG4NLP 2022), pages 22 - 29
July 15, 2022 ©2022 Association for Computational Linguistics

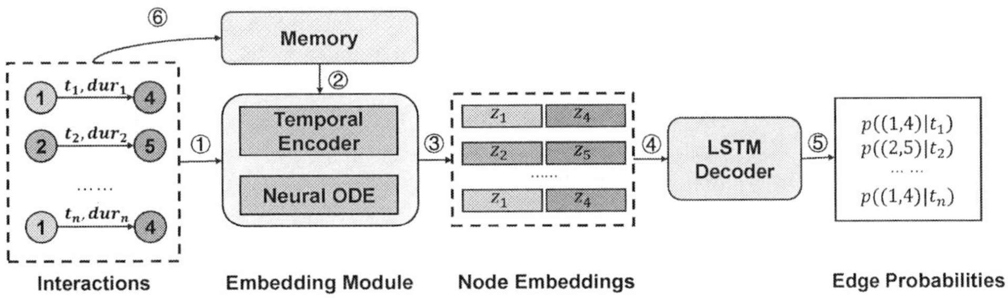

Figure 2: Overview of our Continuous Temporal Graph network.

proximity networks). The event-based dynamic graph includes the time at which the link appeared and the duration of the link. Link duration reflects the degree of association between the two nodes, *e.g.*, user i browses item j for 2 seconds and k for 20 seconds. It means that the user's interest in the two items j, k is different. Ignoring the link duration information can reduce the link prediction ability and even result in questionable inference. Thus, it is crucial to consider the influence of link duration on node relationship prediction (Zhang and Chen, 2018; Li et al., 2020) and knowledge completion (Liu et al., 2021b).

The existing GNN-based methods (Weinan, 2017; Oono and Suzuki, 2019) that learn the node representation over dynamic graphs can be considered discrete dynamical systems. Chen *et al.* (2018) demonstrate that the continuous dynamical systems are more efficient for modeling continuous-time dynamic data. The discrete networks can roughly be regarded as continuous networks by stacking enough layers. However, Onno and Suzuki (2019) point out that graph neural networks (GNNs) exponentially lose expressive power for downstream tasks, which will lead to over-smoothing problems as we add more hidden layers. Therefore, designing effective continuous Graph Neural Networks to model continuous-time dynamics of node representation on dynamic graphs is critical. To this end, many continuous graph neural networks (Chen et al., 2018; Xhonneux et al., 2019) have been proposed recently. Although those mentioned above continuous dynamic neural networks are more efficient to model the graph data, few approaches have been proposed for dealing with dynamic graphs using continuous-time dynamic neural networks.

This paper proposes a general framework of continuous temporal graph networks (CTGNs) to model continuous-time representations for dynamic graph-structured data. We combine Ordinary Differential Equation Systems (ODEs) and graphs methods. Instead of specifying discrete hidden layers, we integrate neural layers over continuous time. Figure 2 illustrates the workflow of the proposed CTGN method. There is an interaction between two nodes. First, a novel temporal graph network (TGN) is applied as the encoder to learn the latent states using the updated memory. Then, the neural ODE module is used to model the node's continuous-time representation. Considering that the link duration reflects the degree of association between the two nodes, we use the link duration as the integration variable to control the weights of different interactions. After that, we use the LSTM (Shi et al., 2015) as the decoder to compute the probability of interaction between the two given nodes. Finally, the memory is updated as the input of the encoder. Memory is a compressed representation of the historical behavior of all nodes defined in Section 3.1. Experimental results on five real-world datasets of link prediction demonstrate the effectiveness of the proposed method over the state-of-art baselines. The main contributions of this paper are:

- We present a novel Continuous Temporal Graph Network (CTGN) inspired by the neural ODE method.
- CTGNs pay attention to the event-based dynamic graph. CTGNs update the node's representation with both the valid discrete timestamps when the link appears and the link duration between two linked nodes as evolving information.
- We show that our model can outperform existing state-of-the-art methods on both transductive and inductive tasks.

2 Background

2.1 Dynamic Graph Methods

The existing dynamic graph representation learning methods can be divided into two categories, discrete-time dynamic graphs and continuous-time dynamic graphs.

Discrete-time dynamic graphs (DTDGs) are a sequence of snapshots at different time intervals.

$$DG = \{G^1, G^2, ..., G^T\}, \tag{1}$$

where T is the number of snapshots. Current dynamic graph methods (Wang et al., 2020a; Trivedi et al., 2017; Xiong et al., 2019) have been mostly designed for discrete-time dynamic graphs (DTDGs).

Continuous-time dynamic graphs (CTDGs) can be viewed as a set of observations/events (Kazemi et al., 2019), and the network evolution information is retained. There are only a few works on CTDG. But recently, more attention has been paid to continuous-time graphs. All three representations of CTDG are described in more detail below.

1. **The contact sequence dynamic graph** is the simplest representation form of CTDG.

$$CS = (u_i, v_i, t_i), \tag{2}$$

where u is the source node, v is the destination node, and t is the timestamp when the link appears. In the contact sequence dynamic graph, the link is permanent (*e.g.*, citation networks) or instantaneous (*e.g.*, email networks). Therefore, this graph has no link duration.

There has been a lot of research on contact sequence dynamic graphs. Trivedi *et al.* (2018) learn the representation of node i by aggregating the node destination's neighborhood information and updating the embedding for the node using a recurrent architecture after an interaction involving node i. Kumar *et al.* (2019) employ two recurrent neural networks to update the embedding of a user and an item at every interaction. TGAT (Xu et al., 2020) proposes a novel functional time encoding method and uses self-attention to inductive representation learning on temporal graphs. Wang *et al.* (2020b) propose the asynchronous propagation attention network (APAN) for real-time temporal graph embedding.

2. **The event-based dynamic graph** consists of the node pairs (u, v), the edge appears timestamp t and the link duration Δt . Link duration indicates how long the edge lasts until it disappears.

$$EB = (u_i, v_i, t_i, \Delta t_i). \tag{3}$$

Rossi et al. (2020) proposes a generic inductive framework operating on contact sequence dynamic graphs by adding a memory module on TGAT (Xu et al., 2020). TGN can also operate on the event-based dynamic graph by simply replacing the timestamp t with link duration Δt in the memory module.

3. **The streams graph** can be viewed as a particular case of the event-based dynamic graph. The streams graph includes the edge label δ, which indicates edge removal or edge addition.

$$GS = (u_i, v_i, t_i, \delta_i), \delta_i \in [-1, 1]. \tag{4}$$

TGN (Rossi et al., 2020) converts the streams graph into an event-based graph for processing. According to the edge label, the event can be reorganized as (u_i, v_i, t', t), which was created at time t' and deleted at time t, then two messages can be computed for the source and target nodes.

The existing CTDG methods model discrete dynamics representations of continuous-time graph data with multiple discrete propagation layers. Our proposed method focuses on the event-based temporal graph and updates the node's representation with both the timestamps and the link duration between the two nodes. CTGN also supports contact sequence dynamic graph. The model details will be slightly different from event-based dynamic graph. We will clarify this point in Chapter 3.

2.2 Continuous-time Dynamical Systems

Continuous-time dynamical systems mean that the system's behavior changes with time development in the continuous-time domain. There have been related works that view data as a continuous object in artificial intelligence, *e.g.*, pictures (Chen et al., 2018) and static graphs (Xhonneux et al., 2019; Poli et al., 2019). The continuous-time dynamic graph (CTDG) we introduced in Section 2.1 is also a continuous-time dynamical system in which nodes' state changes over time. Therefore, it is necessary to model the continuous dynamical system of CTDG data. To the best of our knowledge, our CTGN is the first approach that learn continuous-time dynamics on CTDG.

2.3 Neural Ordinary Differential Equations and Continuous Graph Neural Networks

Considering a residual network:

$$\mathbf{h}_{t+1} = \mathbf{h}_t + f(\mathbf{h}_t, \theta_t) \tag{5}$$

A theoretical method to improve the performance of discrete networks is to stack more neural layers and take smaller steps (Chen et al., 2018). However, this scheme is not feasible because of the limited computer resources and over-fitting problems. Oono and Suzuki (2019) point out that Graph Neural Networks (GNNs) exponentially lose expressive power for downstream tasks when adding more hidden layers because of over-smoothness problems.

Inspired by residual network and ordinary difference, neural ordinary difference is proposed to solve this problem. Neural ODE models continuous-time dynamical systems by parameterizing the hidden state's derivative using a neural network.

$$\frac{d_{\mathbf{z}}}{d_t} = f(\mathbf{z}, t), \mathbf{z}(0) = \mathbf{x}, \tag{6}$$

NeuralODE can be regarded as a discrete network with an infinitesimal learning rate and infinite layers. Weinanl (2017) proposes the idea of using continuous dynamical systems to model hidden layers. Chen *et al.* (2018) introduce neural ODE, a continuous-depth model by parameterization the derivative of the hidden state using a neural network. Neural ODE only focuses on unstructured data. Xhonneux *et al.* (2019) apply continuous dynamical methods to static graph-structured data. They propose Continuous Graph Neural Networks (CGNNs), which solve the over-smoothing caused by stacking more layers and improve the performance of GNNs. Zang and Wang (2019) learn continuous-time dynamics on complex networks. However, continuous graph neural networks (CGNN) can only deal with static data.

3 The Proposed Method: CTGN

In this section, we introduce our proposed approach. The key idea of the CTGN is to build continuous-time hidden layers which can learn continuous informative node representations over event-based dynamic graphs. To characterize the continuous dynamics of node representation, we use ordinary differential equations (ODEs) parameterized by a neural network, which is a continuous function of time. We study both transductive and inductive settings. In the transductive task, we predict future links of the nodes observed during the training phase. In the inductive tasks, we predict future links of the nodes never seen before. We first employ a temporal graph attention layer (Xu et al., 2020) to project each node into a latent space based on its features and neighbors. And then, an ODE module is designed to define the continuous dynamics on the node's latent representation $\mathbf{h}_i(t)$.

3.1 Temporal Graph Network

Memory Passing. Memory $\mathbf{s}_i(t)$ is used to record the historical information of each node i the model has seen so far. It is a compressed representation of the historical behavior of all nodes. Memory $\mathbf{s}_i(t)$ is updated when there is an interaction involving node i. At the end of each batch, we firstly compute memory $\mathbf{s}_i(t)$ using the last time message $\mathbf{m}_i(t^-)$ and memory $\mathbf{s}_i(t^-)$:

$$\mathbf{s}_i(t) = mem(\mathbf{m}_i(t), \mathbf{s}_i(t^-)). \tag{7}$$

Here, $mem(\cdot)$ is a learnable memory update function. In all experiments, we choose the memory function as GRU. $\mathbf{s}_i(0)$ is initialized as a zero vector. At the end of each batch, the message $\mathbf{m}_i(t)$ for the node can be updated to compute i's memory:

$$\begin{aligned}\mathbf{m}_i(t) &= msg_s(\mathbf{s}_i(t^-)||\mathbf{s}_j(t^-)||\Delta t||\mathbf{e}_{ij}(t)),\\ \mathbf{m}_j(t) &= msg_s(\mathbf{s}_j(t^-)||\mathbf{s}_i(t^-)||\Delta t||\mathbf{e}_{ij}(t)).\end{aligned} \tag{8}$$

Here $||$ is the concatenation operator, Δt is the link duration between node i and j, . In the contact sequence dynamic graph, the link duration property is not available. We use $(t - t^-)$ as Δt. There may be multiple events $\mathbf{e}_{i1}(t_1), \ldots, \mathbf{e}_{iN}(t_N)$ involving the same node i in the same batch. In the experiment, we only use the latest interaction $\mathbf{e}_{iN}(t_N)$ to compute i's message. $msg(\cdot)$ is a learnable function, and we use an RNN network in our experiment:

Multi-head Attention. Given an observed event $p = (i, j, t, \Delta t)$, we can compute the node latent representation respectively for i and j using:

$$\mathbf{H}^{(l)}(t) = Attn^{(l)}(\mathbf{Q}^{(l)}(t), \mathbf{K}^{(l)}(t), \mathbf{V}^{(l)}(t)), \tag{9}$$

	Event-based dynamic graph			Contact sequence dynamic graph	
	NetFlix	Mooc	Lastfm	Wikipedia	Reddit
Nodes	18672	13374	7353	9227	10984
Edges	163417	131660	73358	157474	672447
Chronological Split	70%-15%-15%	70%-15%-15%	70%-15%-15%	70%-15%-15%	70%-15%-15%
Unseen nodes	10%	10%	10%	10%	10%
Timespan	2 years	2 years	2 years	30 days	30 days

Table 1: Statistics of the datasets used in our experiments.

$$Attn(\mathbf{Q}, \mathbf{K}, \mathbf{V}) = softmax(\frac{\mathbf{Q}\mathbf{K}^T}{\sqrt{d_k}})\mathbf{V}\,, \quad (10)$$

where $\mathbf{Q}$, $\mathbf{K}$, $\mathbf{V}$ denote the 'querys', 'keys', 'values', respectively. $\mathbf{H}^{(l)} = [\mathbf{h}_1^{(l)}, ..., \mathbf{h}_i^{(l)}]$ are the embedding of the graph nodes of l-th layers. The multi-head attention layer compute the node i's representation by aggregating it's N-hop neighbors.

$$\mathbf{Q}^{(l)}(t) = (\mathbf{H}^{(l-1)}(t) \mid\mid \phi(0))\mathbf{W}_Q\,, \quad (11)$$

$$\mathbf{K}^{(l)}(t) = \mathbf{C}^{(l)}(t)\mathbf{W}_K\,, \quad (12)$$

$$\mathbf{V}^{(l)}(t) = \mathbf{C}^{(l)}(t)\mathbf{W}_V\,, \quad (13)$$

$$\begin{aligned}\mathbf{C}^{(l)}(t) = [&\mathbf{H}_1^{(l-1)}(t) \mid\mid \mathbf{E}_1(t_1) \mid\mid \phi(t-t_1), \\ &\ldots, \mathbf{H}_N^{(l-1)}(t) \mid\mid \mathbf{E}_N(t_N) \mid\mid \phi(t-t_N)]\,.\end{aligned} \quad (14)$$

Here $\phi(\cdot)$ represents a generic time encoder (Xu et al., 2020). $\mathbf{W}_Q, \mathbf{W}_K, \mathbf{W}_V \in \mathbb{R}^{d_k \times d_k}$ are the projection matrices used to generate attention embedding. We define keys and values as the neighbor information. $\mathbf{h}_i^{(0)}(t) = \mathbf{s}_i(t) + \mathbf{v}_i$, $\mathbf{s}_i(t)$ is node i's memory which saves the history information for the node. $\mathbf{E}_n(t) = [e_{1n}(t), ..., e_{in}(t)]$, $e_{in}(t)$ is edge features between node i and it's n-hop neighbor at time t. Temporal graph network is a discrete method that can be thought of as a discretization of the continuous dynamical systems.

3.2 Model Continuous Dynamics of Node Representation

In order to characterize the continuous dynamics of node representations, instead of only specifying a discrete sequence of hidden layers, we parameterize the hidden layers using ordinary differential equations (ODEs), a continuous function of time.

$$\frac{d_{\mathbf{z}}}{d_t} = f(\mathbf{z}, t), \mathbf{z}(0) = \mathbf{x}. \quad (15)$$

Here, $\mathbf{x}$ is an initial vector, f is a learnable function, t is a time interval and $\mathbf{z}$ is a vector.

$$\mathbf{z}(t) = \mathbf{z}(0) + \int_0^t (f(t, z))d\tau. \quad (16)$$

We can compute the node's continuous-time dynamics representation by Equation 16 at arbitrary time t > 0.

Previous work (Zang and Wang, 2019; Poli et al., 2019) model continuous-time dynamics for data by setting integration variable $[0, t]$ as a hyper-parameter. Considering the influence of link duration on the interaction between two nodes, we choose the link duration as the integration variable, in our experiment $t = dur$.

Link duration shows how long it was (in seconds) until that user terminated browsing. Link duration can reflect the user's interest in different items. Take link duration as an integer variable that can control the weights of different interactions.

We parameterize the derivative of the hidden state using a neural network that takes the latent state, computed by the temporal graph network mentioned in Section 3.1 as input.

$$\mathbf{z}_i(t) = ODESolver(f(t, z), \mathbf{h}_i(t), \Delta t_i). \quad (17)$$

Here, $\mathbf{h}_i(t)$ is a discrete latent state computed by temporal graph networks, Δt_i is the link duration between source node i and destination j. $f(t, z)$ is ODE function, we choose $f(t, z)$ as MLP. A black-box ODE solver computes the final node continuous dynamics embedding $\mathbf{z}_i(t)$. We utilize the *torchdiffeq.odeint_adjoint* PyTorch package to solve reverse-time ODE and backpropagate.

3.3 Time Smoothness

The time-encoding method (Xu et al., 2020) used in this paper is an effective method to map timestamp t from the time domain to d-dim vector space.

	NetFlix		Mooc		Lastfm	
	Transductive	Inductive	Transductive	Inductive	Transductive	Inductive
GAT*	96.45 ± 0.2	92.09 ± 0.6	83.33 ± 10	77.39 ± 10	76.77 ± 0.5	62.81 ± 0.6
GraphSAGE*	95.14 ± 0.6	89.84 ± 1.7	82.01 ± 2.4	78.36 ± 2.2	77.41 ± 0.6	62.57 ± 0.3
CGNN*	91.82 ± 0.2	†	96.88 ± 0.2	†	74.93 ± 10	†
NDCN*	90.70 ± 0.9	†	96.07 ± 0.1	†	82.09 ± 1.4	†
DyRep	99.07 ± 0.1	97.36 ± 0.1	83.52 ± 6.5	68.96 ± 4.0	82.96 ± 0.3	68.06 ± 0.3
Jodie	99.20 ± 0.1	97.43 ± 0.1	93.12 ± 0.6	80.85 ± 1.2	84.41 ± 0.3	68.14 ± 0.5
TGAT	96.56 ± 0.2	93.04 ± 0.2	73.69 ± 1.3	68.76 ± 1.2	78.80 ± 0.8	64.19 ± 0.7
TGN	99.05 ± 0.2	97.38 ± 0.4	97.76 ± 0.4	93.86 ± 0.9	87.05 ± 0.1	72.89 ± 0.1
APAN	98.23 ±1.7	†	93.64 ± 1.3	†	82.65 ± 0.1	†
CTGN	**99.27 ± 0.1**	**97.84 ± 0.2**	**97.97 ± 0.4**	**94.89 ± 0.4**	**87.20 ± 0.1**	**74.05 ± 0.1**

Table 2: Experiments on event-based datasets. Average Precision (%) for future edge prediction task in transductive and inductive settings. **First** best performing method. *Static graph method. †Does not support inductive.

	node classification		link prediction-tranductive		link prediction-inductive	
	Wikipedia	Reddit	Wikipedia	Reddit	Wikipedia	Reddit
GAE*	74.85 ± 0.6	58.39 ± 0.5	91.44 ± 0.1	93.23 ± 0.3	†	†
VGAE*	73.67 ± 0.8	57.98 ± 0.6	91.34 ± 0.3	92.92 ± 0.2	†	†
GAT*	82.34 ± 0.8	64.52 ± 0.5	94.73 ± 0.2	97.33 ± 0.2	91.27 ± 0.4	95.37 ± 0.3
GraphSAGE*	82.42 ± 0.7	61.24 ± 0:6	93.56 ± 0.3	97.65 ± 0.2	91.09 ± 0.3	96.27 ± 0.2
DyRep	84.59 ± 2.2	62.91 ± 2.4	94.59 ± 0.2	97.98 ± 0.1	92.05 ± 0.3	95.68 ± 0.2
Jodie	84.84 ± 1.2	61.83 ± 2.7	94.62 ± 0.5	97.11 ± 0.3	93.11 ± 0.4	94.36 ± 1.1
TGAT	83.69 ± 0.7	65.56 ± 0.7	95.34 ± 0.1	98.12 ± 0.2	93.99 ± 0.3	96.62 ± 0.3
TGN	87.81 ± 0.3	67.06 ± 0.9	98.46 ± 0.1	98.70 ± 0.1	97.81 ± 0.1	97.55 ± 0.1
APAN	**89.86 ± 0.3**	65.34 ± 0.4	98.12 ± 0.2	**99.22 ± 0.2**	†	†
CTGN	88.01 ± 1.5	**68.38 ± 3.4**	**98.64 ± 0.1**	98.28 ± 0.2	**98.01 ± 0.1**	**98.05 ± 0.2**

Table 3: Experiments on contact sequence datasets. ROC AUC (%) for the dynamic node classification task, Average Precision (%) for link prediction task. *Static method, †Does not support inductive.

However, the learning process of each timestamp is independent of other timestamps. Independent learning of hyperplanes of adjacent time intervals may cause adjacent times to be farther apart in embedded space. Actually, adjacent states in the graph should be more similar. To avoid the problem mentioned above, we constrained the variation between hyperplanes at adjacent timestamps by minimizing the euclidean distance:

$$L_{smooth}(W) = \sum_{t=1}^{T-1} ||w_{t+1} - w_t||_2 . \quad (18)$$

3.4 Model Learning

We use the link prediction loss function for training CTGN:

$$loss = \alpha L_{smooth}(W) + L_{task} , \quad (19)$$

where α is a tradeoff parameter, l_{task} is a loss function defined as the cross-entropy of the prediction and the ground truth. Our experiment found a parameter α of 0.002 for contact sequence dynamic graphs and 0.7 for event-based dynamic graphs.

4 Experiment and Analysis

In this section, we first introduce datasets, baselines and parameter settings. Then we compare our proposed method with other strong baselines and competing approaches for both the inductive and transductive tasks for two benchmarks contact sequence dynamic graph datasets and three event-based dynamic graph datasets.

We study both transductive and inductive tasks. For event-based dynamic graphs, we learn link prediction tasks. For contact-sequence dynamic graphs, we learn dynamic node classification and link prediction tasks.

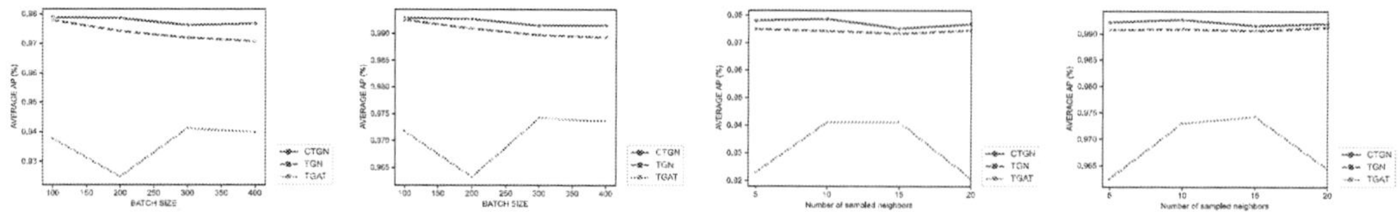

(a) (b) (c) (d)

Figure 3: Ablation studies on the Netflix dataset for both the transductive and inductive setting of the link prediction task. 3(a) Sensitivity study result of batch size in inductive setting. 3(b) Sensitivity study result of batch size in transductive setting. 3(c) The relationship between number of sampled neighbors and the model performance in inductive setting. 3(d) The relationship between number of sampled neighbors and the model performance in transductive setting.

4.1 Datasets

We use five real-world datasets in our experiments, three event-based dynamic graphs: Netflix [1], Mooc (Feng et al., 2019) and Lastfm (Cantador et al., 2011), two contact sequence dynamic graphs: Wikipedia (Kumar et al., 2019), Reddit (Kumar et al., 2019).

The statistics of the datasets used in our experiments are described in detail in Table 1.

4.2 Baseline

We compare our model with four CTDG methods: Jodie (Kumar et al., 2019), Dyrep (Trivedi et al., 2018), TGAT (Xu et al., 2020), TGN (Rossi et al., 2020), APAN (Wang et al., 2020b). And we also include four DTDG methods: GAE (Kipf and Welling, 2016), VGAE (Kipf and Welling, 2016), GAT (Veličković et al., 2018), GraphSAGE (Hamilton et al., 2017) as well as two state-of-the-art static graph neural ODE methods: CGNN (Xhonneux et al., 2019), NDCN (Zang and Wang, 2019).

4.3 Parameter Setup

We set the batch size to 200 for training and patience to 5 for early stopping in all experiments. The node embedding dimension is 172. During training, we used 0.0001 as the learning rate for contact sequence dynamic graph datasets (Wikipedia and Reddit) and 0.00009 for event-based dynamic graph datasets (Netflix, Mooc, Lastfm). The weight of time smoothness loss α is set to 0.002 on Wikipedia , Reddit and 0.7 on Netflix, Mooc, Lastfm. We choose the LSTM layer as the decoder for link prediction task and MLP for node classification task. We report mean and standard deviation across 10 runs.

[1] https://vodclickstream.com/

4.4 Result

To demonstrate the effectiveness of our proposed method, we compare CTGN with competitive baselines on five real-world event-based graph datasets. Table 2 shows the results on link prediction tasks in both transductive and inductive settings for three event-based datasets. It is evident that our approach has achieved better results than the discrete dynamics graph neural networks on almost all datasets, especially in the inductive setting.

Table 3 shows the dynamic node classification and link prediction results on two contact sequence-datasets. CTGN has a solid ability to embed dynamic graphs. The conclusion can be obtained from the Table 2 and Table 3.

Figure 3 shows ablation studies on the Netflix dataset for both the transductive and inductive setting of the link prediction task. As we can see from Figure 3(a) and 3(b), our model is not sensitive to batch size. When the training batch size is 100, CTGN has the same average precision as TGN. With the continuous increase of batch size, the performance of CTGN is more stable.

5 Conclusion

This paper introduces CTGN, a continuous temporal graph neural network for learning representation for event-based dynamic graphs. We build the connection between temporal graph networks and continuous dynamical systems inspired by neural ODE. Our framework allows the user to trade off speed for precision by selecting different learning rates and the weight of time smoothness loss parameters during training. We demonstrate on the link prediction task against competitive baselines that our model can outperform many existing state-of-the-art methods.

References

James Atwood and Don Towsley. 2015. Search-convolutional neural networks. *CoRR*, abs/1511.02136.

Iván Cantador, Peter Brusilovsky, and Tsvi Kuflik. 2011. 2nd workshop on information heterogeneity and fusion in recommender systems (hetrec 2011). In *Proceedings of the 5th ACM conference on Recommender systems*, RecSys 2011, New York, NY, USA. ACM.

Tian Qi Chen, Yulia Rubanova, Jesse Bettencourt, and David Duvenaud. 2018. Neural ordinary differential equations. *CoRR*, abs/1806.07366.

Zifeng Ding, Zhen Han, Yunpu Ma, and Volker Tresp. 2021. Temporal knowledge graph forecasting with neural ODE. *CoRR*, abs/2101.05151.

Wenqi Fan, Yao Ma, Qing Li, Yuan He, Yihong Eric Zhao, Jiliang Tang, and Dawei Yin. 2019. Graph neural networks for social recommendation. *CoRR*, abs/1902.07243.

W. Feng, J. Tang, and T. X. Liu. 2019. Understanding dropouts in moocs. *Proceedings of the AAAI Conference on Artificial Intelligence*, 33:517–524.

William L. Hamilton, Rex Ying, and Jure Leskovec. 2017. Inductive representation learning on large graphs. *CoRR*, abs/1706.02216.

S. M. Kazemi, R. Goel, K. Jain, I. Kobyzev, A. Sethi, P. Forsyth, and P. Poupart. 2019. Representation learning for dynamic graphs: A survey.

Thomas N. Kipf and Max Welling. 2016. Variational graph auto-encoders.

Srijan Kumar, Xikun Zhang, and Jure Leskovec. 2019. Predicting dynamic embedding trajectory in temporal interaction networks. *Proceedings of the 25th ACM SIGKDD International Conference on Knowledge Discovery Data Mining*.

X Li, Y. Shang, Y. Cao, Y. Li, and Y. Liu. 2020. Type-aware anchor link prediction across heterogeneous networks based on graph attention network. *Proceedings of the AAAI Conference on Artificial Intelligence*, 34(1):147–155.

Shangqing Liu, Yu Chen, Xiaofei Xie, Jing Kai Siow, and Yang Liu. 2021a. Retrieval-augmented generation for code summarization via hybrid GNN. In *International Conference on Learning Representations*.

Xiyang Liu, Huobin Tan, Qinghong Chen, and Guangyan Lin. 2021b. Ragat: Relation aware graph attention network for knowledge graph completion. *IEEE Access*, 9:20840–20849.

Kenta Oono and Taiji Suzuki. 2019. Graph neural networks exponentially lose expressive power for node classification.

Michael Poli, Stefano Massaroli, Junyoung Park, Atsushi Yamashita, Hajime Asama, and Jinkyoo Park. 2019. Graph neural ordinary differential equations. *CoRR*, abs/1911.07532.

E. Rossi, B. Chamberlain, F. Frasca, D. Eynard, F. Monti, and M. Bronstein. 2020. Temporal graph networks for deep learning on dynamic graphs.

Xingjian Shi, Zhourong Chen, Hao Wang, Dit-Yan Yeung, Wai-Kin Wong, and Wang-chun Woo. 2015. Convolutional LSTM network: A machine learning approach for precipitation nowcasting. *CoRR*, abs/1506.04214.

R. Trivedi, M. Farajtabar, Y. Wang, H. Dai, and S. Le. 2017. Know-evolve: Deep reasoning in temporal knowledge graphs.

Rakshit Trivedi, Mehrdad Farajtabar, Prasenjeet Biswal, and Hongyuan Zha. 2018. Representation learning over dynamic graphs. *CoRR*, abs/1803.04051.

Petar Veličković, Guillem Cucurull, Arantxa Casanova, Adriana Romero, Pietro Liò, and Yoshua Bengio. 2018. Graph attention networks.

J. Wang, Y. Jin, G. Song, and X. Ma. 2020a. Epne: Evolutionary pattern preserving network embedding.

X. Wang, D. Lyu, M. Li, Y. Xia, Q. Yang, X. Wang, X. Wang, P. Cui, Y. Yang, and B. Sun. 2020b. Apan: Asynchronous propagation attention network for real-time temporal graph embedding.

Weinan. 2017. A proposal on machine learning via dynamical systems. *Communications in Mathematics amp; Statistics*, 5(1):1–11.

Lpac Xhonneux, M. Qu, and J Tang. 2019. Continuous graph neural networks.

Y. Xiong, Y. Zhang, H. Fu, W. Wang, and P. S. Yu. 2019. *DynGraphGAN: Dynamic Graph Embedding via Generative Adversarial Networks.* Grundlagen des MA-Geschäftes.

D. Xu, C. Ruan, E. Korpeoglu, S. Kumar, and K. Achan. 2020. Inductive representation learning on temporal graphs.

Chengxi Zang and Fei Wang. 2019. Neural dynamics on complex networks. *CoRR*, abs/1908.06491.

Muhan Zhang and Yixin Chen. 2018. Link prediction based on graph neural networks. *CoRR*, abs/1802.09691.

Scene Graph Parsing via Abstract Meaning Representation in Pre-trained Language Models

Woo Suk Choi[1], Yu-Jung Heo[1,3], Dharani Punitan[1], and Byoung-Tak Zhang[1,2]
[1] Seoul National University [2] AI Institute (AIIS), Seoul National University [3] Surromind
{wschoi, yjheo}@bi.snu.ac.kr, punithan.dharani@gmail.com, btzhang@bi.snu.ac.kr

Abstract

In this work, we propose the application of abstract meaning representation (AMR) based semantic parsing models to parse textual descriptions of a visual scene into scene graphs, which is the first work to the best of our knowledge. Previous works examined scene graph parsing from textual descriptions using dependency parsing and left the AMR parsing approach as future work since sophisticated methods are required to apply AMR. Hence, we use pre-trained AMR parsing models to parse the region descriptions of visual scenes (i.e. images) into AMR graphs and pre-trained language models (PLM), BART and T5, to parse AMR graphs into scene graphs. The experimental results show that our approach explicitly captures high-level semantics from textual descriptions of visual scenes, such as objects, attributes of objects, and relationships between objects. Our textual scene graph parsing approach outperforms the previous state-of-the-art results by 9.3% in the SPICE metric score.

1 Introduction

Understanding and representing a scene is straightforward for humans, but an AI system requires various techniques to implement it. One such technique is scene graph proposed by (Johnson et al., 2015). Scene graph is a graph-structured representation that captures high-level semantics of visual scenes (i.e. images) by explicitly modeling objects along with their attributes and relationships with other objects. Scene graph is demonstrated effective in various tasks including semantic image retrieval (Wang et al., 2020; Schroeder and Tripathi, 2020), image captioning (Yang et al., 2019; Zhong et al., 2020), and visual question answering (Hildebrandt et al., 2020; Damodaran et al., 2021).

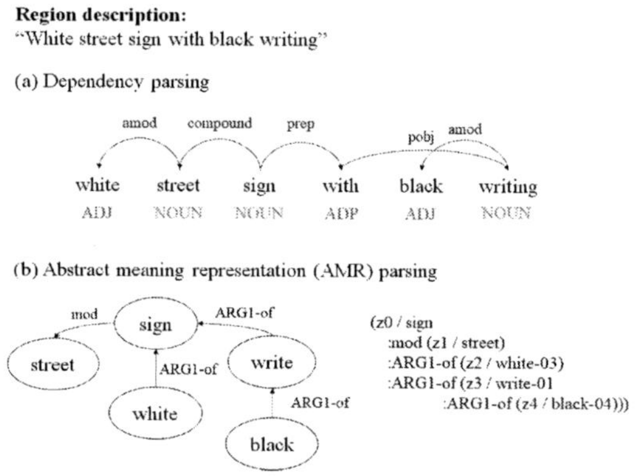

Figure 1: An example of (a) dependency parsing and (b) abstract meaning representation (AMR) parsing from textual description (i.e. region description) of "White street sign with black writing".

Approaches for scene graph generation are classified into two categories: 1) scene graph generation based on image as input and 2) scene graph generation based on text (i.e. image caption) as input. Various approaches (Xu et al., 2017; Zellers et al., 2018; Gu et al., 2019; Zhong et al., 2021) are proposed for the former category. On the other hand, only a fewer approaches (Schuster et al., 2015; Anderson et al., 2016; Wang et al., 2018; Andrews et al., 2019) are proposed for the latter. In this paper, we focus on the latter category, which is also called textual scene graph parsing. Textual scene graph parsing has the advantage of being able to capture the high-level meaning of the image scene from the text.

Most of previous works (Schuster et al., 2015; Anderson et al., 2016; Wang et al., 2018) for scene graph parsing generated scene graphs using dependency parsing to acquire the dependency relationships for all words in a text, as shown in Figure 1 (a). Apart from dependency parsing, there is also another approach for parsing semantic graphs from textual descriptions, which is called abstract mean-

Proceedings of the 2nd Workshop on Deep Learning on Graphs for Natural Language Processing (DLG4NLP 2022), pages 30 - 35
July 15, 2022 ©2022 Association for Computational Linguistics

ing representation (AMR) proposed by (Banarescu et al., 2013). AMR abstracts semantic concepts from words, and we therefore consider AMR is more suitable for scene graph parsing. However, the use of dependency parsing appeared to be a common theme in the literature rather than AMR, hence scene graph parsing with AMR has been left as future work in (Anderson et al., 2016; Wang et al., 2018).

To this end, we investigate the use of AMR with pre-trained language models (PLM), such as BART (Lewis et al., 2020) and T5 (Raffel et al., 2020), for parsing scene graphs from textual descriptions of visual scenes. We first parse sentences to AMR graphs using a pre-trained AMR parsing model, and then we generate scene graphs from AMR graphs using the PLM.

Our contributions are the following: i) To the best of our knowledge, ours is the first work for parsing scene graphs from texts using abstract meaning representation (AMR) contrary to the previous works (Schuster et al., 2015; Anderson et al., 2016; Wang et al., 2018). ii) We extend pre-trained language models such as BART and T5 to generate scene graphs from texts and AMR graphs. iii) Our approach outperforms the previous state-of-the-art result by 9.3% on SPICE metric for scene graph parsing task on intersection of Visual Genome and MS COCO datasets.

2 Related Works

2.1 Abstract Meaning Representation

Abstract meaning representation (AMR) (Banarescu et al., 2013) is a graph-based semantic representation which captures semantics "*who is doing what to whom*" in a sentence. Each sentence is represented as a rooted, directed, acyclic graph with labels on nodes (e.g. semantic concepts) and edges (e.g. semantic relations). Representative tasks for AMR are *Text-to-AMR*, capturing the meaning of a sentence within a semantic graph, and *AMR-to-Text*, generating text from such a graph. AMR2.0 (LDC2017T10) and AMR3.0 (LDC2020T02) datasets are currently actively used, which contain a semantic treebank of over $39,260$ and $59,255$ English natural language sentences, respectively from broadcast conversations, newswire, weblogs and web discussion forums.

To address these tasks, earlier studies used statistical methods. With the development of deep learning, researchers have proposed neural models such as graph-to-sequence (Zhu et al., 2019), sequence-to-graph (Cai and Lam, 2020), and neural transition-based parser models (Zhou et al., 2021). Recently, with the advent of pre-trained language models (PLM), AMR-based models incorporating the generation capability of PLM have been proposed and shown interesting results for various NLP tasks such as information extraction (Huang et al., 2018; Zhang and Ji, 2021), text summarization (Liu et al., 2015; Dohare and Karnick, 2017), and dialogue systems (Bonial et al., 2020).

(Lam et al., 2021) proposed an efficient heuristic algorithm to approximate the optimal solution by formalizing ensemble graph prediction as mining the largest graph that is the most supported by a collection of graph predictions. (Bevilacqua et al., 2021) proposed symmetric parsing and generation (SPRING), which casts AMR tasks as a symmetric transduction task by devising graph linearization and extending the pre-trained encoder-decoder model, BART. In this paper, we utilize pre-trained AMR parsing (i.e. Text-to-AMR) models from (Bevilacqua et al., 2021) to parse AMR graph from sentences since the SPRING model has the best performance among the publicly available pre-trained AMR parsing models[1].

2.2 Scene Graph Parsing

Scene graph proposed by (Johnson et al., 2015) is a graph-structured representation that represents rich structured semantics of visual scenes (i.e. images). Nodes in the scene graph represent either an object, an attribute for an object, or a relationship between objects. Edges depict the connection between two nodes. In this subsection, we introduce the study of scene graph parsing based on text. Most of the previous studies (Schuster et al., 2015; Anderson et al., 2016; Wang et al., 2018) used dependency parsing as a common theme. (Schuster et al., 2015) proposed a rule-based and a learned classifier with dependency parsing. (Wang et al., 2018) proposed a customized dependency parser with end-to-end training to parse scene graph. (Andrews et al., 2019) proposed a customized attention graph mechanism using the OpenAI Transformer[2] (Radford and Narasimhan, 2018). Unlike these studies, we use the AMR approach to parse scene graphs and demonstrate better quantitative

[1] https://github.com/SapienzaNLP/spring

[2] This model consists of a BPE (Byte-Pair-Encoding) subword embedding layer followed by 12-layers of decoder-only transformer with masked self-attention heads.

performance.

2.3 Pre-trained Language Model

BART (Lewis et al., 2020) is a denoising autoencoder for pretraining sequence-to-sequence (seq2seq) models. It uses the standard Transformer (Vaswani et al., 2017)-based neural machine translation (NMT) architecture. It is constructed based on seq2seq/NMT architecture by combining a bidirectional encoder (Devlin et al., 2019) and a left-to-right decoder (Radford et al., 2019). BART is trained by corrupting text with an arbitrary noising function (i.e. token masking, infilling, deletion, and sentence permutation) and learning a model to reconstruct the original text. We use both BART-base (BART model with 6 encoder and decoder layers and around 140M parameters) and BART-large (BART model with 12 encoder and decoder layers and nearly 400M parameters) models for our investigation.

T5 (Raffel et al., 2020) is an encoder-decoder unified framework that is pre-trained on a multi-task mixture of unsupervised and supervised tasks and for which a wide range of NLP tasks such as translation, classification, and question answering are cast as feeding the model text as input and training it to generate some target text. We use both T5-base (T5 model with 12 encoder and decoder layers and nearly 220M parameters) and T5-large (T5 model with 24 encoder and decoder layers and nearly 770M parameters) models for our examination.

3 Methodology

In this section, we use pre-trained language models (PLM), BART (Lewis et al., 2020) and T5 (Raffel et al., 2020), as baselines to parse scene graph (SG) from text directly (Text-to-SG). We then describe how to generate scene graphs from AMR graphs (AMR-to-SG) using PLM models.

3.1 Text-to-SG Parsing

We train the pre-trained language models to take each region description of an image as input and generate scene graphs. The PLM models take text as input and map it into a task-specific output sequence. For instance, if the region description *"White street sign with black writing"* is an input, the parsed output, {*(street sign, writing), (white-street sign, black-writing), (street sign-with-writing)*} will be in the form of *{(objects), (attribute-object), (object-relationship-object)}*.

3.2 AMR-to-SG Parsing

First, we parse the region descriptions into AMR graphs. Then, we parse the AMR graphs into the scene graphs. For this, we use the two AMR parsing models of SPRING (Bevilacqua et al., 2021), which are pre-trained on AMR2.0 (LDC2017T10) and AMR3.0 (LDC2020T02) datasets.

We linearize the AMR graph into a sequence of symbols which will be the input to pre-trained language models, BART and T5, for training. For the linearization technique, we adopt the depth-first search (DFS) based algorithm used in (Konstas et al., 2017), as it is closely related to the way how natural language syntactic trees are linearized (Bevilacqua et al., 2021). Thus, as shown in Figure 1 (b), the input of BART and T5 will be *"(z0 / sign :mod (z1 / street) :ARG1-of (z2 / white-03) :ARG1-of (z3 / write-01 :ARG1-of (z4 / black-04)))"*, where *zo, z1, z2, z3* and *z4* are special tokens to handle co-referring nodes, and the output will be in the same format as Text-to-SG parsing output.

4 Experiments

4.1 Implementation Details

Datasets For fair comparisons with the existing models, we train and validate our models with the subsets of Visual Genome (VG) (Krishna et al., 2016) and MS COCO (Lin et al., 2014) datasets. The training set is the intersection of the VG and MS COCO train2014 set (34,027 images with 1,070,145 regions). The evaluation set is the intersection of VG and MS COCO val2014 set (17,471 images with 547,795 regions). We follow the same preprocessing steps as in (Wang et al., 2018) for setting the training/test splits.

Evaluation To evaluate parsed scene graphs from region descriptions with the ground truth region scene graphs, we use SPICE metric (Anderson et al., 2016) which calculates a F-score over tuples. As mentioned in (Wang et al., 2018), there is an issue that a node in one graph could be matched to several nodes in the other when SPICE calculates the F-score. Thus, following previous works, we enforce one-to-one matching while calculating the F-score and report the average F-score for all regions.

Scene graph parser		F-score
Text-to-SG		
Stanford (Schuster et al., 2015)		0.3549
SPICE (Anderson et al., 2016)		0.4469
CDP (Wang et al., 2018)		0.4967
AG (Andrews et al., 2019)		0.5221
BART-base		0.5071
BART-large		0.5073
T5-base		0.5093
T5-large		0.5101
AMR-to-SG		
BART-base	AMR2.0	0.6112
	AMR3.0	0.6096
BART-large	AMR2.0	0.6062
	AMR3.0	0.6092
T5-base	AMR2.0	0.6128
	AMR3.0	0.6114
T5-large	AMR2.0	**0.6151**
	AMR3.0	0.6149

Table 1: F-score (i.e. SPICE metric) comparison between pre-trained language models (for Text-to-SG and AMR-to-SG) and existing parsers on the intersection of VG (Krishna et al., 2016) and MS COCO (Lin et al., 2014) validation set. CDP and AG are abbreviations of Customized Dependency Parser and Attention Graph, respectively.

Experimental Settings In our experiments, We set the number of epoch to 5, the batch size to 32, and learning rate to 0.0005 with a weight decay of 0.004. It takes about a day to train BART-base, BART-large, and T5-base models and around four days to train T5-large model using two Tesla V100 with 32 GB graphic memory.

4.2 Results and Analysis

Table 1 shows results of the F-score comparison between pre-trained language models (PLM) with both Text-to-SG and AMR-to-SG and existing parsers on the intersection of VG and MS COCO validation set.

Text-to-SG We observe that the performance of PLM models is relatively higher than dependency parsing based models (i.e. Stanford, SPICE and Customized Dependency Parser) and shows comparable results with the previous state-of-the-art model, Attention Graph (AG), which used customized attention graph with pre-trained transformer model. Furthermore, we find that the larger the model size, the better the performance. We expect to improve the performance of PLM models with hyperparameter tuning, which we perform as our future work.

AMR-to-SG All parsing models using AMR (AMR-to-SG) not only outperform the previous state-of-the-art model, Attention Graph (AG), but also show better performance than Text-to-SG PLM-based models. All of AMR-to-SG models for AMR 2.0 achieves an average of 8.92% performance improvement, and 8.91% for AMR 3.0. In particular, our best model (T5-large for AMR 2.0) outperforms the previous state-of-the-art model by 9.3%. Interestingly, despite the same PLM model, when comparing the case where AMR graph is input instead of text, BART shows an average of 10.32% performance improvement for AMR 2.0 and 10.22% for AMR 3.0, respectively. T5 shows an average of 10.43% performance improvement for AMR 2.0 and 12.87% for AMR 3.0, respectively. In consequence, we find that the AMR based approach captures high-level abstract semantics of text better than dependency parsers and the other baseline models.

5 Conclusion

In this work, we investigate the application of abstract meaning representation (AMR) for parsing scene graph by using pre-trained language models (PLM), BART and T5, with AMR parsing model of SPRING. We conducted two sets of experiments: 1) scene graph parsing using PLM models, directly from region descriptions, and 2) scene graph parsing using PLM models from AMR graphs parsed from region descriptions via AMR parsing pre-trained models. Our results show AMR graphs capture high-level abstract semantics of region descriptions. We evaluate our approach using the SPICE metric score. The results of Text-to AMR are comparable and of AMR-to-Text outperform the existing state-of-the-art models by 9.3%.

In our future work, we will investigate an adapter-based method (Ribeiro et al., 2021) to encode graph structures into PLM models to improve the performance of textual scene graph parsing. Furthermore, we will examine our approach based on the lately published, pre-trained AMR parsing model, AMRBART[3] (Bai et al., 2022). As our scene graph parser performance improves further, we expect to be able to use it to automatically generate either an image scene graph or video scene graph datasets with less biased and more diverse labels.

[3]https://github.com/muyeby/AMRBART

Acknowledgements

This work was partly supported by the Institute of Information Communications Technology Planning Evaluation (2015-0-00310-SW.StarLab/20%, 2019-0-01371-BabyMind/20%, 2021-0-02068-AIHub/10%, 2021-0-01343-GSAI/10%, 2022-0-00951-LBA/20%, 2022-0-00166-PICA/20%) grant funded by the Korean government.

References

Peter Anderson, Basura Fernando, Mark Johnson, and Stephen Gould. 2016. Spice: Semantic propositional image caption evaluation. In *Computer Vision – ECCV 2016*, pages 382–398, Cham. Springer International Publishing.

Martin Andrews, Yew Ken Chia, and Sam Witteveen. 2019. Scene graph parsing by attention graph. *CoRR*, abs/1909.06273.

Xuefeng Bai, Yulong Chen, and Yue Zhang. 2022. Graph pre-training for amr parsing and generation. *ArXiv*, abs/2203.07836.

Laura Banarescu, Claire Bonial, Shu Cai, Madalina Georgescu, Kira Griffitt, Ulf Hermjakob, Kevin Knight, Philipp Koehn, Martha Palmer, and Nathan Schneider. 2013. Abstract Meaning Representation for sembanking. In *Proceedings of the 7th Linguistic Annotation Workshop and Interoperability with Discourse*, pages 178–186, Sofia, Bulgaria. Association for Computational Linguistics.

Michele Bevilacqua, Rexhina Blloshmi, and Roberto Navigli. 2021. One SPRING to rule them both: Symmetric AMR semantic parsing and generation without a complex pipeline. In *Proceedings of AAAI*.

Claire Bonial, Lucia Donatelli, Mitchell Abrams, Stephanie M. Lukin, Stephen Tratz, Matthew Marge, Ron Artstein, David Traum, and Clare Voss. 2020. Dialogue-AMR: Abstract Meaning Representation for dialogue. In *Proceedings of the 12th Language Resources and Evaluation Conference*, pages 684–695, Marseille, France. European Language Resources Association.

Deng Cai and Wai Lam. 2020. AMR parsing via graph-sequence iterative inference. In *Proceedings of the 58th Annual Meeting of the Association for Computational Linguistics*, pages 1290–1301, Online. Association for Computational Linguistics.

Vinay Damodaran, Sharanya Chakravarthy, Akshay Kumar, Anjana Umapathy, Teruko Mitamura, Yuta Nakashima, Noa García, and Chenhui Chu. 2021. Understanding the role of scene graphs in visual question answering. *ArXiv*, abs/2101.05479.

Jacob Devlin, Ming-Wei Chang, Kenton Lee, and Kristina Toutanova. 2019. Bert: Pre-training of deep bidirectional transformers for language understanding. In *NAACL*.

Shibhansh Dohare and Harish Karnick. 2017. Text summarization using abstract meaning representation. *ArXiv*, abs/1706.01678.

Jiuxiang Gu, Handong Zhao, Zhe Lin, Sheng Li, Jianfei Cai, and Mingyang Ling. 2019. Scene graph generation with external knowledge and image reconstruction. In *Proceedings of the IEEE/CVF Conference on Computer Vision and Pattern Recognition (CVPR)*.

Marcel Hildebrandt, Hang Li, Rajat Koner, Volker Tresp, and Stephan Günnemann. 2020. Scene graph reasoning for visual question answering. *ArXiv*, abs/2007.01072.

Lifu Huang, Heng Ji, Kyunghyun Cho, Ido Dagan, Sebastian Riedel, and Clare Voss. 2018. Zero-shot transfer learning for event extraction. In *Proceedings of the 56th Annual Meeting of the Association for Computational Linguistics (Volume 1: Long Papers)*, pages 2160–2170, Melbourne, Australia. Association for Computational Linguistics.

Justin Johnson, Ranjay Krishna, Michael Stark, Li-Jia Li, David Shamma, Michael Bernstein, and Li Fei-Fei. 2015. Image retrieval using scene graphs. In *Proceedings of the IEEE Conference on Computer Vision and Pattern Recognition (CVPR)*.

Ioannis Konstas, Srinivasan Iyer, Mark Yatskar, Yejin Choi, and Luke Zettlemoyer. 2017. Neural AMR: Sequence-to-sequence models for parsing and generation. In *Proceedings of the 55th Annual Meeting of the Association for Computational Linguistics (Volume 1: Long Papers)*, pages 146–157, Vancouver, Canada. Association for Computational Linguistics.

Ranjay Krishna, Yuke Zhu, Oliver Groth, Justin Johnson, Kenji Hata, Joshua Kravitz, Stephanie Chen, Yannis Kalantidis, Li-Jia Li, David A Shamma, Michael Bernstein, and Li Fei-Fei. 2016. Visual genome: Connecting language and vision using crowdsourced dense image annotations.

Hoang Thanh Lam, Gabriele Picco, Yufang Hou, Young-Suk Lee, Lam M. Nguyen, Dzung T. Phan, Vanessa López, and Ramon Fernandez Astudillo. 2021. Ensembling graph predictions for amr parsing. In *Advances in Neural Information Processing Systems 35: Annual Conference on Neural Information Processing Systems 2021, NeurIPS 2021, December 6-14, 2021, virtual*.

Mike Lewis, Yinhan Liu, Naman Goyal, Marjan Ghazvininejad, Abdelrahman Mohamed, Omer Levy, Veselin Stoyanov, and Luke Zettlemoyer. 2020. BART: Denoising sequence-to-sequence pre-training for natural language generation, translation, and comprehension. In *Proceedings of the 58th Annual Meeting of the Association for Computational Linguistics*, pages 7871–7880, Online. Association for Computational Linguistics.

Tsung-Yi Lin, Michael Maire, Serge J. Belongie, James Hays, Pietro Perona, Deva Ramanan, Piotr Dollár, and C. Lawrence Zitnick. 2014. Microsoft coco: Common objects in context. In *ECCV*.

Fei Liu, Jeffrey Flanigan, Sam Thomson, Norman M. Sadeh, and Noah A. Smith. 2015. Toward abstractive summarization using semantic representations. In *NAACL*.

Alec Radford and Karthik Narasimhan. 2018. Improving language understanding by generative pre-training.

Alec Radford, Jeff Wu, Rewon Child, David Luan, Dario Amodei, and Ilya Sutskever. 2019. Language models are unsupervised multitask learners.

Colin Raffel, Noam Shazeer, Adam Roberts, Katherine Lee, Sharan Narang, Michael Matena, Yanqi Zhou, Wei Li, and Peter J. Liu. 2020. Exploring the limits of transfer learning with a unified text-to-text transformer. *Journal of Machine Learning Research*, 21(140):1–67.

Leonardo F. R. Ribeiro, Yue Zhang, and Iryna Gurevych. 2021. Structural adapters in pretrained language models for AMR-to-Text generation. In *Proceedings of the 2021 Conference on Empirical Methods in Natural Language Processing*, pages 4269–4282, Online and Punta Cana, Dominican Republic. Association for Computational Linguistics.

Brigit Schroeder and Subarna Tripathi. 2020. Structured query-based image retrieval using scene graphs. *2020 IEEE/CVF Conference on Computer Vision and Pattern Recognition Workshops (CVPRW)*, pages 680–684.

Sebastian Schuster, Ranjay Krishna, Angel Chang, Li Fei-Fei, and Christopher D. Manning. 2015. Generating semantically precise scene graphs from textual descriptions for improved image retrieval. In *Proceedings of the Fourth Workshop on Vision and Language*, pages 70–80, Lisbon, Portugal. Association for Computational Linguistics.

Ashish Vaswani, Noam Shazeer, Niki Parmar, Jakob Uszkoreit, Llion Jones, Aidan N Gomez, Ł ukasz Kaiser, and Illia Polosukhin. 2017. Attention is all you need. In *Advances in Neural Information Processing Systems*, volume 30. Curran Associates, Inc.

Sijin Wang, Ruiping Wang, Ziwei Yao, Shiguang Shan, and Xilin Chen. 2020. Cross-modal scene graph matching for relationship-aware image-text retrieval. In *2020 IEEE Winter Conference on Applications of Computer Vision (WACV)*, pages 1497–1506.

Yu-Siang Wang, Chenxi Liu, Xiaohui Zeng, and Alan Yuille. 2018. Scene graph parsing as dependency parsing. In *Proceedings of the 2018 Conference of the North American Chapter of the Association for Computational Linguistics: Human Language Technologies, Volume 1 (Long Papers)*, pages 397–407, New Orleans, Louisiana. Association for Computational Linguistics.

Danfei Xu, Yuke Zhu, Christopher Choy, and Li Fei-Fei. 2017. Scene graph generation by iterative message passing. In *Computer Vision and Pattern Recognition (CVPR)*.

Xu Yang, Kaihua Tang, Hanwang Zhang, and Jianfei Cai. 2019. Auto-encoding scene graphs for image captioning. In *2019 IEEE/CVF Conference on Computer Vision and Pattern Recognition (CVPR)*, pages 10677–10686.

Rowan Zellers, Mark Yatskar, Sam Thomson, and Yejin Choi. 2018. Neural motifs: Scene graph parsing with global context. In *Conference on Computer Vision and Pattern Recognition*.

Zixuan Zhang and Heng Ji. 2021. Abstract Meaning Representation guided graph encoding and decoding for joint information extraction. In *Proceedings of the 2021 Conference of the North American Chapter of the Association for Computational Linguistics: Human Language Technologies*, pages 39–49, Online. Association for Computational Linguistics.

Yiwu Zhong, Jing Shi, Jianwei Yang, Chenliang Xu, and Yin Li. 2021. Learning to generate scene graph from natural language supervision. In *ICCV*.

Yiwu Zhong, Liwei Wang, Jianshu Chen, Dong Yu, and Yin Li. 2020. Comprehensive image captioning via scene graph decomposition. In *ECCV*.

Jiawei Zhou, Tahira Naseem, Ramón Fernandez Astudillo, and Radu Florian. 2021. AMR parsing with action-pointer transformer. In *Proceedings of the 2021 Conference of the North American Chapter of the Association for Computational Linguistics: Human Language Technologies*, pages 5585–5598, Online. Association for Computational Linguistics.

Jie Zhu, Junhui Li, Muhua Zhu, Longhua Qian, Min Zhang, and Guodong Zhou. 2019. Modeling graph structure in transformer for better AMR-to-text generation. In *Proceedings of the 2019 Conference on Empirical Methods in Natural Language Processing and the 9th International Joint Conference on Natural Language Processing (EMNLP-IJCNLP)*, pages 5459–5468, Hong Kong, China. Association for Computational Linguistics.

Graph Neural Networks for Adapting Off-the-shelf General Domain Language Models to Low-Resource Specialised Domains

Merieme Bouhandi[1], **Emmanuel Morin**[1] and **Thierry Hamon**[2]
[1]LS2N, UMR CNRS 6004, Nantes Université, Nantes, France
[2]LISN, Université Paris-Saclay & Université Sorbonne Paris Nord, France
{merieme.bouhandi, emmanuel.morin}@ls2n.fr
thierry.hamon@limsi.fr

Abstract

Language models encode linguistic proprieties and are used as input for more specific models. Using their word representations as-is for specialised and low-resource domains might be less efficient. Methods of adapting them exist, but these models often overlook global information about how words, terms, and concepts relate to each other in a corpus due to their strong reliance on attention. We consider that global information can influence the results of the downstream tasks, and combination with contextual information is performed using graph convolution networks or GCN built on vocabulary graphs. By outperforming baselines, we show that this architecture is profitable for domain-specific tasks.

1 Introduction

Numerous types of word vectors are used as word representations for NLP tasks. These vectors encode useful semantic proprieties and are often used as weights or input of generic task models. For quite some time, Word2Vec (Mikolov et al., 2013) and GloVe (Pennington et al., 2014) were the go-to off-the-shelf embeddings that many systems used. FastText (Bojanowski et al., 2017) came as a way to deal with OOV words and still offers a better representation for words than most systems since it takes into account the morphological complexity of words by dealing with n-grams instead of whole words. Over the last few years, a new generation of deep neural approaches brought forth by transformers has brought significant improvements in many downstream applications. Language models, like BERT (Devlin et al., 2019), already encode so much knowledge and can capture semantic and syntactic information remarkably well (Coenen et al., 2019). They can be further trained on new tasks for adapting it to a new task or more specialised domains and further improve the quality of the representations (Peters et al., 2019).

Language models are trained over massive general domain corpora (Graff et al., 2003; Zhu et al., 2015) by optimising an objective that predicts the local contexts, captures linguistic units' distributional properties along the way, and address polysemy issues. Their quality can thus be arguably correlated to the volume of data available. However, in the case of specialised domains, the corpora are generally relatively modest in size, and these methods might be less efficient. It must be noted that if this claim is not always valid for all domains, especially for the English language, it is undoubtedly almost always true for other much less-resourced languages (Eisenschlos et al., 2019).

When using neural-based models, the conventional way of integrating further knowledge about specialised domains into models pre-trained on general corpora is to leverage pre-training by doing transfer learning and fine-tuning the model, tweaking its original weights to suit the tasks at hand better. If fine-tuning BERT is the most used adaptation method, it will rapidly hit a performance ceiling if the domain is too specialised or small, and some methods (Schick and Schütze, 2020) exist to tackle this problem. BERT will heavily rely on the context to build representations of too specialised or rare words. Each layer of the encoder's attention mechanism enriches the new representation of the input data with contextual information by paying attention to different parts of the text. Nonetheless, this particular feature of BERT may make it more challenging for it to consider the more global place a word occupies within a corpus's vocabulary, especially for these words.

Many data structures are hierarchical or graph structures in nature, such as social networks, paper citation networks, ontologies and semantic relations, such as hypernymy of hyponymy. Global relations between words within a sentence, a document or a corpus can be represented as a graph. Using such graphs as inputs, Graph Neural Net-

Proceedings of the 2nd Workshop on Deep Learning on Graphs for Natural Language Processing (DLG4NLP 2022), pages 36 - 42
July 15, 2022 ©2022 Association for Computational Linguistics

work (GNN) (Wu et al., 2021) captures general knowledge about the words and how they interact in a corpus. Several variants of GNN for text classification tasks exist. As presented by (Kipf and Welling, 2017), Graph Convolutional networks (GCN) is an approach for semi-supervised learning on graph-structured data based on an efficient variant of convolutional neural networks that operate directly on graphs. GCN is typically built using an adjacency matrix (based on a given relationship graph). The GCN's central idea is to take the weighted average of a node and all its neighbours during the convolution operation and uses both node features and the structure for the training. Text GCN (Yao et al., 2019) is a particular version of GCN, jointly learning both words and documents embeddings, and suited for situations with less training data. Graph methods do not encode positional information, and when information about position or context is needed, it might not be enough. Hence, pairing a GCN with a model that can grasp contextual information, like BERT, seems necessary.

There has not been much work trying to combine BERT and GNN. Since experts make inferences with relevant domain knowledge when performing domain-specific tasks, previous work has been conducted to integrate this knowledge into language models using knowledge graphs. Knowledge-enabled language representation model K-BERT (Liu et al., 2019) injects triples from a knowledge graph into the sentences as domain knowledge. BERT-MK (He et al., 2020) also takes into account knowledge graph contextualised knowledge. (Shang et al., 2019) embedded a medical ontology with Graph Attention Networks (GAT) and combined it with BERT for medication recommendation. (Jeong et al., 2020) concatenates the output of GCN and the output of BERT for citation recommendation tasks. Obviously, these methods presuppose the existence of a knowledge graph or an ontology. These resources are expensive to build and do not always exist for the domain and task at hand. Vocabulary graphs, on the other hand, are easy to build. (Lu et al., 2020) propose VGCN-BERT, a model which combines BERT with a Vocabulary GCN (VGCN), and where local and global information interacts from the first layer of BERT down, building an augmented representation jointly.

We build upon their work to adapt BERT to our specialised tasks and corpora. As (Lu et al., 2020) conveniently pointed out in their work, the utility of capturing global dependencies with a graph embedding instead of conventional non-contextualised embedding models (Mikolov et al., 2013; Pennington et al., 2014; Bojanowski et al., 2017) can be questioned (Srinivasan and Ribeiro, 2020). These methods provide additional information, but these models' small text window limits the connections between words. Long-range connections are more easily captured with GCN. In addition, by building a graph on a task-specific corpus, task-dependent dependencies are captured, in addition to the general dependencies already encoded in the pre-trained models.

2 Intrintic Evaluation Tasks

I2B2 (Uzuner et al., 2011) deals with automatic medical concept extraction and deals with the extraction of concepts (problems, tests and treatments) from anonymised medical reports. This task was proposed by the 2010 edition of the I2B2/VA Natural Language Processing Challenges for Clinical Records [1]. Medical reports tend to be unstructured, arbitrarily expressed, and sometimes roughly thrown together, leading the NLP practitioner to deal with noisy documents.

Concept	Training	Test
Problem	7,073	12,592
Test	4,608	9,225
Treatment	4,844	9,344
Total	16,525	31,161

Table 1: Frequencies of concept types in the I2B2 2010 annotated corpus

BioCreative V CDR (BC5CDR) is a collection of 1,500 PubMed titles and abstracts selected from the CTD-Pfizer corpus and was used in the BioCreative V chemical-disease relation task. We use the standard training and test set in the BC5CDR shared task to extract the entities, and we do not perform entity linking.

3 Experimental Methodology

Transfer Learning Pre-trained word vectors have been an essential component in many NLP systems. Word representations are fed into a task-specific model, often improving the results. Re-

[1] https://portal.dbmi.hms.harvard.edu/projects/n2c2-nlp/

Dataset	Training	Dev	Test
Disease	4,182	4,244	4,424
Chemical	5,203	5,347	5,385
Total	9,385	9,591	9,809

Table 2: Frequencies of entities in BC5CDR (chemical and disease) annotated corpus

cently, contextual word representations have significantly improved state of the art over non-contextual vectors. Transfer learning is leveraged here with the usage of BERT embeddings.

Domain Adaptation Adaptation can often take two forms: feature extraction, where the model's weights are used as-is as inputs of another system in a similar fashion to classic feature-based models and fine-tuning, where the model's weights continue to be trained on the new data for a specific task.

Graph Convolutional Networks Graph Convolutional Networks (GCNs) are often used for hierarchical representation problems. By performing convolution operations on neighbouring nodes (words) in the graph, a representation of a word will be enriched with information about its neighbours, which will allow the integration of information about the global context of the word. Since we are using the vocabulary to build the graph, we use VGCN (Lu et al., 2020). VGCN are able to take into account more global information about the vocabulary but often fail to capture some of the local information, which is why we use them combined with BERT. This paper considers lexical relations in a language, namely, the vocabulary graph, to be global information about the task-specific language. This vocabulary graph is constructed using both wordpieces (Wu et al., 2016) and word's co-occurrences alongside documents. We first select the relevant part of the global vocabulary graph according to the input token or sentence and transform it into an embedding representation. We then combine it with BERT token embedding and use multiple layers of attention mechanism to fuse the two.

The vocabulary graph is constructed using weighted positive point-wise mutual information (PPMI) (Levy and Goldberg, 2014). A higher PPMI indicate a higher semantic correlation between words. For each pair of words (w, c), we have:

$$P_\alpha(c) = \frac{count(c)^\alpha}{\sum_c count(c)^\alpha}$$

with the context probabilities raised to $\alpha = 0.75$, giving rare words are slightly higher probability.

$$PMI_\alpha(w,c) = max(log_2 \frac{P(w,c)}{P(w)P_\alpha(c)}, 0)$$

With this subword segmentation method, the word *epistaxis*, for example, will be represented as five tokens by BERT: *ep*, *##ista*, *##xi* and *##s*), since it is not in the model's training vocabulary. We are left with having to average or sum these embeddings to get a final embedding for our word. It puts us at a disadvantage when dealing with domain-specific corpora because most of the words in the area do not exist in the model's vocabulary. The model will rely heavier on the context to get embeddings for these wordpieces. We use both full words and wordpieces to build the vocabulary graphs in order to counteract this.

Given an undirected graph $G = (V, E)$ with a set N nodes $v_i \in V$, a set of edges (v_i, v_j), respectively, an adjacency matrix $A \in \mathbb{R}^{N \times N}$, a degree matrix $D_{ii} = \sum_j A_{ij}$ and a feature matrix $X \in \mathbb{R}^{N \times C}$, with C the number of dimensions of a feature vector, a forward 2-layer GCN model is computed as follow :

$$Z = f(X, A)$$

$$f(X, A) = softmax(\hat{A} \cdot ReLU(\hat{A}XW^0)W^{(1)})$$

with $\hat{A} = (\tilde{D}^{-\frac{1}{2}}\tilde{A})(\tilde{D}^{-\frac{1}{2}}X)$, the average of all neighbours feature vectors, scaled over both the rows and the columns of the matrix, putting more weights on low-degree nodes and reducing the impact of high-degree ones, and computed using $\tilde{A} = A + \lambda I_N$ (usually, $\lambda = 1$, but it can be treated as a trainable parameter) and $\tilde{D}$, its degree matrix. The adjacency matrix A corresponds to the weighted PPMI as the vocabulary graph and the feature matrix X to pre-trained embedding from BERT.

In the equation aforementioned, the GCN has two layers, as it is usually the standard (Kipf and Welling, 2017; Lu et al., 2020). With one layer GCN, each node can only get the information from its immediate neighbours. By adding another convolutional layer on top of it, we repeat the aggregation (or pooling process), but this time, the neighbours already have information about their

Model	I2B2 P	I2B2 R	I2B2 F1	BC5CDR P	BC5CDR R	BC5CDR F1
BiLSTM-CRF	81.2 ± 0.4	84.4 ± 0.6	82.0 ± 0.3	78.2 ± 0.1	80.1 ± 0.8	79.2 ± 0.2
GCN	71.4 ± 0.5	52.1 ± 0.2	63.7 ± 0.1	79.9 ± 0.9	77.2 ± 1.0	78.6 ± 0.9
BERT	87.4 ± 0.3	87.0 ± 0.1	87.2 ± 0.8	86.0 ± 0.7	85.0 ± 0.8	85.5 ± 0.1
+ $\text{GCN}_{\text{vanilla}}$	87.7 ± 1.2	86.5 ± 0.2	87.4 ± 0.2	86.3 ± 0.6	**86.1 ± 0.7**	86.2 ± 0.3
+ GCN_{add}	**89.7 ± 0.4**	86.0 ± 0.7	87.7 ± 0.1	87.7 ± 0.4	85.7 ± 0.3	86.3 ± 0.2
+ $\text{GCN}_{\text{embedding}}$	89.0 ± 0.2	**88.8 ± 1.0**	**88.9 ± 0.2**	**87.9 ± 0.5**	85.7 ± 0.1	**86.7 ± 0.4**

Table 3: Analysis (in % F1-Score) of the outputs of our different models for the sequence labelling. This is an averaging of 3 runs for each experiment.

neighbours from the previous step. The number of layers is really the maximum number of hops that each node can reach to capture global information. However, we usually do not want to go too far in the graph. Otherwise, we may smooth out the graph, erasing important information entirely, making the representation less meaningful and resulting in a drop of performance (Kipf and Welling, 2017). Since the GCN's nodes are task entities, such as words, wordpieces or documents, this architecture requires all entities, including those from the training set, validation set, and test set, to be present in the graph during all the phases [2].

In the same fashion as (Lu et al., 2020), to combine these representations with BERT and to leverage both local and global information, we combine the vocabulary graph embedding obtained by our GCN and the BERT embedding and feed them to the first encoder. It will allow for the words' order in the sentence to be maintained and local information to be used, all the while the global information obtained by GCN will interact with BERT representation over the 12 layers of encoders. We also test two other combination methods: as for the first one, instead of integrating the GCN into the BERT embedding module, we simply add it to BERT embedding before passing it to the encoder. The second one consists of producing two outputs, one of the GCN and one of BERT, concatenating it just before applying a RELU and feeding it to the fully connected classification layer.

To summarise, multiple models are tested here, with several baselines in addition to the BERT and GCN combinations:

- **Bi-LSTM model**: BERT embeddings are used as input of a 256 hidden units and 2-layers bidirectional LSTM with an additional CRF layer.
- **GCN**: 2-layer GCN with BERT embeddings as input, with a simple fully-connected layer as output. This model only leverages global informations.
- **BERT**: pre-trained BERT for token classification, with a simple fully-connected layer as output. For all tasks, *bert-base-cased* is used.
- **BERT+GCN_{add}** or **BERT with added graph embedding**: Two representations are generated using BERT and GCN and are then summed. The combined representation is passed through a fully-connected layer for classification.
- **BERT+$\text{GCN}_{\text{embedding}}$** or **BERT with integrated graph embedding**: Instead of only using the regular BERT embeddings as input, we feed both the graph embedding obtained by the GCN and the BERT embedding to the BERT encoders.
- **BERT+$\text{GCN}_{\text{vanilla}}$** or **BERT with concatenated graph embedding**: Two representations are generated using BERT and GCN and are then concatenated. The combined representation is passed through a fully-connected layer for classification.

3.1 Pre-processings and Experimental settings

For all tasks, non-ASCII values, special characters and HTML tags are removed. Tokens from I2B2 and BC5CDR are then represented in the Inside–Outside–Beginning (IOB) tagging format for token classification. For the experimental settings,

[2] Masks are used during training to only use training nodes.

we implemented the models in PyTorch and PyTorch Geometric for the GCN part. All our experiments were run on a single GPU GEFORCE GTX 1080 for about $\pm$ 40 minutes per run (on average, over all the experiments).

4 Results

The results of the experiments are shown in Table 3. Performance is measured in macro-averaged scores (exact match). We report our results for the standard approaches first, and we contrast them with different combinations and architectures. Overall, all the BERT models with additional GCN global information perform better than the other baseline models, namely, the BiLSTM-CRF, the simple GCN and BERT. This confirms our intuitions and shows that it is beneficial to merge local and global information, and those resulting representations seem more worthwhile for the downstream tasks. A tendency seems to be showing (see Table 3): while getting a better F1-score, most of the boost in the overall score for the BERT with added global information goes to have better precision than the vanilla BERT and a lower recall simultaneously. This indicates an actual decrease in false positives, and these tendencies are similar across the board.

Future analysis can also be conducted on subwords since BERT breaks words down into wordpieces. The problem for specialised domains is that a more domain-oriented subword tokenisation method is probably more appropriate. For example, with BERT wordpieces tokeniser, *"adenocarcinoma"* will be broken into *"aden"*, *"oca"*, *"rc"*, *"ino"*, *"ma"* and, surprisingly, *"carcinoma"* will be broken into *"car"*, *"cino"*, *"ma"*, making *"ma"* the only subword that they share, even if the two words are semantically very close. Some methods have been developed, particularly for clinical text (Nguyen et al., 2019). However, using them means that we have to retrain the whole BERT model (similar to ClinicalBERT, for example), which defeats the purpose of adaptation. We rely on the GCN to fetch these missing pieces of information, connect them and integrate them back into the BERT model.

In this work, we wanted to examine if we can improve results for languages and domains for which there are no BioBERT and Clinical BERT, e.g. there are no WindBERT or PoliticalBERT for hypothetical wind energy or politics related tasks. This step of adaptation to the domain would make sense and even be necessary. Using a graph neural network constructed over the corpus' vocabulary exclusively follows the same logic. It comes from our decision to find a way to improve the model intrinsically without using external resources. Even if many resources exist for the English language, it is still crucial to explore ways to adapt existing models to our downstream specialised tasks where the volume of data is often insufficient. There is still a lot of room for improvement. One major limitation of this work — and work on graph neural networks in general, is the need to use all entities, including those from the training set, validation set, and test set, to build the vocabulary graph.

5 Conclusion

The quality of word representations obtained through language models is often correlated to the volume of data available. In the case of specialised domains, these methods might be less efficient due to the usually modest size of the corpora. This is particularly exacerbated in the case of specialised and low-resource domains, and the models might need to go through an adaptation phase. This work seeks to understand how these methods can be adapted on the fly by using additional features from GCN. The achieved results outperform the baselines across the board. It shows that it is beneficial to merge local and global information, and those resulting representations yield some additional advantages and are more worthwhile for the downstream task. Future work will cover analysis of attention layers before and after adding more global information. It will also involve considering more sophisticated relations than simple mutual information into the GCN, such as exploiting oriented graphs to encode dependencies, synonymy, hypo- and hyperonymy, and different architecture such as Graph Attention Networks.

Acknowledgements

This work has been funded by the French National Research Agency (ANR) and is under the ADDICTE project (ANR-17-CE23-0001).

References

Piotr Bojanowski, Edouard Grave, Armand Joulin, and Tomas Mikolov. 2017. Enriching Word Vectors with Subword Information. *Transactions of the Association for Computational Linguistics*, 5:135–146.

Andy Coenen, Emily Reif, Ann Yuan, Been Kim, Adam Pearce, Fernanda B. Viégas, and Martin Wattenberg. 2019. Visualizing and Measuring the Geometry of BERT. In H. Wallach, H. Larochelle, A. Beygelzimer, F. d'Alché Buc, E. Fox, and R. Garnett, editors, *Advances in Neural Information Processing Systems 32*, pages 8594–8603. Curran Associates, Inc.

Jacob Devlin, Ming-Wei Chang, Kenton Lee, and Kristina Toutanova. 2019. BERT: Pre-training of Deep Bidirectional Transformers for Language Understanding. In *Proceedings of the 2019 Conference of the North American Chapter of the Association for Computational Linguistics: Human Language Technologies (NAACL-HLT'18)*, pages 4171–4186, Minneapolis, MN, USA.

Julian Eisenschlos, Sebastian Ruder, Piotr Czapla, Marcin Kadras, Sylvain Gugger, and Jeremy Howard. 2019. MultiFiT: Efficient multi-lingual language model fine-tuning. In *Proceedings of the 2019 Conference on Empirical Methods in Natural Language Processing and the 9th International Joint Conference on Natural Language Processing (EMNLP-IJCNLP)*, pages 5702–5707, Hong Kong, China. Association for Computational Linguistics.

David Graff, Junbo Kong, Ke Chen, and Kazuaki Maeda. 2003. English gigaword. *Linguistic Data Consortium, Philadelphia*, 4(1):34.

Bin He, Di Zhou, Jinghui Xiao, Xin Jiang, Qun Liu, Nicholas Jing Yuan, and Tong Xu. 2020. BERT-MK: Integrating graph contextualized knowledge into pretrained language models. In *Findings of the Association for Computational Linguistics: EMNLP 2020*, pages 2281–2290, Online. Association for Computational Linguistics.

Chanwoo Jeong, Sion Jang, Eunjeong Park, and Sungchul Choi. 2020. A context-aware citation recommendation model with bert and graph convolutional networks. *Scientometrics*, 124(3):1907–1922.

Thomas N. Kipf and Max Welling. 2017. Semi-supervised classification with graph convolutional networks. In *International Conference on Learning Representations (ICLR)*.

Omer Levy and Yoav Goldberg. 2014. Neural word embedding as implicit matrix factorization. In *Advances in Neural Information Processing Systems*, volume 27. Curran Associates, Inc.

Weijie Liu, Peng Zhou, Zhe Zhao, Zhiruo Wang, Qi Ju, Haotang Deng, and Ping Wang. 2019. K-bert: Enabling language representation with knowledge graph.

Zhibin Lu, Pan Du, and Jian-Yun Nie. 2020. Vgcn-bert: Augmenting bert with graph embedding for text classification. In *Advances in Information Retrieval - 42nd European Conference on IR Research, ECIR 2020, Lisbon, Portugal, April 14-17, 2020, Proceedings, Part I*, volume 12035 of *Lecture Notes in Computer Science*, pages 369–382. Springer.

Tomas Mikolov, Ilya Sutskever, Kai Chen, Greg S Corrado, and Jeff Dean. 2013. Distributed representations of words and phrases and their compositionality. In C. J. C. Burges, L. Bottou, M. Welling, Z. Ghahramani, and K. Q. Weinberger, editors, *Advances in Neural Information Processing Systems 26*, pages 3111–3119. Curran Associates, Inc.

Vincent Nguyen, Sarvnaz Karimi, and Zhenchang Xing. 2019. Investigating the effect of lexical segmentation in transformer-based models on medical datasets. In *Proceedings of the The 17th Annual Workshop of the Australasian Language Technology Association*, pages 165–171, Sydney, Australia. Australasian Language Technology Association.

Jeffrey Pennington, Richard Socher, and Christopher Manning. 2014. Glove: Global vectors for word representation. In *Proceedings of the 2014 Conference on Empirical Methods in Natural Language Processing (EMNLP'14)*, pages 1532–1543, Doha, Qatar.

Matthew E. Peters, Sebastian Ruder, and Noah A. Smith. 2019. To Tune or Not to Tune? Adapting Pretrained Representations to Diverse Tasks. In *Proceedings of the 4th Workshop on Representation Learning for NLP (RepL4NLP'19)*, volume abs/1903.05987, pages 7–14, Florence, Italy.

Timo Schick and Hinrich Schütze. 2020. BERTRAM: Improved word embeddings have big impact on contextualized model performance. pages 3996–4007.

Junyuan Shang, Tengfei Ma, Cao Xiao, and Jimeng Sun. 2019. Pre-training of graph augmented transformers for medication recommendation. In *Proceedings of the Twenty-Eighth International Joint Conference on Artificial Intelligence, IJCAI-19*, pages 5953–5959. International Joint Conferences on Artificial Intelligence Organization.

Balasubramaniam Srinivasan and Bruno Ribeiro. 2020. On the equivalence between positional node embeddings and structural graph representations. In *International Conference on Learning Representations*.

Ozlem Uzuner, Brett South, Shuying Shen, and Scott DuVall. 2011. 2010 i2b2/va challenge on concepts, assertions, and relations in clinical text. *Journal of the American Medical Informatics Association : JAMIA*, 18:552–6.

Yonghui Wu, Mike Schuster, Z. Chen, Quoc V. Le, Mohammad Norouzi, Wolfgang Macherey, Maxim Krikun, Yuan Cao, Qin Gao, Klaus Macherey, Jeff Klingner, Apurva Shah, Melvin Johnson, Xiaobing Liu, Lukasz Kaiser, Stephan Gouws, Yoshikiyo Kato, Taku Kudo, Hideto Kazawa, Keith Stevens, George Kurian, Nishant Patil, Wei Wang, Cliff Young, Jason R. Smith, Jason Riesa, Alex Rudnick, Oriol Vinyals, Gregory S. Corrado, Macduff Hughes, and Jeffrey Dean. 2016. Google's neural machine translation system: Bridging the gap between human and machine translation. *ArXiv*, abs/1609.08144.

Zonghan Wu, Shirui Pan, Fengwen Chen, Guodong Long, Chengqi Zhang, and Philip S. Yu. 2021. A comprehensive survey on graph neural networks. *IEEE Transactions on Neural Networks and Learning Systems*, 32(1):4–24.

Liang Yao, Chengsheng Mao, and Yuan Luo. 2019. Graph convolutional networks for text classification. *Proceedings of the AAAI Conference on Artificial Intelligence*, 33(01):7370–7377.

Yukun Zhu, Ryan Kiros, Rich Zemel, Ruslan Salakhutdinov, Raquel Urtasun, Antonio Torralba, and Sanja Fidler. 2015. Aligning books and movies: Towards story-like visual explanations by watching movies and reading books. In *Proceedings of the 2015 IEEE International Conference on Computer Vision (ICCV)*, ICCV '15, page 19–27, USA. IEEE Computer Society.

GRADA: Graph Generative Data Augmentation for Commonsense Reasoning

Adyasha Maharana **Mohit Bansal**
Department of Computer Science
University of North Carolina at Chapel Hill
{adyasha,mbansal}@cs.unc.edu

Abstract

Recent advances in commonsense reasoning have been fueled by the availability of large-scale human annotated datasets. Manual annotation of such datasets, many of which are based on existing knowledge bases, is expensive and not scalable. Moreover, it is challenging to build augmentation data for commonsense reasoning because the synthetic questions need to adhere to real-world scenarios. Hence, we present GRADA, a graph-generative data augmentation framework to synthesize factual data samples from knowledge graphs for commonsense reasoning datasets. First, we train a graph-to-text model for conditional generation of questions from graph entities and relations. Then, we train a generator with GAN loss to generate distractors for synthetic questions. Our approach improves performance for SocialIQA, CODAH, HellaSwag and CommonsenseQA, and works well for generative tasks like ProtoQA. We show improvement in robustness to semantic adversaries after training with GRADA and provide human evaluation of the quality of synthetic datasets in terms of factuality and answerability. Our work provides evidence and encourages future research into graph-based generative data augmentation. [1]

1 Introduction

Recent work has seen the emergence of several datasets for improving commonsense reasoning of language models through tasks like question answering (QA) (Sap et al., 2019b; Talmor et al., 2019; Bisk et al., 2020) and natural language inference (Bhagavatula et al., 2020; Zellers et al., 2019; Sakaguchi et al., 2020). Some of these datasets are based on existing knowledge graphs that represent different aspects of commonsense through entities and relations. For example, annotators for SocialIQA (Sap et al., 2019b) were shown an event from the inferential knowledge graph ATOMIC (Sap et al., 2019a) and instructed to turn it into a sentence by adding names, filling placeholders and adding context, etc. For multiple-choice QA datasets, annotators are also instructed to write distractor choices for each question. These useful datasets are collected through a time-taking and money-intensive crowdsourcing process which is hard to scale. Large pretrained models like GPT2 (Radford et al., 2018) can be finetuned to generate sentences from narrow data distributions, and it has recently been leveraged to augment datasets for text classification (Anaby-Tavor et al., 2020) and question answering (Puri et al., 2020; Yang et al., 2020). However, it is challenging to generate augmentation data for commonsense reasoning because the generated questions and answers (referred to as "synthetic" in rest of the paper) need to depict plausible real-world scenarios accurately. Hence, we develop GRADA, a graph-based generative data augmentation framework to generate

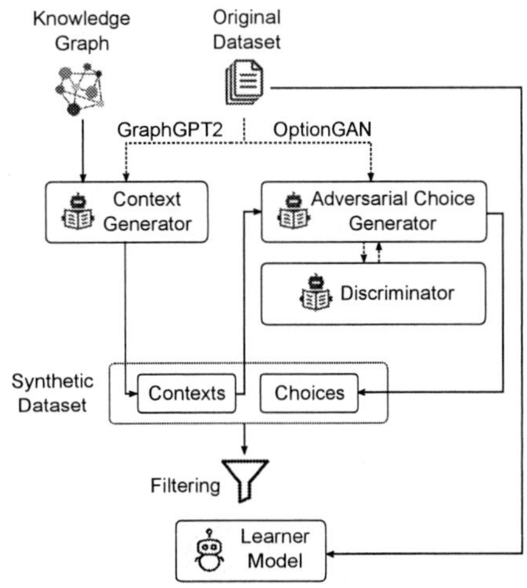

Figure 1: GRADA framework: The original dataset is used to train GraphGPT2, a graph-to-text question generator and OptionGAN, a distractor generator. The synthetic dataset is subjected to filtering and used to train the model in combniation with the original dataset.

[1]Code and synthetic data files are available at https://github.com/adymaharana/GraDA.

Proceedings of the 2nd Workshop on Deep Learning on Graphs for Natural Language Processing (DLG4NLP 2022), pages 43 - 59
July 15, 2022 ©2022 Association for Computational Linguistics

synthetic samples from existing knowledge graphs that encode information about the real world.

Each sample in commonsense reasoning datasets comprises a question which describes a real-world scenario and can be mapped to a set of predefined entities and relations from knowledge bases like ConceptNet and ATOMIC. For instance, the question "Besides a mattress, name something people sleep on." from the ProtoQA dataset (Boratko et al., 2020) can be mapped to the single-hop path (mattress, *RelatedTo*, people) using ConceptNet. If a pretrained language model is trained to conditionally generate questions from such input paths, we can expect it to generate sensible questions when it is provided new paths with similar relations. The model will likely generalize to unseen entity nodes and generate questions containing unique commonsense knowledge. Following this intuition, we finetune GPT2 (Radford et al., 2019) to generate questions which explicitly depict the entities and relations in input path. When trained on the aforementioned example (alongside other similar examples) and provided with the new path (mattress, *RelatedTo*, soft), our model generates "Besides a mattress, name something that's soft.", which is a valid question for probing real-world commonsense. Usually, these paths contain multiple nodes with several hops and hence are referred to as graphs in rest of the paper. In order to represent the graph, we explore both (a) encoding of linearized graph and (b) augmentation of linear encodings with structure-aware encoding of graph, and find that the latter improves the transfer of semantic knowledge from graph to text.

Synthetic questions need to be accompanied by synthetic answers and distractor choices (for multiple-choice datasets), which are similarly generated by finetuning GPT2 for conditional generation of answers/distractors from the question. However, Yang et al. (2020) report that human annotators find it hard to pick a unique/unambiguous answer in more than 50% of the synthetic dataset generated in this manner. Therefore, we explore an alternative where we finetune the generative model within a GAN framework (Nie et al., 2019a) where it is continuously challenged by a discriminator model to generate unique distractors that can fool the discriminator (see OptionGAN, Figure 1). The synthetic questions and answers thus generated are assembled into synthetic samples which are then used in a two-stage training pipeline (Mitra et al., 2019). Additionally, since the generative pipeline is only an approximate imitation of the human annotation process, we are left with several ambiguous and inaccurate samples in the synthetic pool. Hence, we retain the most informative data samples from the synthetic pool by using Question Answering Probability (Zhang and Bansal, 2019) to measure accuracy by answerability. Our contributions can be summarized as follows:

- We present a generative framework consisting of (i) a graph-to-text model to convert knowledge graphs to questions, (ii) a model finetuned with GAN loss to generate distractors for commonsense reasoning QA datasets, and (iii) combined with a filter for selecting the most informative samples from synthetic datasets.
- We improve performance on commonsense reasoning datasets, and perform ablation analysis to show the impact of various modules in our framework as well as human evaluation of synthetic dataset quality.

2 Related Work

Explicit reasoning over knowledge graphs has been a popular approach for improving commonsense understanding of QA models. Bauer et al. (2018); Lin et al. (2019); De Cao et al. (2019); Feng et al. (2020) and Lv et al. (2020) extract relevant multi-hop relational commonsense from knowledge graphs and show significant improvements over models that operate solely on text. Devlin et al. (2019); Yang et al. (2019); Ye et al. (2019) expand the rich latent knowledge of large pretrained models by finetuning on similar corpora (Havasi et al., 2010) before finetuning on the target dataset. Mitra et al. (2019) convert external resources (Koupaee and Wang, 2018) to QA samples for data augmentation. Yang et al. (2020) generate randomly initialized samples from finetuned GPT2 as augmentation data for target datasets. We ground the generated samples to real-world facts by providing knowledge graphs as input to the model.

There has been a surge of efforts in neural graph-to-text modeling in the recent years. Marcheggiani and Perez-Beltrachini (2018) encode input graphs using a graph convolutional encoder (Kipf and Welling, 2017). Koncel-Kedziorski et al. (2019) propose the model GraphWriter which improves on the graph attention networks presented in Velickovic et al. (2018) by replacing self-attention encoder with Transformer blocks (Vaswani et al.,

2017). Several recent works have shown that pretrained generative models can be finetuned with or without structure-aware graph encoding to improve graph-to-text generation (Mager et al., 2020; Ribeiro et al., 2020; Hoyle et al., 2020; He et al., 2020; Ke et al., 2021). Query or question generation has also been shown to benefit from knowledge graphs in Shen et al. (2022); Bi et al. (2020). We combine the structure-aware encoding capabilities of graph-to-text models with the rich contextual knowledge of pretrained models in GraphGPT2 and generate rich real-world scenarios from sparse sub-graphs (Shen et al., 2022; Chen et al., 2020; Kumar et al., 2019).

Good distractors are necessary for a task model to learn the right reasoning towards answering multiple-choice datasets. To this end, Liang et al. (2018) rank distractors using feature-based ensemble methods. Offerijns et al. (2020); Yang et al. (2020) finetune GPT2 to generate distractors. Chung et al. (2020) approach distractor generation as a coverage problem and select distractors for maximizing sample difficulty. Cai and Wang (2018) use adversarial training to sample high quality negative training examples for knowledge graph embeddings. In a similar line of work, we use generative adversarial networks (GANs) (Goodfellow et al., 2014) with the Gumbel-Softmax relaxation (Kusner and Hernández-Lobato, 2016; Nie et al., 2019b) and train a generator with GAN loss to imitate the creation of human-authored tricky, incorrect answer options. Most NLP applications use REINFORCE (Sutton et al., 2000) algorithm and its variants (Yu et al., 2017; Cai and Wang, 2018; Qin et al., 2018; Zhang et al., 2018) to circumvent the discrete sampling issue for text-based GANs.

3 Methods

In this section, we describe the various modules in the GRADA framework.

3.1 Graph-to-Text Generation

In the first module of our pipeline, we generate synthetic questions by using knowledge graphs as input. Given a dataset of input graphs (g_i), we finetune GPT2 with cross-entropy loss for conditional generation of questions (q_i) from the graphs i.e., $L_q = \sum_{i=1}^{N} log\, p(q_i|f(g_i))$, where $f(.)$ is the function for encoding the graph and $p(.)$ represents the probabilities. We explore linearized graph encoding as well as structure-aware encoding of graph.

Linearized Graph Input. Graph linearization is a simple way to use graphs like text when finetuning GPT2. We adopt depth-first-search to linearize the input graphs and preserve edge information to some extent by augmenting GPT2 vocabulary with special tokens for edges. GPT2 is finetuned for conditional generation of target question from this linearized graph input.

Using linearized graphs with pretrained language models (PTLMs) surpasses graph-based architectures at data-to-text generation by a large margin (Ribeiro et al., 2020). However, Mager et al. (2020) show that omitting the edge information from linearized graphs notably degrades performance, implying that graph structure is beneficial for generation. Hence, we propose GraphGPT2.

GraphGPT2 for Structure-aware Graph Input. Instead of linearizing the input graph, we encode the graph using a Transformer-based graph encoder $f_s(.)$ which preserves the graph structure by performing masked self-attention over edges and nodes. We use the Transformer-based graph encoder from Graph Writer (Koncel-Kedziorski et al., 2019) for structure-preserving encoding of graphs. First, we convert the input graphs g_i into unlabeled connected bipartite graphs $G_i = (v_i, e_i)$, where v_i is the list of entities, relations and global vertex, and e_i is the adjacency matrix describing the directed edges (Beck et al., 2018). The global vertex is connected to all entity vertices and promotes global context modelling by allowing information flow between all parts of the graph. Next, v_i is projected to a dense, continuous embedding space V_i and is sent as input to the graph encoder (see Figure 2). The encoder is composed of L stacked Transformer blocks; each Transformer block consists of a N-headed self-attention layer followed by normalization and a two-layer feed-forward network. The resulting encodings i.e. $f_s(g_i)$, are referred to as graph contextualized vertex encodings. These encodings are prepended to the embedded representation of linearized graph in the form of past key values, and sent as input to the decoder. The decoder i.e., pretrained GPT2, is finetuned to generate a coherent question from the combined embeddings. The graph encoder is initialized with GPT2 embeddings to force continuity in word representation across modules. Figure 2 shows the integration of graph contextualized encodings with

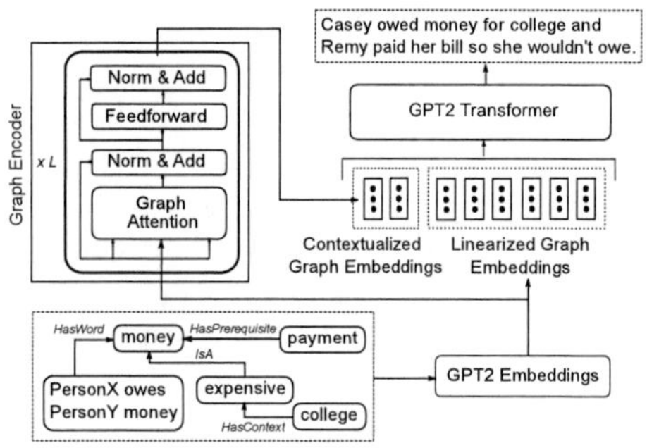

Figure 2: GraphGPT2: The Graph Encoder is composed of L Transformer blocks and its output is concatenated with GPT2 embeddings for input to GPT2.

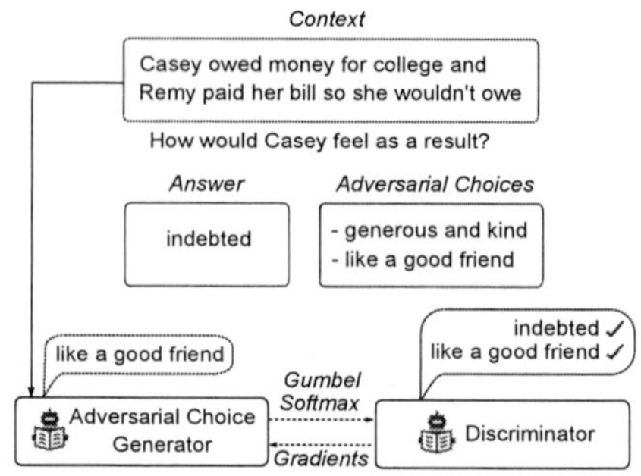

Figure 3: Training process for OptionGAN.

GPT2 in GraphGPT2. The combined generative model is finetuned end-to-end for maximizing the conditional log-likelihood of target question q_i i.e. $L_q = \sum_{i=1}^{N} log\, p(q_i \mid [f_l(g_i); f_s(g_i)])$, where $f_l(.)$ represents the linearized graph embeddings.

During inference, both of the above models are provided with graphs that do not appear in training dataset to generate synthetic questions containing new knowledge. See Sec. 4.1 for details on creation of training and inference datasets.

3.2 Answer & Distractor Generation

We finetune a GPT2 model for conditional generation of answers from questions i.e., $L_a = \sum_{i=1}^{N} log\, p(a_i|q_i)$. However, as we discussed in Sec. 1, a similar method for conditional generation of distractors does not guarantee good distractors. Hence, we finetune GPT2 within a GAN framework to generate maximally adversarial distractors, in a bid to imitate the best human annotator.

OptionGAN for Adversarial Choices. We train a model to generate distractors (in the multiple-choice QA task) for the synthetic questions obtained from GraphGPT2 (see Figure 1) using a generator-discriminator adversarial framework. The discriminator D is a sequential classification model that takes the question q_i, concatenated with the ground truth correct answer a_i i.e., $[q_i; a_i]$ or the distractor $\hat{d}_i$ generated by generator G i.e., $[q_i; \hat{d}_i]$ as input and classifies the pair as correct or otherwise. While training, the generator runs the risk of learning to generate correct answers instead of distractors, since it's goal is to be able to fool the discriminator into classifying the question-distractor pair $[q_i; \hat{d}_i]$ as correct. To prevent this, we heavily bias the model by first pretraining it to generate only distractors using the conditional cross-entropy loss and then continue with adversarial training from the saved weights. Mathematically, we pretrain the generator G with the loss $L_g = \sum_{i=1}^{N} log\, p(d_i|q_i)$, where q_i, d_i are question and distractor, respectively. We use the question as input instead of the knowledge sub-graph, since most generated questions contain additional semantics from the latent knowledge of the pretrained generative model which is not present in the original sub-graph. Then, the pretrained generator is finetuned within an adversarial framework to produce distractors that successfully fool the discriminator, so that we get adversarial options that are as tricky as human-annotated options (see Figure 3). We use the Gumbel-Softmax relaxation (Nie et al., 2019a) while sampling from generator to allow flow of gradients through the discriminator model i.e. $z = softmax(\frac{1}{\tau}(h + g))$, where h, g and τ are the logits generated from G, Gumbel distribution sample and temperature respectively. The temperature is annealed using an exponential function during training. Following RelGAN (Nie et al., 2019a), we use the Relativistic standard GAN loss for the adversarial training i.e. $\min_{G} \max_{D} log\, sigmoid(D([q_i; a_i]) - D([q_i; \hat{d}_i]))$. Generator G is trained to minimize the loss while discriminator D is trained to maximize the loss. In practice, we use GPT2 for both roles i.e., generator as well as discriminator.

3.3 Filtering and Selection of Samples

Inspite of the careful construction of synthetic samples using knowledge graphs, the pool of synthetic samples can be noisy and may consist of incoherent text, incorrect question-answer pairs or out-of-distribution samples. Hence, we use Question Answering Probability (QAP) (Zhang and Bansal, 2019) to measure accuracy of synthetic samples.

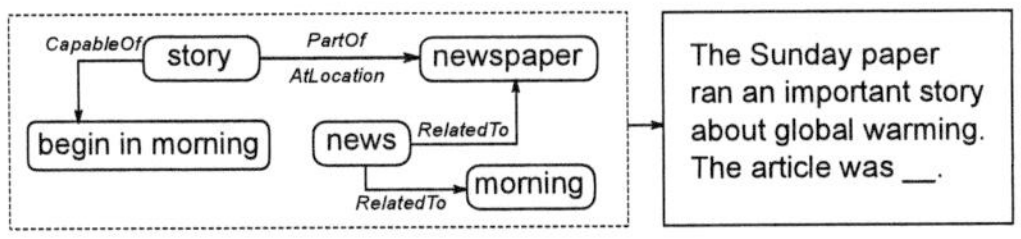

Figure 4: Example of synthetic context generated from GraphGPT2 for the CODAH dataset.

The QAP score (μ) is the prediction probability of the true class by a model with parameters θ which has been trained on the original dataset i.e. $\mu_i = p_\theta(a_i|x_i)$. Samples with low prediction probabilities for the correct choices are either annotated incorrectly or are especially difficult instances for the model. We define a low and high threshold for the QAP filter and samples lying within this range are retained in the dataset.

See supplementary for a comparison of QAP with two other methods for filtering i.e. Energy (Liu et al., 2020) and Model Confidence & Variability (Swayamdipta et al., 2020).

4 Experimental Setup

4.1 Datasets

SocialIQA (Sap et al., 2019b) and CommonsenseQA (Talmor et al., 2019) are annotated using knowledge graphs, making them a suitable choice for testing our approach. SocialIQA is a question answering dataset based on ATOMIC (Sap et al., 2019a), containing 33,410/1954/2224 samples in training, development and test set, resp. CommonsenseQA (CQA) is a similarly crowd-sourced dataset based on ConceptNet (Speer et al., 2017) containing an official split of 9741/1221/1241 samples. Following Yang et al. (2020), we also test our method on HellaSwag-2K (Zellers et al., 2019) and CODAH (Chen et al., 2019) for low-resource scenario. HellaSwag-2K is created by sampling 2000/1000/1000 examples from HellaSWAG training and validation sets. We test our approach on the CoDAH folds (2.8k samples) released by Yang et al. (2020) for comparison. Apart from these four MCQ datasets, we also experiment with the generative QA dataset ProtoQA (9762/52/102) (Boratko et al., 2020) and find that our approach works especially well with it. See Appendix for details.

Data Preparation. To prepare graph-to-text datasets for training GraphGPT2, we map the questions to multi-hop paths in ConceptNet (Bauer et al., 2018). We use Spacy[2] to tag the questions with part-of-speech and extract verbs and nouns as concepts, retaining those that appear in ConceptNet as entities and the connecting relations (see example in Fig. 4).[3] We remove inverse relations from the set of triples. The graphs extracted in this manner are acyclic and can be linearized with a depth-first search. For SocialIQA, we map the questions to a combination of ATOMIC and ConceptNet. ATOMIC events contain nouns and verbs which are representative of the social scenario being described in the event and are further extended in the context by SocialIQA annotators. We tokenize and stem the events and contexts to extract these representative words, and compute the percentage of overlapping words in the context with respect to each event. The event with maximum overlap with context is selected as the corresponding ATOMIC subject. The ATOMIC relation is selected from the predefined map of ATOMIC relations to SocialIQA questions. This way, we recover the ATOMIC alignments of nearly 20,000 samples from training set of SocialIQA (88% acc.).

Generation of Synthetic Data. In order to prepare synthetic datasets, we create a dataset of unseen input graphs by mutating the graphs from training sets of graph-to-text datasets. One or two entities are replaced by a randomly selected entity (or relation-entity pair) with similar adjacency to other entities in the input graph, to create a mutated graph. The maximum sequence length of graph contextualized embeddings is set to 64, while that of GPT2 is set to 128. The synthetic dataset size (pre-filtering) is 100k/50k/10k/10k/50k for SocialIQA, CQA, HellaSwag-2K, Codah, and ProtoQA respectively. For generation of synthetic data for SocialIQA, we use the set of tuples from ATOMIC that do not appear in the original dataset. To prepare the synthetic dataset for CommonsenseQA, we select two adversarial choices from ConceptNet and two choices generated by OptionGAN. For ProtoQA, we find accurate answers by generating 30 sets of answers for each synthetic question, ranking the answer choices by frequency and retaining the ones that appear at least 5 times in the 30 sets. See example of synthetic context generation in Fig. 4.

Evaluation. To evaluate graph-to-text generation, we define an ORACLE score which measures the semantic relevance of synthetic question when

[2] `https://spacy.io/`

[3] We use the question concept present in CQA annotations as additional concept for the questions.

paired with the original answer options. We replace the original question in validation set samples with the synthetic question and re-evaluate models on this modified dataset. In addition, we adopt the following NLG metrics: BLEU-4 (Papineni et al., 2002), METEOR (Banerjee and Lavie, 2005), CIDEr[4] (Vedantam et al., 2015) and BERTScore (F1 score) (Zhang et al., 2020). Models trained on the synthetic and original commmonsense reasoning datasets are evaluated using their respective task-specific accuracies (see Appendix). For ProtoQA, we report the accuracy in top-k answers where $k = 1, 3, 5$. We also perform human evaluation of the samples generated using GraphGPT2 and OptionGAN.

5 Results & Analysis

First, we present results from the complete GRADA framework followed by results from ablation experiments. Then, we discuss evaluation of the various generative models in GRADA using automated metrics as well as human annotators. Finally, we evaluate the robustness of models trained with and without GRADA to semantic adversaries and discuss upper bounds of our data augmentation pipeline. See Appendix for visualization of the quality of the synthetic datasets.

5.1 Data Augmentation Results

Results from the best GRADA model are presented in Table 1.[5] The baseline row represents results from the same task models used for GRADA but trained without any data augmentation i.e. T5-3B for ProtoQA and RoBERTa for all other datasets. We see 1-2% improvements over baseline across all multiple-choice datasets using GRADA. For the best GRADA models (selected using validation results), synthetic samples are generated from structured GraphGPT2 and OptionGAN, and filtered using QAP.[6] GRADA results in large improvements for ProtoQA i.e. 4-6% higher values on the Max Answers 1/3/5 metrics (see Appendix), suggesting the effectiveness of our approach for similar generative tasks. We see 0.3%, 0.3% and 0.26% improvement with GRADA over G-DAUG for CQA, Codah and HellaSwag-2K respectively. Our approach also performs similar to the Option Comparison Network in HyKAS (Ma et al., 2019) for CQA (row 3 in Table 1). Our approach is orthogonal to HyKAS, KG-Fusion as their instance-level approach retrieves information for each sample while GRADA augments knowledge on a global level.

Ablation results from the GRADA framework on validation sets are presented in Table 2. The first row of Table 2 presents results from baseline task models i.e., trained without data augmentation. Next, we compare results from two-stage training and see upto 1.7% (p<0.05 for all datasets) improvements (row 1 vs. 4 in Table 2) with the addition of synthetic data without filtering.[7] Using structured GraphGPT2 leads to 0.47% (p=0.043), 0.39% (p=0.078), 1.46% (p=0.12)[8] improvements over linearized GraphGPT2 for SocialIQA, CQA, ProtoQA and diminishing improvements for the smaller datasets. We see consistent but modest improvements which are not significant, from addition of distractors generated from OptionGAN. Even though improvements with OptionGAN are marginal, it is necessary for the completeness of the pipeline for synthetic generation. Next, adding filter to denoise the synthetic pool unequivocally improves results by large margins for all datasets except CQA. Filtering by QAP (row 5 in Table 2) provides additional benefit (p=0.069 and p=0.093 for SocialIQA and CQA, p<0.05 for other datasets) to downstream task models over unfiltered synthetic data augmentation (row 4).[9] See examples of high and low quality synthetic data samples filtered using QAP in Table 7. Smaller datasets benefit the most from GRADA.

Single-hop vs. Multi-hop Paths. Additionally, we finetune GraphGPT2 with sub-graphs made of single-hop paths only to generate the context. We perform data augmentation using the synthetic questions generated through this approach and compare to the GRADA results on validation sets. See results in Table 4. We observe 0.92%, 0.08%, 1.48% and 1.05% drops in performance for validation sets of SocialIQA, CQA, CODAH and HellaSwag respectively. The larger drops for smaller datasets suggest that multi-hop paths are effective in low-resource scenarios.

[4] https://github.com/Maluuba/nlg-eval

[5] It should be noted that the state-of-the-art UnifiedQA has 30x parameters in $\text{RoBERTa}_{\text{LARGE}}$

[6] ProtoQA is not a multiple-choice dataset, so OptionGAN is not used and we use sample perplexity as the only filter.

[7] Statistical significance is computed with 100K samples using bootstrap (Noreen, 1989; Tibshirani and Efron, 1993).

[8] p-values are larger for improvements on ProtoQA validation set which has only 52 samples.

[9] We also ran experiments with MLM pretraining (ATOMIC for SocialIQA and OMCS corpus for the rest) before finetuning on target dataset and saw <1% improvements.

Method	SocialIQA	CQA	Codah	HellaSwag-2K	ProtoQA
UnifiedQA-11B (Khashabi et al., 2020)	81.45	79.1	-	-	41.49 / 24.95 / 21.77
RoBERTa + KG Fusion (Mitra et al., 2019)	78.00	-	-	-	-
RoBERTa + HyKAS (Ma et al., 2019)	-	73.2			
BACKTRANSLATION (Yang et al., 2020)		70.2	81.8		-
G-DAUG (Yang et al., 2020)	-	72.6	84.3	75.70	-
Baseline* (No Augmentation)	76.74	72.1	82.3	73.40	35.77 / 43.81 / 49.88
GRADA	77.85	72.9	84.7	75.96	42.02 / 48.90 / 54.23

Table 1: Results on test sets of commonsense datasets and comparative results from other approaches taken from leaderboards. *We use T5-3B for ProtoQA baseline and GRADA results and RoBERTa for all other datasets.

Method	SIQA	CQA	CDH	H2K	PQA
Baseline	77.78	77.23	84.48	75.10	41.1
Synthetic Data Augmentation					
Linearized	78.21	77.55	86.07	76.40	45.63
+ Structured	78.68	77.94	86.13	76.70	46.09
+ OptionGAN	78.82	78.02	86.19	76.70	-
Filtering					
QAP*	79.12	78.06	86.81	77.60	50.34

Table 2: Ablation results on validation set of commonsense reasoning datasets. *We use sample perplexity for filtering ProtoQA samples.

Dataset	Original	GraphGPT2	
		Linearized	*Structured*
SocialIQA	75.92	55.18	57.34
CQA	77.23	57.63	58.71
CODAH	82.19	46.23	46.78
HellaSWAG-2K	76.58	41.35	41.74
ProtoQA	41.10	28.21	23.47

Table 3: ORACLE scores for question generation. Original represents the performance of baseline task models on original dataset. The columns GPT2 and GraphGPT2 represent similar evaluation with synthetic questions generated from linearized graphs and structure-aware graph encoder respectively.

Generalization to Unseen Concepts. We looked for %overlap of entity nodes and single-hop paths (subject– relation– object) between the multi-hop KGs spanning the questions of correctly answered samples after GraDA training and the questions of synthetic data, and observed 5-60% entity overlap and <20% path overlap. This suggests GRADA also promotes reasoning capabilities of the downstream models for unseen concepts.

5.2 Generative Model Evaluation Results

ORACLE scores for the two variations of GraphGPT2 are presented in Table 3. The scores in first column refer to the validation set performance of baseline models on original datasets. These models are re-evaluated on the questions generated by GraphGPT2 (as described in Sec. 4.1). The largest improvement i.e. 2.16% (p=0.068) is observed for SocialIQA, which may be attributed to its large dataset size. We see diminishing improvements for low-resource scenarios i.e. Codah and HellaSwag-2K. We observe a similar trend when the synthetic questions are evaluated using NLG metrics (see Appendix). More importantly, since phrase-matching metrics are not ideal for NLG evaluation (Novikova et al., 2017), we also perform human evaluation to judge the quality of generation for SocialIQA and CQA as we see significant improvements from structured GraphGPT2 vs. linearized GraphGPT2. We ask annotators on Amazon Mechanical Turk[10] (AMT) to select the sentence which is more representative of the information encoded in input graph, for 100 samples from validation set. Questions generated from GraphGPT2 are preferred 46% and 53% of the times for SocialIQA and CQA resp., compared to those from linearized inputs only, showing that the addition of graph encoder improves integration of knowledge in generated text.

Method	SIQA	CQA	CDH	H2K	PQA
Baseline	77.78	77.23	84.48	75.10	41.1
GraDA (single-hop)	78.70	77.31	85.96	76.05	45.67
GraDA (multi-hop)	79.12	78.06	86.81	77.60	50.34

Table 4: Results on validation set of commonsense reasoning datasets using single-hop vs. multi-hop graphs for GRADA pipeline.

Dataset	Question	Answer	Distractors
SocialIQA	96.1%	86.0%	50.0%
CommonsenseQA	100.0%	97.2%	25.0%
HellaSwag-2K	92.0%	88.1%	25.8%
CODAH	90.3	83.4%	30.6%
ProtoQA	97.2%	75.0%	-

Table 5: Results from human evaluation of generated questions, answers and distractors.

We perform human evaluation (AMT) of answerability of the generated questions/answers/distractors on 50 randomly selected samples from the filtered augmentation

[10]Located in United States, HIT Approval Rate>98%, Number of HITs Approved>10K, $15 per hour (approx.).

G-Daug (Yang et al., 2020)	GRADA	
	Knowledge-Graph Tuple	Generated Data
A human enjoys putting rubber on furniture. They should do this before .. front of the mirror. There was a large, cold bite of ice on my where? He hated flying, the controls were what?	*S*: PersonX provides ___ for PersonY's children *R*: xIntent *O*: To be helpful	Taylor provided meals for Kendall's children and they all enjoyed it greatly. Why did Taylor do this? [A] to be a bad friend [B] to be helpful [C] to be rude
What is a square leg made of made out of? What country does a cow go to make a milk run?	*S*: weasel *R*: AtLocation *O*: mafia organization	The man was a weasel, he was part of a powerful what? [A] out of doors [b] terrarium [c] mafia organization [D] farmyard [E] backyard

Table 6: Comparison of randomly generated synthetic data from G-Daug (Yang et al., 2020) (left) and knowledge-grounded synthetic data generated using GRADA (right). (S=Subject, R=Relation, O=Object)

	High-quality synthetic samples
SIQA	Riley provided help to the community through his many charity events over the years. How would Others feel as a result? [A] selfish [B] appreciative [C] bored
CQA	When a child is upset by something, what may they do? [A] fall down [B] wish to fly [C] start crying [D] play tag [E] boy or girl
PQA	Name something you worry you're still doing when you're not supposed to. drinking, smoking, sleeping, working, using cell phone
	Low-quality synthetic samples
SIQA	Tracy raised her arm to her face to cover her eyes during the scary movie. What does Tracy need to dobefore this? [A] scared [B] be scared of the movie [C] to have a fundraiser
CQA	What will you do if you want to go public? [A] prepare for worst [B] tell family first [C] own private company [D] telegram [E] charming
PQA	Name a family tradition that has deep roots in the dialect of suzh. cooking, caroling, knitting, hunting, fishing

Table 7: High and low quality synthetic samples generated through GRADA for SIQA, CQA, ProtoQA (PQA) and ranked using QAP scores (and perplexity for PQA). Labels are marked in green.

data (see Table 5). Annotators were provided with the question, answer and distractors, and asked to evaluate a) if the question can be answered in a few words (b) if the question can be answered by the given answer and (c) if the distractors are wrong answers for the question. More than 90% of the questions were judged as answerable, 75-90% of the answers were judged as correct answers for the respective questions. The quality of distractors ranged from 50% for SocialIQA to 20-30% for smaller datasets. However, the overall quality of distractors is high enough to benefit data augmentation. See examples in Table 7. We also perform human evaluation for the factuality of samples generated using our method GraDA and GDaug (Yang et al., 2020). We picked a randomly sampled set of 100 synthetic

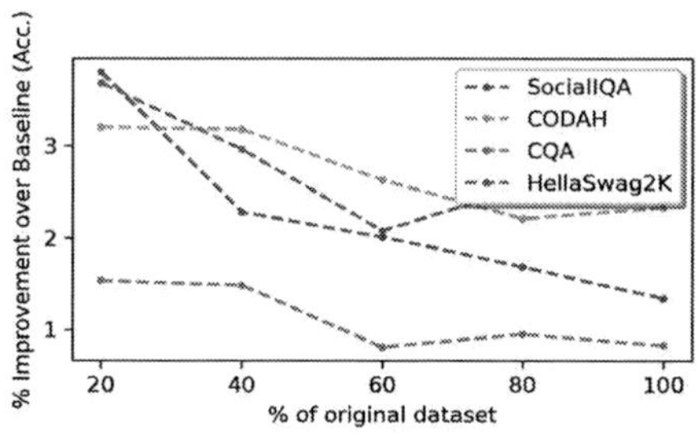

Figure 5: % improvement in accuracy over baseline with different % of original dataset. Baseline is RoBERTa finetuned on the same % of original dataset.

QA pairs from G-Daug for the datasets CQA, Codah and HellaSWAG-2K. For a fair comparison, we collected 100 synthetic pairs from GraDA for the same datasets. We asked an annotator to evaluate if each of the synthetic QA pair adheres to a plausible real-world scenario, and found that 56% G-Daug samples were judged as factual as compared to 68% of the GraDA samples (see examples in Table 6).

5.3 Upper Bounds

We ran experiments for augmentation with 20%, 40%, 60%, 80% and 100% training data from the original set (see Fig. 5). The improvement margins from the augmentation dataset is upto 4% at 20% of the original SocialIQA dataset. We see similar trends for CODAH, HellaSwag and ProtoQA, while the improvements for CQA were <1.5%.

5.4 Robustness Evaluation

We expect that data augmentation exposes the task model to diverse language and improves its robustness to semantic adversaries in addition to boosting its performance on the target task. To evaluate this, we use the TextFooler system (Jin et al., 2020; Yang et al., 2020; Wei and Zou, 2019) to generate adversarial text by computing word importance ranking and replacing the most influential words

Method	SIQA	CQA	CDH	H2K	PQA
Baseline	21.7/10.3	14.9/12.5	31.3/16.1	19.4/10.6	5.1/16.2
GRADA	22.4/10.8	15.8/12.9	34.8/18.2	20.5/11.5	6.3/16.8

Table 8: Robustness Evaluation. Failure rate / perturbation ratio (higher is better) from TextFooler experiments are shown on development sets.

with their synonym in the vector space. Overall, GRADA benefits the robustness of task models and improves their failure rate by 1-3% (see Table 8).

6 Conclusion

We present GRADA, a graph-based data augmentation framework for commonsense reasoning QA datasets. We train a graph-to-text question generator and GAN-based adversarial choice generator for creating synthetic data samples, which are used to augment the original datasets. GRADA promotes factuality in synthetic samples and improves results on five downstream datasets.

7 Ethical Considerations

The usage of pretrained generative models in any downstream application requires careful consideration of the real-world impact of generated text. In our approach, we provide concrete inputs for grounding the generated text to specific entities and relations which encode real-world facts, thereby reducing the possibility of propagating unintended stereotypical and social biases embedded within the pretrained models. However, since these entities and relations are derived from existing knowledge bases like ConceptNet (Speer et al., 2017), there is potential for transfer of bias present in these resources to the generated texts. Additionally, the graph-to-text generative models in GRADA pose the same risk as other data-to-text generative models (Ribeiro et al., 2020; Hoyle et al., 2020; Mager et al., 2020) i.e. the models can be made to generate incorrect facts by providing incorrect data as input. Therefore, we recommend restricting the use of GRADA to low-risk, unbiased graphs inputs.

Acknowledgments

We thank the reviewers for their useful feedback. This work was supported by DARPA MCS Grant N66001-19-2-403, ONR Grant N00014-18-1-2871, and NSF-CAREER Award 1846185. The views are those of the authors and not of the funding agency.

References

Ateret Anaby-Tavor, Boaz Carmeli, Esther Goldbraich, Amir Kantor, George Kour, Segev Shlomov, Naama Tepper, and Naama Zwerdling. 2020. Not enough data? deep learning to the rescue! In *Thirty-Fourth AAAI Conference on Artificial Intelligence*.

Satanjeev Banerjee and Alon Lavie. 2005. Meteor: An automatic metric for mt evaluation with improved correlation with human judgments. In *Proceedings of the acl workshop on intrinsic and extrinsic evaluation measures for machine translation and/or summarization*, pages 65–72.

Lisa Bauer, Yicheng Wang, and Mohit Bansal. 2018. Commonsense for generative multi-hop question answering tasks. In *Proceedings of the 2018 Conference on EMNLP*, pages 4220–4230.

Daniel Beck, Gholamreza Haffari, and Trevor Cohn. 2018. Graph-to-sequence learning using gated graph neural networks. In *Proceedings of the 56th Annual Meeting of the Association for Computational Linguistics (Volume 1: Long Papers)*, pages 273–283.

Chandra Bhagavatula, Ronan Le Bras, Chaitanya Malaviya, Keisuke Sakaguchi, Ari Holtzman, Hannah Rashkin, Doug Downey, Wen-tau Yih, and Yejin Choi. 2020. Abductive commonsense reasoning. In *8th International Conference on Learning Representations, ICLR 2020, Addis Ababa, Ethiopia, April 26-30, 2020*. OpenReview.net.

Sheng Bi, Xiya Cheng, Yuan-Fang Li, Yongzhen Wang, and Guilin Qi. 2020. Knowledge-enriched, type-constrained and grammar-guided question generation over knowledge bases. In *Proceedings of the 28th International Conference on Computational Linguistics*, pages 2776–2786.

Yonatan Bisk, Rowan Zellers, Ronan Le Bras, Jianfeng Gao, and Yejin Choi. 2020. Piqa: Reasoning about physical commonsense in natural language. In *Proceedings of the AAAI Conference on Artificial Intelligence*, volume 34, pages 3027–3035.

Michael Boratko, Xiang Li, Tim O'Gorman, Rajarshi Das, Dan Le, and Andrew McCallum. 2020. Protoqa: A question answering dataset for prototypical common-sense reasoning. In *Proceedings of the 2020 Conference on Empirical Methods in Natural Language Processing (EMNLP)*, pages 1122–1136.

Antoine Bosselut, Hannah Rashkin, Maarten Sap, Chaitanya Malaviya, Asli Celikyilmaz, and Yejin Choi. 2019. Comet: Commonsense transformers for automatic knowledge graph construction. In *Proceedings of the 57th Annual Meeting of the Association for Computational Linguistics*, pages 4762–4779.

Liwei Cai and William Yang Wang. 2018. Kbgan: Adversarial learning for knowledge graph embeddings. In *Proceedings of NAACL-HLT*, pages 1470–1480.

Michael Chen, Mike D'Arcy, Alisa Liu, Jared Fernandez, and Doug Downey. 2019. Codah: An adversarially authored question-answer dataset for common sense. In *Proceedings of the 3rd Workshop on Evaluating Vector Space Representations for NLP*.

Yu Chen, Lingfei Wu, and Mohammed J Zaki. 2020. Toward subgraph guided knowledge graph question generation with graph neural networks. *arXiv preprint arXiv:2004.06015*.

Ho-Lam Chung, Ying-Hong Chan, and Yao-Chung Fan. 2020. A bert-based distractor generation scheme with multi-tasking and negative answer training strategies. *arXiv preprint arXiv:2010.05384*.

Nicola De Cao, Wilker Aziz, and Ivan Titov. 2019. Question answering by reasoning across documents with graph convolutional networks. In *Proceedings of NAACL-HLT*, pages 2306–2317.

Jacob Devlin, Ming-Wei Chang, Kenton Lee, and Kristina Toutanova. 2019. Bert: Pre-training of deep bidirectional transformers for language understanding. In *Proceedings of the 2019 Conference of the North American Chapter of the Association for Computational Linguistics: Human Language Technologies, Volume 1 (Long and Short Papers)*, pages 4171–4186.

Yanlin Feng, Xinyue Chen, Bill Yuchen Lin, Peifeng Wang, Jun Yan, and Xiang Ren. 2020. Scalable multi-hop relational reasoning for knowledge-aware question answering. In *Proceedings of the 2020 Conference on Empirical Methods in Natural Language Processing (EMNLP)*, pages 1295–1309.

Ian Goodfellow, Jean Pouget-Abadie, Mehdi Mirza, Bing Xu, David Warde-Farley, Sherjil Ozair, Aaron Courville, and Yoshua Bengio. 2014. Generative adversarial nets. In *Advances in neural information processing systems*, pages 2672–2680.

Catherine Havasi, Robert Speer, Kenneth Arnold, Henry Lieberman, Jason Alonso, and Jesse Moeller. 2010. Open mind common sense: Crowd-sourcing for common sense. In *Workshops at the Twenty-Fourth AAAI Conference on Artificial Intelligence*.

Bin He, Di Zhou, Jinghui Xiao, Xin Jiang, Qun Liu, Nicholas Jing Yuan, and Tong Xu. 2020. Integrating graph contextualized knowledge into pre-trained language models. In *Proceedings of the 2020 Conference on Empirical Methods in Natural Language Processing: Findings*, pages 2281–2290.

Alexander Hoyle, Ana Marasović, and Noah Smith. 2020. Promoting graph awareness in linearized graph-to-text generation. *arXiv preprint arXiv:2012.15793*.

Di Jin, Zhijing Jin, Joey Tianyi Zhou, and Peter Szolovits. 2020. Is bert really robust? natural language attack on text classification and entailment. In *AAAI*.

Pei Ke, Haozhe Ji, Yu Ran, Xin Cui, Liwei Wang, Linfeng Song, Xiaoyan Zhu, and Minlie Huang. 2021. Jointgt: Graph-text joint representation learning for text generation from knowledge graphs. In *Findings of the Association for Computational Linguistics: ACL-IJCNLP 2021*, pages 2526–2538.

Daniel Khashabi, Sewon Min, Tushar Khot, Ashish Sabharwal, Oyvind Tafjord, Peter Clark, and Hannaneh Hajishirzi. 2020. Unifiedqa: Crossing format boundaries with a single qa system. In *Proceedings of the 2020 Conference on Empirical Methods in Natural Language Processing: Findings*, pages 1896–1907.

Thomas N Kipf and Max Welling. 2017. Semi-supervised classification with graph convolutional networks. In *ICLR*. OpenReview.net.

Rik Koncel-Kedziorski, Dhanush Bekal, Yi Luan, Mirella Lapata, and Hannaneh Hajishirzi. 2019. Text generation from knowledge graphs with graph transformers. In *Proceedings of the 2019 Conference of the NAACL: HLT, Volume 1 (Long and Short Papers)*, pages 2284–2293.

Mahnaz Koupaee and William Yang Wang. 2018. Wikihow: A large scale text summarization dataset. *arXiv preprint arXiv:1810.09305*.

Vishwajeet Kumar, Yuncheng Hua, Ganesh Ramakrishnan, Guilin Qi, Lianli Gao, and Yuan-Fang Li. 2019. Difficulty-controllable multi-hop question generation from knowledge graphs. In *International Semantic Web Conference*, pages 382–398. Springer.

Matt J Kusner and José Miguel Hernández-Lobato. 2016. GANs for sequences of discrete elements with the gumbel-softmax distribution. *arXiv preprint arXiv:1611.04051*.

Chen Liang, Xiao Yang, Neisarg Dave, Drew Wham, Bart Pursel, and C Lee Giles. 2018. Distractor generation for multiple choice questions using learning to rank. In *Proceedings of the thirteenth workshop on innovative use of NLP for building educational applications*, pages 284–290.

Bill Yuchen Lin, Xinyue Chen, Jamin Chen, and Xiang Ren. 2019. Kagnet: Knowledge-aware graph networks for commonsense reasoning. In *Proceedings of the 2019 Conference on Empirical Methods in Natural Language Processing and the 9th International Joint Conference on Natural Language Processing (EMNLP-IJCNLP)*, pages 2822–2832.

Weitang Liu, Xiaoyun Wang, John Owens, and Yixuan Li. 2020. Energy-based out-of-distribution detection. *Advances in Neural Information Processing Systems*, 33.

Yinhan Liu, Myle Ott, Naman Goyal, Jingfei Du, Mandar Joshi, Danqi Chen, Omer Levy, Mike Lewis, Luke Zettlemoyer, and Veselin Stoyanov. 2019. Roberta: A robustly optimized bert pretraining approach. *arXiv preprint arXiv:1907.11692*.

Shangwen Lv, Daya Guo, Jingjing Xu, Duyu Tang, Nan Duan, Ming Gong, Linjun Shou, Daxin Jiang, Guihong Cao, and Songlin Hu. 2020. Graph-based reasoning over heterogeneous external knowledge for commonsense question answering. In *Proceedings of the Thirty-Fourth Conference on Association for the Advancement of Artificial Intelligence (AAAI)*.

Kaixin Ma, Jonathan Francis, Quanyang Lu, Eric Nyberg, and Alessandro Oltramari. 2019. Towards generalizable neuro-symbolic systems for commonsense question answering. In *Proceedings of the First Workshop on Commonsense Inference in Natural Language Processing*, pages 22–32.

Manuel Mager, Ramón Fernandez Astudillo, Tahira Naseem, Md Arafat Sultan, Young-Suk Lee, Radu Florian, and Salim Roukos. 2020. Gpt-too: A language-model-first approach for amr-to-text generation. In *Proceedings of the 58th Annual Meeting of the Association for Computational Linguistics*, pages 1846–1852.

Diego Marcheggiani and Laura Perez-Beltrachini. 2018. Deep graph convolutional encoders for structured data to text generation. In *Proceedings of the 11th International Conference on Natural Language Generation*, pages 1–9.

Arindam Mitra, Pratyay Banerjee, Kuntal Kumar Pal, Swaroop Mishra, and Chitta Baral. 2019. Exploring ways to incorporate additional knowledge to improve natural language commonsense question answering. *arXiv preprint arXiv:1909.08855*.

Weili Nie, Nina Narodytska, and Ankit Patel. 2019a. Relgan: Relational generative adversarial networks for text generation. In *7th International Conference on Learning Representations, ICLR 2019, New Orleans, LA, USA, May 6-9, 2019*. OpenReview.net.

Weili Nie, Nina Narodytska, and Ankit Patel. 2019b. Relgan: Relational generative adversarial networks for text generation. In *7th International Conference on Learning Representations, ICLR 2019, New Orleans, LA, USA, May 6-9, 2019*. OpenReview.net.

Eric W Noreen. 1989. *Computer-intensive methods for testing hypotheses*. Wiley New York.

Jekaterina Novikova, Ondřej Dušek, Amanda Cercas Curry, and Verena Rieser. 2017. Why we need new evaluation metrics for NLG. In *Proceedings of the 2017 Conference on Empirical Methods in Natural Language Processing*, pages 2241–2252, Copenhagen, Denmark. Association for Computational Linguistics.

Jeroen Offerijns, Suzan Verberne, and Tessa Verhoef. 2020. Better distractions: Transformer-based distractor generation and multiple choice question filtering. *arXiv preprint arXiv:2010.09598*.

Kishore Papineni, Salim Roukos, Todd Ward, and Wei-Jing Zhu. 2002. Bleu: a method for automatic evaluation of machine translation. In *Proceedings of the 40th annual meeting on association for computational linguistics*, pages 311–318. Association for Computational Linguistics.

Raul Puri, Ryan Spring, Mostofa Patwary, Mohammad Shoeybi, and Bryan Catanzaro. 2020. Training question answering models from synthetic data. *arXiv preprint arXiv:2002.09599*.

Pengda Qin, Weiran Xu, and William Yang Wang. 2018. Dsgan: Generative adversarial training for distant supervision relation extraction. In *Proceedings of the 56th Annual Meeting of the Association for Computational Linguistics (Volume 1: Long Papers)*, pages 496–505.

Alec Radford, Karthik Narasimhan, Tim Salimans, and Ilya Sutskever. 2018. Improving language understanding by generative pre-training. *OpenAI Technical Report*.

Alec Radford, Jeffrey Wu, Rewon Child, David Luan, Dario Amodei, and Ilya Sutskever. 2019. Language models are unsupervised multitask learners.

Colin Raffel, Noam Shazeer, Adam Roberts, Katherine Lee, Sharan Narang, Michael Matena, Yanqi Zhou, Wei Li, and Peter J Liu. 2020. Exploring the limits of transfer learning with a unified text-to-text transformer. *Journal of Machine Learning Research*, 21:1–67.

Leonardo FR Ribeiro, Martin Schmitt, Hinrich Schütze, and Iryna Gurevych. 2020. Investigating pretrained language models for graph-to-text generation. *arXiv preprint arXiv:2007.08426*.

Keisuke Sakaguchi, Ronan Le Bras, Chandra Bhagavatula, and Yejin Choi. 2020. Winogrande: An adversarial winograd schema challenge at scale. In *Proceedings of the AAAI Conference on Artificial Intelligence*, volume 34.

Maarten Sap, Ronan Le Bras, Emily Allaway, Chandra Bhagavatula, Nicholas Lourie, Hannah Rashkin, Brendan Roof, Noah A Smith, and Yejin Choi. 2019a. Atomic: An atlas of machine commonsense for if-then reasoning. In *Proceedings of the AAAI Conference on Artificial Intelligence*, volume 33, pages 3027–3035.

Maarten Sap, Hannah Rashkin, Derek Chen, Ronan Le Bras, and Yejin Choi. 2019b. Social iqa: Commonsense reasoning about social interactions. In *Proceedings of the 2019 Conference on EMNLP and the 9th IJCNLP*, pages 4453–4463.

Xinyao Shen, Jiangjie Chen, Jiaze Chen, Chun Zeng, and Yanghua Xiao. 2022. Diversified query generation guided by knowledge graph. In *Proceedings of the Fifteenth ACM International Conference on Web Search and Data Mining*, pages 897–907.

Jasper Snoek, Hugo Larochelle, and Ryan P Adams. 2012. Practical bayesian optimization of machine learning algorithms. In *Advances in neural information processing systems*, pages 2951–2959.

Robyn Speer, Joshua Chin, and Catherine Havasi. 2017. Conceptnet 5.5: An open multilingual graph of general knowledge. In *Thirty-First AAAI Conference on Artificial Intelligence*.

Richard S Sutton, David A McAllester, Satinder P Singh, and Yishay Mansour. 2000. Policy gradient methods for reinforcement learning with function approximation. In *Advances in neural information processing systems*, pages 1057–1063.

Swabha Swayamdipta, Roy Schwartz, Nicholas Lourie, Yizhong Wang, Hannaneh Hajishirzi, Noah A Smith, and Yejin Choi. 2020. Dataset cartography: Mapping and diagnosing datasets with training dynamics. In *Proceedings of the 2020 Conference on Empirical Methods in Natural Language Processing (EMNLP)*, pages 9275–9293.

Christian Szegedy, Vincent Vanhoucke, Sergey Ioffe, Jon Shlens, and Zbigniew Wojna. 2016. Rethinking the inception architecture for computer vision. In *Proceedings of the IEEE conference on computer vision and pattern recognition*, pages 2818–2826.

Alon Talmor, Jonathan Herzig, Nicholas Lourie, and Jonathan Berant. 2019. Commonsenseqa: A question answering challenge targeting commonsense knowledge. In *Proceedings of the 2019 Conference of the NAACL: HLT, Volume 1 (Long and Short Papers)*, pages 4149–4158.

Robert J Tibshirani and Bradley Efron. 1993. An introduction to the bootstrap. *Monographs on statistics and applied probability*, 57:1–436.

Ashish Vaswani, Noam Shazeer, Niki Parmar, Jakob Uszkoreit, Llion Jones, Aidan N Gomez, Łukasz Kaiser, and Illia Polosukhin. 2017. Attention is all you need. In *Advances in neural information processing systems*, pages 5998–6008.

Ramakrishna Vedantam, C Lawrence Zitnick, and Devi Parikh. 2015. Cider: Consensus-based image description evaluation. In *Proceedings of the IEEE conference on computer vision and pattern recognition*, pages 4566–4575.

Petar Velickovic, Guillem Cucurull, Arantxa Casanova, Adriana Romero, Pietro Liò, and Yoshua Bengio. 2018. Graph attention networks. In *6th International Conference on Learning Representations, ICLR 2018, Vancouver, BC, Canada, April 30 - May 3, 2018, Conference Track Proceedings*. OpenReview.net.

Jason Wei and Kai Zou. 2019. Eda: Easy data augmentation techniques for boosting performance on text classification tasks. In *Proceedings of the 2019 Conference on Empirical Methods in Natural Language Processing and the 9th International Joint Conference on Natural Language Processing (EMNLP-IJCNLP)*, pages 6383–6389.

Yiben Yang, Chaitanya Malaviya, Jared Fernandez, Swabha Swayamdipta, Ronan Le Bras, Ji-Ping Wang, Chandra Bhagavatula, Yejin Choi, and Doug Downey. 2020. G-daug: Generative data augmentation for commonsense reasoning. In *Proceedings of the 2020 Conference on Empirical Methods in Natural Language Processing: Findings*, pages 1008–1025.

Zhilin Yang, Zihang Dai, Yiming Yang, Jaime Carbonell, Russ R Salakhutdinov, and Quoc V Le. 2019. Xlnet: Generalized autoregressive pretraining for language understanding. In *Advances in neural information processing systems*, pages 5754–5764.

Zhi-Xiu Ye, Qian Chen, Wen Wang, and Zhen-Hua Ling. 2019. Align, mask and select: A simple method for incorporating commonsense knowledge into language representation models. *arXiv preprint arXiv:1908.06725*.

Lantao Yu, Weinan Zhang, Jun Wang, and Yong Yu. 2017. Seqgan: Sequence generative adversarial nets with policy gradient. In *Thirty-First AAAI Conference on Artificial Intelligence*.

Rowan Zellers, Ari Holtzman, Yonatan Bisk, Ali Farhadi, and Yejin Choi. 2019. Hellaswag: Can a machine really finish your sentence? In *Proceedings of the 57th Annual Meeting of the Association for Computational Linguistics*, pages 4791–4800.

Shiyue Zhang and Mohit Bansal. 2019. Addressing semantic drift in question generation for semi-supervised question answering. In *Proceedings of the 2019 Conference on Empirical Methods in Natural Language Processing and the 9th International Joint Conference on Natural Language Processing (EMNLP-IJCNLP)*, pages 2495–2509.

Tianyi Zhang, Varsha Kishore, Felix Wu, Kilian Q Weinberger, and Yoav Artzi. 2020. Bertscore: Evaluating text generation with bert. In *8th International Conference on Learning Representations, ICLR 2020, Addis Ababa, Ethiopia, April 26-30, 2020*. OpenReview.net.

Zhirui Zhang, Shujie Liu, Mu Li, Ming Zhou, and Enhong Chen. 2018. Bidirectional generative adversarial networks for neural machine translation. In *Proceedings of the 22nd Conference on Computational Natural Language Learning*, pages 190–199. Association for Computational Linguistics.

A Experiment Setup

Datasets: Social IQA (Sap et al., 2019b) and CommonsenseQA (Talmor et al., 2019) are popular datasets based on knowledge graphs, making them a suitable choice for testing our approach. Social IQA is a multiple-choice question answering dataset. Each sample consists of a context, question and three multiple choices. CommonsenseQA is also a multiple-choice QA dataset, wherein each sample consists of a context and five multiple choices. Of those 5 choices, three are taken from ConceptNet and the other two are authored by annotators. We only use the human-authored incorrect choices to train our adversarial choice generator OptionGAN. The ATOMIC knowledge graph contains 24K base events and 877K tuples describing a variety of social scenarios. We use the 710K training split introduced in Bosselut et al. (2019) to randomly sample 100K tuples as the seed subgraphs for generation of synthetic data dataset for Social IQA. For CommonsenseQA, we use the entire ConceptNet knowledge graph, subject to pruning as outlined in Talmor et al. (2019), to sample seed tuples for synthetic dataset generation. For SocialIQA, CQA, Codah and HellaSwag-2K, we use simple accuracy for model evaluation.

ProtoQA (Boratko et al., 2020) is a generative QA dataset which is evaluated by 7 different metrics[11]. We report the first 3 metrics i.e. Max Answers 1/3/5. For tables showing only one number for ProtoQA, such as the ablation table in main text, we report the Max Answer 1 metric. In order to train T5-3B for ProtoQA, we concatenate the ranked choices for each question and finetune the model for conditional generation of this concatenated string from the input question.

All of the above datasets are being for their intended purposes i.e. research only, in our work. All of these datasets are in the English language.

Data Preparation: To prepare graph-to-text datasets for training GraphGPT2, we map the questions to multi-hop paths in ConceptNet (Bauer et al., 2018). We use Spacy[12] to tag the questions with part-of-speech and extract verbs and nouns as concepts, retaining those that appear in ConceptNet as entities[13]. For SocialIQA, we map the questions to a combination of ATOMIC and ConceptNet. ATOMIC events contain nouns and verbs which are representative of the social scenario being described in the event and are further extended in the context by Social IQA annotators (see Table 6). We tokenize and stem the events and contexts to extract these representative words, and compute the percentage of overlapping words in the context with respect to each event. The event with maximum overlap with context is selected as the corresponding ATOMIC subject. The ATOMIC relation is selected from the predefined map of ATOMIC relations to Social IQA questions. This way, we recover the ATOMIC alignments of 20,000 samples from training set of SocialIQA with 88% accuracy.

Synthetic Data Generation. In order to prepare synthetic datasets, we create a dataset of unseen input graphs by mutating the graphs from training sets of graph-to-text datasets. One or two entities are replaced by a randomly selected entity (or relation-entity pair) with similar adjacency to other entities in the input graph, to create a mutated graph. The synthetic dataset size (prefitering) is 100k/50k/10k/10k/50k for SocialIQA, CQA, HellaSwag-2K, Codah, and ProtoQA respectively. For generation of synthetic data, we use the set of tuples from ATOMIC and ConceptNet that do not appear in SocialIQA and CommonsenseQA datasets respectively. To prepare the synthetic dataset for CommonsenseQA, we select two adversarial choices from ConceptNet and two choices generated by OptionGAN. For ProtoQA, we find accurate answers by generating 30 samples of answers for each synthetic question, ranking the answer choices by frequency and retaining the ones that appear atleast 5 times in the 30 samples. After this, the synthetic question and answer (concatenation of high-frequency answer choices) is subjected to filtering. Due to lack of option for supplementary in this submission, we have included a sample of the generated synthetic examples in Table 9.

A.1 Filtering and Selection of Samples

Inspite of the careful construction of synthetic samples using knowledge graphs, the pool of synthetic samples can be noisy and may consist of incoherent text, incorrect question-answer pairs or out-of-distribution samples. Hence, we compare the effect of three different methods to filter samples on downstream task performance.

Question Answering Probability (QAP). The QAP score (μ) (Zhang and Bansal, 2019) is the prediction probability of the true class by a model with parameters θ which has been trained on the original dataset i.e. $\mu_i = p_\theta(y_i^*|x_i)$. Samples with low prediction probabilities for the correct choices are either annotated incorrectly or are especially difficult instances for the model. We define a low and high threshold for the QAP filter and samples lying within this range are retained in the dataset.

Model Confidence and Variability. Swayamdipta et al. (2020) propose the model confidence ($\hat{\mu}_i$) and variability ($\hat{\sigma}_i$) measures to identify

[11] https://github.com/iesl/protoqa-evaluator

[12] https://spacy.io/

[13] We use the question concept present in CQA annotations as additional concept for the questions.

HellaSWAG-2K	
Question	*Answer*
A close up of a gymnast is shown. a gymnast balances on beam as she sweeps __	(a) over obstacles. (b) around with other gymnast. (c) performs a front squat and a flip, and crosses her arms. (d) performing multiple back and forth moves.
"We then search for a car by its model and make. Once we get the car model __	(a) we determine what the tires are for. (b) we either buy a new or recycle it. If we want to recycle the car, we simply (c) click the buy now button. The seller will then provide a description of the car and (d) we'll add it to the computer so we can make a list of the different models we'll
A man in black robes is walking into a bar. He __	(a) is telling several anecdotes about how he has been following other people around and talking to them. (b) speaks to a group of workers and they all rise and raise their arms in the air. (c) starts singing into the microphone. (D) begins a beat down on a man standing behind him.
CODAH	
Question	*Answer*
I am feeling very hungry. I think that __	(a) I will have dinner. (b) I will drink some milk. (c) I will sleep a lot. (d) I will play catch with my grandpa.
A man with no body hair was peacefully wallowing in the sea of ocean. The man then __	(a) was surrounded by a flock of birds. (b) hung from the ceiling and sang (c) began to carpet the beach. (d) watched a movie with his headphones on.
A man excitedly planned a surprise party for his friend. He __	(a) got a shotgun. (b) put up a giant neon sign with his own hand painted on it. (c) decided to end his life in front of his friend. (d) planned to brew a cup of coffee and play chess.
ProtoQA	
Question	*Answer*
Name something you worry you're still doing when you're not supposed to.	drinking, smoking, sleeping, working, using cell phone
Besides milk, name a popular product in the dairy market.	cheese, ice cream, yogurt, butter
Name something you can disagree about.	religion, politics, parenting, weight, money
If you sent a postcard from china what would be pictured on the front?	great wall, temple, dragon
Name something a knight needs for a good day's work.	horse, armour, sword, lance, shield

Table 9: Examples of synthetic samples generated for HellaSWAG-2K, CODAH and ProtoQA datasets from the GRADA pipeline. Correct answers for multiple-choice questions are marked in green.

the effect of data samples on the model's generalization error. Specifically, $\hat{\mu_i} = \frac{1}{E}\sum_{e=1}^{E} p_\theta(y_i^*|x_i)$ and $\hat{\sigma_i} = \sqrt{\frac{\sum_{e=1}^{E}(p_\theta(y_i^*|x_i)-\hat{\mu_i})^2}{E}}$, where E is training epochs. They find that ambiguous samples i.e., high variability and mid-range confidence, contribute the most to test performance on downstream task. Following this, we define low and high thresholds for both confidence and variability in order to find the most informative samples.

Energy. Liu et al. (2020) show that the energy score can be reliably used for distinguishing between in- and out-of-distribution (OOD) samples, as compared to the traditional approach of using the softmax scores. We introduce an energy threshold to select samples which are out-of-distribution i.e. $E_i = -log\sum_j^C e^{p_\theta(y_i^j|x)}$ where C is the number of choices in the QA sample, and measure the effect of using OOD samples as augmentation data.

A.2 Training Details

Baselines: We use pretrained RoBERTa$_{\text{LARGE}}$ (Liu et al., 2019) for multiple-choice datasets and T5-3B (Raffel et al., 2020) for ProtoQA as the task models. The baseline task model is finetuned on original datasets with no data augmentation, and is used as scoring model for filtering. We use GPT2$_{\text{MEDIUM}}$ for GraphGPT2, GPT2$_{\text{SMALL}}$ as the pretrained generator and discriminator for OptionGAN. For GRADA, the model is first finetuned on synthetic samples using label smoothing (Szegedy et al., 2016) and then on original dataset. We refer the reader to Koncel-Kedziorski et al. (2019) for full implementation details of the Graph Encoder in GraphGPT2.

OptionGAN: It is tricky to train GAN models, especially with discrete data like text. We follow the training method in Nie et al. (2019a) to finetune the adversarial choice generator in a minimax

Parameter	Bounds
Filter Parameters	
QAP/Model Confidence Lower Threshold	[0.0, 0.49]
QAP/Model Confidence Higher Threshold	[0.51, 1.0]
Energy Lower Threhsold	[0.0, 1.0]
Energy Higher Threshold	[0.0, 1.0]
Model Variability Lower Threshold	[0.0, 0.5]
Model Variability Higher Threshold	[0.0, 0.5]
Training Parameters	
Learning Rate	[1, 10]*1e-6
Batch Size (*inc*)	[4, 8, 16]
Total Train Epochs	[3, 5]

Table 10: Optimization bounds for grid-search based tuning of training hyperparameters.

Method	BLEU4	METEOR	CIDEr	BERTScore
Social IQA				
GPT2	14.58	26.41	132.84	89.12
GraphGPT2	15.37	26.95	135.91	91.83
CommonsenseQA				
GPT2	1.71	12.78	30.89	85.76
GraphGPT2	1.90	13.64	33.76	87.34

Table 11: Comparison of performance for GPT2 and GraphGPT2 on development sets.

game with discriminator. In addition to the training parameters mentioned in Table 17, we restrict the number of training iterations to 5000, and perform one gradient descent step on generator for every 5 gradient descent steps on discriminator.

Training & Hyperparameter Tuning. After generation of synthetic examples, we perform two-stage training of the task models. In the first phase, the model is finetuned on synthetic data only, In the second phase, the model is finetuned on the original dataset. The model trained in first phase is subject to bayesian optimization (Snoek et al., 2012) of filter parameters.

A.3 Human Evaluation

Generative source of the sentences are omitted when presented to annotators. The input graphs are seed tuples from ATOMIC and ConceptNet for samples from the development sets of Social IQA and CommonsenseQA respectively. The annotators can pick both the sentences if either of them are equally relevant in their subjective opinion. We allow for a single hit for each assignment in Amazon Mechanical Turk.

Dataset	Wins	Loses	Tie
SocialIQA	46%	37%	17%
CommonsenseQA	53%	31%	16%

Table 12: Results from comparative human evaluation of generated questions. Wins and Loses refer to the %times synthetic question generated from structured graph input was chosen over linearized graph.

B Results

B.1 Generative Model Evaluation

As shown in Table 11, we see small improvements for BLEU-4 and METEOR, but larger improvements in other metrics from GraphGPT2 i.e., 3.07% (p=0.027), 2.87% (p=0.035) in CIDEr, and 2.71% (p=0.042), 1.58% (p=0.056) in BERTScore for Social IQA and CQA, resp. The phrase-matching metric scores are low for CQA, which may be attributed to its small sample size. However, BERTScore for CQA lies between 85-88%, showing that the model manages to convey similar meaning as human-annotated context albeit with different words.

More importantly, since phrase-matching metrics are not ideal for NLG evaluation (Novikova et al., 2017), we also perform human evaluation to judge the quality of generation for SocialIQA and CommonsenseQA as we see significant improvements from structured GraphGPT2 vs. linearized GraphGPT2. We ask annotators on Amazon Mechanical Turk[14] to select the sentence which is more representative of the information encoded in input graph, for 100 samples from validation set. Results are shown in Table 12. Samples generated from structured input are selected significantly more times than those from linearized inputs, for both SocialIQA and CQA, showing that addition of a graph encoder improves representation of knowledge in generated sample.

Additionally, we perform human evaluation of the samples generated using GraphGPT2 and OptionGAN. We randomly select 50 samples from the filtered augmentation datasets for each of the five datasets, and ask 2 annotators to answer 3 yes/no questions about the quality of the question, answer and distractors respectively. We present results from the survey in Table 5. More than 90% of the questions in each dataset were judged as answerable, showing the effectiveness of GraphGPT2 as well as the QAP-based filtering method. Simi-

[14]Located in United States, HIT Approval Rate>98%, Number of HITs Approved>10K.

Method	SIQA	CQA	CDH	H2K	PQA
Baseline	77.78	77.23	84.48	75.10	41.1
		Filtering			
QAP*	79.12	78.06	86.81	77.60	50.34
Confidence	79.05	77.83	86.59	77.40	-
Energy	78.76	77.79	86.38	77.10	-

Table 13: Ablation results on validation set of commonsense reasoning datasets using various filtering methods. *We use sample perplexity for filtering ProtoQA samples.

larly, 75-90% of the answers were judged as correct answers for the respective questions. The quality of distractors were relatively lower, ranging from 50% for larger datasets like SocialIQA to 20-30% for rest of the datasets. The inter-annotator agreement was also low (<0.6) for distractor judgements, suggesting the general difficulty of both tasks: distractor generation and measurement of distractor quality. However, the overall quality of distractors in our datasets is high enough to benefit data augmentation.

For both human evaluation annotation tasks, it was made clear in the instructions that the data is being collected for research purposes only.

B.2 Comparison of Filtering Methods

Table 13 demonstrates the effect of using various methods of filtering i.e. QAP, Energy and Model Confidence/Variability. Results are shown on the validation sets the commonsense reasoning datasets. We see largest improvements with using QAP as the filter. Similar improvements are seen with the confidence/variability scores; however, it requires scores from multiple finetuned models from various training checkpoints.

B.3 Robustness Evaluation

We expect that data augmentation exposes the task model to diverse language and improves its robustness to semantic adversaries in addition to boosting its performance on the target task. To evaluate this, we use the TextFooler system (Jin et al., 2020; Yang et al., 2020; Wei and Zou, 2019) to generate adversarial text by computing word importance ranking and replacing the most influential words with their synonym in the vector space. Failure rate is the %examples for which TextFooler fails to change the original model prediction, and average perturbation ratio is the average % of words replaced when TextFooler succeeds at changing the prediction. We use our best GRADA models in comparison with baseline models (Table 8). Overall, GRADA positively impacts the robustness of task models to TextFooler and improves the failure rate by >3% for Codah and upto 1% for all other datasets. We observe similar trends for the perturbation ratios too. This shows that GRADA improves semantic robustness of the models. It is also worthwhile noting that generative task models like T5-3B for ProtoQA are especially prone to adversarial attacks like TextFooler with a mere 5-6% failure rate and there needs to be more research towards improving their robustness.

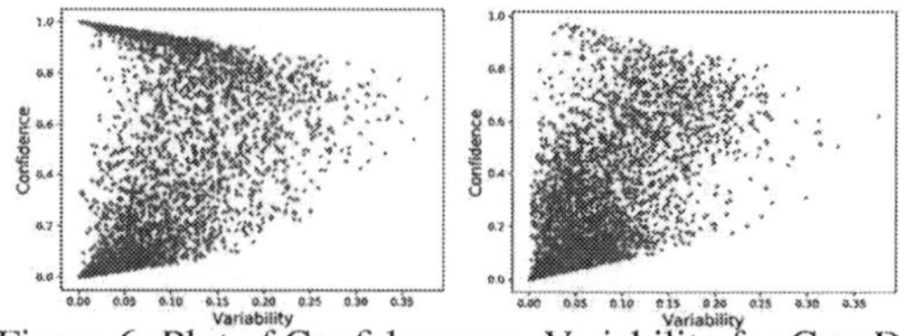

Figure 6: Plot of Confidence vs. Variability for GRADA synthetic samples for CQA (left) and H2K (right).

B.4 Cartography Quality Evaluation

We use dataset cartography Swayamdipta et al. (2020) to visualize the quality of our synthetic datasets. Samples in top left of figure are easy, while samples towards bottom and right of the figure are difficult and ambiguous respectively. We can observe from the figure that the synthetic dataset for CQA (left) has a higher % of easy samples than HellaSwag-2K, suggesting that the quality of synthetic samples generated by GRADA improves with original dataset size. Moreover, when applying QAP filtering, using the entire synthetic dataset yields largest improvements for CQA whereas for HellaSwag-2K (right), the lower cutoff for QAP is 0.3 which filters out most of the samples present in bottom part of the plot. This suggests that in low-resource scenarios, it is important to remove inaccurate samples, while larger datasets benefit from ambiguous and inaccurate samples.

Best Parameters	Social IQA	CQA	Codah	HellaSwag-2K	ProtoQA
QAP Lower Threshold	0.49	0.32	0.43	0.49	0.27
QAP Higher Threshold	1.0	1.0	1.0	1.0	1.0

Table 14: Best Filter Hyperparameters.

	Social IQA			CommonsenseQA		
Hyperparameter	**Baseline**	**GRADA Phase 1**	**GRADA Phase 2**	**Baseline**	**GRADA Phase 1**	**GRADA Phase 2**
Learning Rate	5e-6	4e-6	3e-6	1e-5	5e-6	1e-5
Epochs	3	1	3	5	1	5
Max Gradient Norm	1.0	1.0	1.0	None	None	None
Weight Decay	0.01	0.01	0.01	0.01	0.01	0.01
Batch Size	8	8	8	16	16	16
Max Length	128	128	128	70	70	70
Warmup Ratio	0.0	0.0	0.0	0.06	0.06	0.0
LR Decay	Linear	Linear	Linear	Linear	Linear	Linear
Optimizer	AdamW	AdamW	AdamW	AdamW	AdamW	AdamW
Hardware	RTX 2080Ti	RTX 2080Ti	RTX 2080Ti	RTX 2080Ti	RTX 2080Ti	RTX 2080Ti
Single GPU Hours	5 hrs	1.5 hrs	5 hrs	2 hrs	0.5 hrs	2 hrs

Table 15: Training hyperparameters for baseline and two-stage GRADA training of SocialIQA and CQA

	CODAH			HellaSwag-2K		
Hyperparameter	**Baseline**	**GRADA Phase 1**	**GRADA Phase 2**	**Baseline**	**GRADA Phase 1**	**GRADA Phase 2**
Learning Rate	1e-5	4e-6	3e-6	5e-5	5e-6	1e-5
Epochs	5	1	5	5	1	5
Max Gradient Norm	1.0	1.0	1.0	None	None	None
Weight Decay	0.01	0.01	0.01	0.01	0.01	0.01
Batch Size	16	8	16	8	8	8
Max Length	90	90	90	128	128	128
Warmup Ratio	0.06	0.06	0.06	0.06	0.06	0.06
LR Decay	Linear	Linear	Linear	Linear	Linear	Linear
Optimizer	AdamW	AdamW	AdamW	AdamW	AdamW	AdamW
Hardware	RTX 2080Ti	RTX 2080Ti	RTX 2080Ti	RTX 2080Ti	RTX 2080Ti	RTX 2080Ti
Single GPU Hours	2 hrs*	1 hr* hrs	2 hrs*	0.5 hr	0.2 hr	0.5 hr

Table 16: Training hyperparameters for baseline and two-stage GraDA training of RoBERTa models for HellaSwag-2K and CODAH. *values reported for five-fold training

		OptionGAN		
Hyperparameter	**GraphGPT2**	**Generator**	**Discriminator**	**GAN**
Learning Rate	4e-5	1e-5	1e-5	1e-6
Epochs	5	5	3	-
Max Gradient Norm	1.0	1.0	1.0	None
Weight Decay	0.0	0.01	0.01	0.01
Batch Size	8	8	8	4
Max Length	128	128	128	128
Warmup Ratio	0.0	0.0	0.0	0.06
LR Decay	Linear	Linear	Linear	Linear
Optimizer	AdamW	AdamW	AdamW	AdamW

Table 17: Training hyperparameters for GraphGPT2, Generator, Discriminator and OptionGAN

LiGCN: Label-interpretable Graph Convolutional Networks for Multi-label Text Classification

Irene Li[1], **Aosong Feng**[1], **Hao Wu**[2], **Tianxiao Li**[1], **Toyotaro Suzumura**[3,4], **Ruihai Dong**[5]

[1]Yale University, USA, [2]Trinity College Dublin, Ireland
[3]Barcelona Supercomputing Center (BSC), Spain
[4]University of Tokyo, Japan
[5]University College Dublin, Ireland

Abstract

Multi-label text classification (MLTC) is an attractive and challenging task in natural language processing (NLP). Compared with single-label text classification, MLTC has a wider range of applications in practice. In this paper, we propose a label-interpretable graph convolutional network model to solve the MLTC problem by modeling tokens and labels as nodes in a heterogeneous graph. In this way, we are able to take into account multiple relationships including token-level relationships. Besides, the model allows better interpretability for predicted labels as the token-label edges are exposed. We evaluate our method on four real-world datasets and it achieves competitive scores against selected baseline methods. Specifically, this model achieves a gain of 0.14 on the F1 score in the small label set MLTC, and 0.07 in the large label set scenario.

1 Introduction

In the real world, we have seen an explosion of information on the internet, such as tweets, micro-blogs, articles, blog posts, etc. A practical issue is to assign classification labels to those instances. Such labels may be emotion tags for tweets and micro-blogs (Wang et al., 2016; Li et al., 2020b), or topic category tags for news, articles and blog posts (Yao et al., 2019). Multi-label text classification (MLTC) is the problem of assigning one or more labels to each instance.

Deep learning has been applied for MLTC due to their strong representation capacity in NLP tasks. It has been shown that convolutional neural networks (CNNs) (Kim, 2014) achieve satisfying results for multi-label emotion classification (Wang et al., 2016; Feng et al., 2018). Besides, many recurrent neural networks (RNNs)-based models (Tang et al., 2015) are also playing an important role (Huang et al., 2019; Yang et al., 2018). Recent breakthrough of pre-trained models, i.e., BERT (Devlin et al., 2019) and RoBERTa (Liu et al., 2019a), achieved large performance gains in many NLP tasks. Existing work has applied BERT to solve MLTC problem successfully with very competitive performances (Li et al., 2019c). Moreover, as a new type of neural network architecture with growing research interest, graph convolutional networks (GCNs) (Kipf and Welling, 2017) have been applied to multiple NLP tasks. Different from CNN and RNN-based models, GCNs could capture the relations between words and texts if modeled as graphs (Yao et al., 2019; Li et al., 2019a, 2020a). In the paper, we focus on emphasising a GCN-based model to solve MLTC task.

	Text	Labels
S1	我不知道类似这样的困惑到底还要持续多久。 (I don't know how long the confusion like this will last.)	Anxiety
S2	nothing happened to **make me sad** but i almost **burst into tears** like 3 times today	Pessimism, Sadness
S3	...The price of BASF AG shares improved on Thursday due to its better than expected half year results. At 0900 GMT BASF was up 51 pfennigs at 42.75 marks...	C15, C151, C152, CCAT

Table 1: Examples of multi-label emotion classification. Data source is explained in Sec. 4. Note that in S3, the labels are: C15 (Performance), C151 (Accounts/Earnings), C152 (Comment/Forecasts), CCAT (Corporate/Industrial).

A major challenge for MLTC is the class imbalance. In practice, the number of labels may vary across the training data, and the frequency of each label may differ as well, bringing difficulties to model training (Quan and Ren, 2010). In Table 1, we show some examples of tweet, micro-blog and news article, labeled with emotion tags or news topics. As can be seen from those examples, there is a various number of coexisting labels. Another challenge is the interpretation of assigned class labels by figuring out the trigger words and phrases

Proceedings of the 2nd Workshop on Deep Learning on Graphs for Natural Language Processing (DLG4NLP 2022), pages 60 - 70
July 15, 2022 ©2022 Association for Computational Linguistics

to corresponding labels. In the table, it is easy to tell that in S1, the emotion *Anxiety* is very likely to be triggered by the word *confusion*. However, S2 might be more complicated, with two possible triggering phrases *makes me sad* and *burst into tears* and two emotion labels. There might be different opinions on which phrase triggers which emotion.

To tackle the mentioned challenges and investigate different perspectives, we propose label-interpretable graph convolutional networks for MLTC. We model each token and class label as nodes in a heterogeneous graph, considering various types of edges: token-token, token-label, and label-label. Then we apply graph convolution to graph-level classification. As GCN works well in semi-supervised learning (Ghorbani et al., 2019), we can then ease the impact of data imbalance. Finally, since the token-label relationships are exposed in the graph, one can easily identify the triggering tokens to a specific class, providing a good interpretability for multi-label classification.

The **contributions** of our work are as follows: (1) We transfer the MLTC task to a link prediction task within a constructed graph to predict output labels. In this way, our model is able to provide token-level interpretation for classification. (2) To the best of our knowledge, this is the first work that considers token-label relationships within a manner of a graph neural network for MLTC, allowing label interpretability. (3) We conduct extensive experiments on four representative datasets and achieve competitive results. We also demonstrate comprehensive analysis and ablation studies to show the effectiveness of our proposed model for label nodes and token-label edges. We release our code in `https://github.com/IreneZihuiLi/LiGCN`.

2 Related Work

Multi-label Text Classification Many existing works focus on single-label text classification, while limited literature is available for multi-label text classification. In general, these methods fall into three categories: problem transformation, label adaptation and transfer learning. Problem transformation is to transform the muli-label classification task into a set of single-label tasks (Jabreel and Moreno, 2019; Fei et al., 2020), but this method is not scalable when the label set is large. Label adaptation is to rank the predicted classes or set a threshold to filter the candidate classes. Chen et al. (2017) proposed a novel method to apply an RNN for multi-label generation with the help of text features learned using CNNs. Transfer learning focuses on utilizing knowledge learned to unknown entries. Xiao et al. (2021) proposed a model which transfers the meta-knowledge from data-rich labels to data-poor labels. Moreover, some models also take label correlations into consideration, such as Seq2Emo (Huang et al., 2019) and EmoGraph (Xu et al., 2020). However, some of them may ignore the relationships between input tokens and class labels, making them less interpretable. Please note that there is a research topic named extreme multi-label text classification (Liu et al., 2017), where the pool of candidate labels is extremely large. However, we do not target on the extreme case.

Graph Neural Networks in NLP Previous research has introduced GCN-based methods for NLP tasks by formulating them as graph-structured data tasks. A fundamental task is text classification. Many works show that it is possible to utilize interrelations of documents or tokens to infer the labels (Yao et al., 2019; Zhang et al., 2019). Besides, some NLP tasks focus on learning relationships between nodes in a graph, such as concept prerequisites (Li et al., 2019a) and leveraging dependency trees predicted by GCNs for machine translation (Bastings et al., 2017). Recently, variations of GCN models have been investigated for general text classification tasks (Linmei et al., 2019; Tayal et al., 2019; Ragesh et al., 2021). Limited efforts have been made to apply GCNs for multi-label text classification. For example, EmoGraph (Xu et al., 2020) is a model that captures the dependencies among emotions through graph networks.

3 Method

In this section, we first provide task definition and preliminary, then we introduce the proposed model for multi-label text classification.

3.1 Task Definition

In multi-label text classification task, we are given the training data $\{D, Y\}$. For the i-th sample, D^i contains a list of tokens $D^i = \{w_1, w_2, ...w_m\}$ and Y^i is a list of binary labels $Y^i = \{y_1, y_2, ...y_n\}$, y is 1 if the class label is positive, 0 otherwise. The size of label set n can be small or large. In testing, we predict labels $\hat{Y}^i_{test}$ given D^i_{test} .

3.2 Preliminary

Graph convolutional network (GCN) (Kipf and Welling, 2017) is a type of deep architecture for graph-structured data. In a typical GCN model, we define a graph as $G = (\mathcal{V}, \mathcal{E})$, where $\mathcal{V}$ is a set of nodes and $\mathcal{E}$ is a set of edges. Normally, the edges are represented as an adjacency matrix A, and the node representation is defined as X. In a multi-layer GCN, the propagation rule for layer l is defined as:

$$H^{(l)} = \sigma\left(norm(A^{(l-1)})H^{(l-1)}W^{(l-1)}\right), \quad (1)$$

where $norm(A) = \tilde{D}^{-\frac{1}{2}}\tilde{A}\tilde{D}^{-\frac{1}{2}}$ is a normalization function, H denotes the node representation, and W is the parameter matrix to be learned. $\tilde{A} = A + I_{|\mathcal{V}|}$, $\tilde{D}$ denotes the degree matrix of $\tilde{A}$, In general, in the very first layer, we have $H^{(0)} = X$.

3.3 Label-interpretable Graph Convolutional Networks

In this paper, we propose the LiGCN model, which allows interpretation on the labels when doing MLTC. For each training sample, we construct an undirected graph. We define two types of nodes: token node and label node, and the node representations are X_{token} and X_{label}. Therefore, there are three types of relations between the nodes, defined by the adjacency matrices: A_{token} (between token nodes), A_{label} (between label nodes) and A_{token_label} (between token nodes and label nodes).

We show the model overview in Figure 1. It consists of two main components: a pre-trained BERT/RoBERTa encoder[1] and label-node graph convolutional layers. In the LiGCN model, we have a list of token nodes X_{token} in orange ellipses, and a list of label nodes X_{label} in blue ellipses. Besides, there are edges between token nodes A_{token}, edges between label nodes A_{label}, and edges between token and label nodes A_{token_label}. We explain them in greater details below.

Node Representations X: In the very first layer, to initialize token nodes, we encode the input data $D^i = \{w_1, w_2, ...w_m\}$ using a pre-trained BERT or RoBERTa model and possible other BERT-based ones, where we take the representation of each token including `[CLS]` token as X_{token}. For the label nodes, we initialize them using one-hot vectors.

[1]https://huggingface.co/bert-base-multilingual-cased, https://huggingface.co/roberta-base

Adjacency Matrix A: In our experiments, to initialize token node adjacency matrix A_{token}, we use the token nodes to construct an undirected chain graph, where we consider an input sequence as its natural order, i.e., in A_{token}: $A_{i,i+1} = 1$. Since it is an undirected graph, the adjacency matrix is symmetric, i.e., $A_{i+1,i} = 1$. We also add self-loop to each token: $A_{i,i} = 1$. In other words, A_{token} is a symmetric m-by-m matrix with an upper bandwidth of 1, where m is the number of token nodes.

We initialize A_{label} with an identity matrix, and A_{token_label} with a zero matrix. In the later layers, we reconstruct A_{token_label} for layer l by applying cosine similarity between X_{token} and X_{label} of the current layer:

$$A^l_{token\_label} = cosine(X^l_{token}, X^l_{label}). \quad (2)$$

The value is normalized into the range of [0,1]. After this update, the model conducts graph convolution operation as in Eq. 1.

In Figure 1, we are not showing self-loops, so A_{label} is not visible. We show only a subset of edges from A_{token} and A_{token_label}. Note that we use dashed lines at the first LiGCN layer because A_{token_label} is a zero matrix.

We also investigate other possible ways to build A_{token} including dependency parsing trees (Huang et al., 2020) and random initialization, but our method gives the best result. Such ways may not bring useful information to the graph: the help from dependency relations may be limited in the case of classification, and random initialization brings noises. As we focus more on the network convolution, we leave investigating more methods for initialization as future work.

Predictions In the last LiGCN layer, we are able to reconstruct $A^{last}_{token\_label}$ using Eq. 2. For each label node j, we sum up the edge weights from $A^{last}_{token\_label}$ to get a score,

$$score(j) = \sum_{v_i \in \mathcal{V}_{token}} A^{last}_{i,j}, \quad (3)$$

where $\mathcal{V}_{token}$ is the set of all token nodes in the last LiGCN layer. Then we apply a softmax function over all the labels, so that the scores are transformed to probabilities of labels. Finally, to make the prediction, we rank the probabilities in a descending order, and keep the top k labels from the ranking as predictions. As the predictions are in forms of probabilities, we also convert the ground

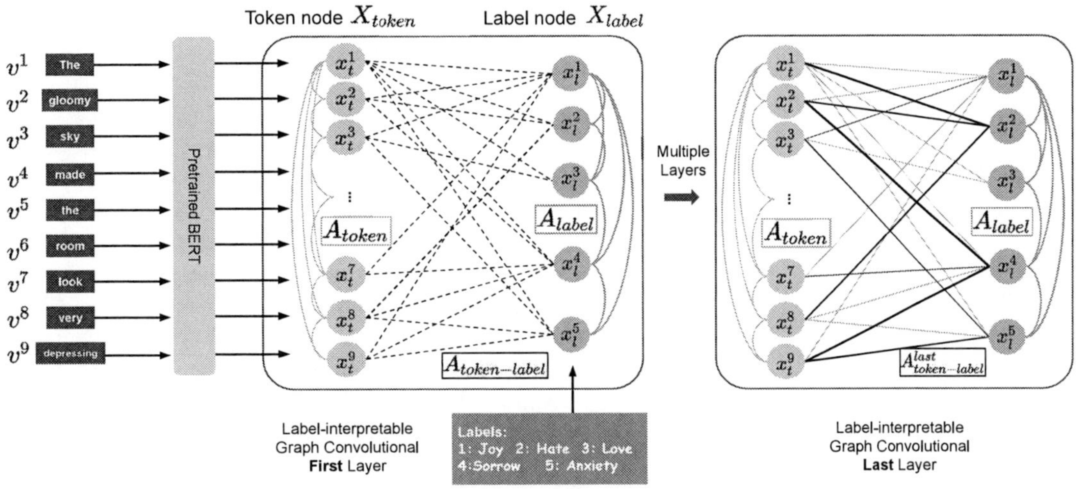

Figure 1: LiGCN model overview. (Best viewed in color.)

Dataset	#train	#dev	#test	#class	#avg label	#token max	#token median	#token mean
SemEval	6,839	887	3,260	11	2.37	499	26	32.08
RenCECps	27,299	-	7,739	8	1.37	36	17	16.42
RCV1	20,647	3,000	783,144	103	3.20	9,380	198	259.06
AAPD	54,840	-	1,000	54	2.41	500	157	166.41

Table 2: Dataset statistics on four selected corpora.

truths into probability distribution. We use the mean square error (MSE) as the loss function. Another way is to apply the normal cross-entropy for classification, but it achieves slightly worse results, so we do not include it.

4 Experimental Results

We evaluate on four public datasets, summarized in Table 2 and 3: **SemEval** (Mohammad et al., 2018) contains a list of subtasks on labeled tweets data. In our experiments, we focus on Task1 (E-c) challenge on English corpus: multi-label classification tweets on 11 emotions. **RenCECps** (Quan and Ren, 2010) is a Chinese blog corpus which contains manual annotation of eight emotional categories. It not only provides sentence-level emotion annotations, but also contains word-level annotations, where in each sentence, emotional words are highlighted. **RCV1** (Lewis et al., 2004) consists of manually-labeled English news articles from Reuters Ltd. Each news article has a list of topic class labels, i.e., CCAT for Corporate/industrial, G12 for Internal politics. We follow the same setting of Yang et al. (2018) and Nam et al. (2017), and do MLTC on the top 103 classes. **AAPD** (Yang et al., 2018) is a set of English computer science paper abstracts and corresponding subjects from `arxiv.org`.

#label	SemEval	RenCEPcs	RCV1	AAPD
0	293	2,755	0	0
1	1,481	**18,858**	35,591	0
2	**4,491**	11,417	203,030	**38,763**
3	3,459	1,815	**362,124**	12,782
4	1,073	172	85,527	3,229
≥ 5	186	21	120,518	1,066
Avg.	2.37	1.37	3.20	2.41

Table 3: Label number distributions.

We report the following evaluation metrics:

Micro/Macro F1, Jaccard Index We report micro-average and macro-average F1 scores as did by previous works (Baziotis et al., 2018; Huang et al., 2019) if the label set is small. Besides, we follow the Jaccard index used by (Mohammad et al., 2018; Baziotis et al., 2018; Huang et al., 2019), as always referred as multi-label accuracy. The definition is given below:

$$J = \frac{1}{N}\sum_{i=1}^{N}\frac{\left|Y^i \cap \hat{Y}^i\right|}{\left|Y^i \cup \hat{Y}^i\right|},$$

where N is the number of samples, Y^i denotes the ground truth labels and $\hat{Y}^i$ denotes system predicted labels.

	SemEval	RenCECPs	RCV1	AAPD
seq length	17	32	256	256
hid dim1	64	64	256	256
hid dim2	16	16	64	64
epoch num	5	3	10	10
top-k	2	1	5	5

Table 4: Hyper-parameters chosen in our experiments.

P@k and nDCG@k When the label set is large, we also report widely-applied metrics P@K and nDCG@K ($k = 1, 3, 5$).

We apply two graph convolutional layers for all datasets by default for our LiGCN model. In Table 4, we show the hyper-parameters conducted in our experiments. We use 4.00E-06 as the learning rate for all experiments. Since we use two LiGCN layers, `hid dim1` is the first layer hidden dimension number, and `hid dim2` is the second layer hidden dimension number. These hyper-parameters were selected by dev sets (if exist), otherwise selected by manual tuning with about 5-10 rounds for search trials.

4.1 Small Label Sets

We first evaluate the proposed model on SemEval and RenCECps in Table 5. Both of them have a small label set, so we report Macro, Micro F1 and Jaccard. We select the following baselines: SGM (Yang et al., 2018) applies a sequence generation model and a decoder structure; Seq2Emo (Huang et al., 2019) is an LSTM-based model that takes into account the correlations among target labels; TECap (Fei et al., 2020) is a topic-enhanced capsule network, which contains a variational autoencoder and a capsule module for multi-label emotion detection; MEDA (Deng and Ren, 2020) is a multi-label emotion detection architecture that focuses on detecting all emotions shown in the text, and it takes BERT for sentence encoding. Finally, EmoGraph (Xu et al., 2020) is a graph-based method that learns dependencies among emotion nodes using GCNs. The result presented is based on our implementation with optimized parameters, and is slightly better than their original paper. We also compare with a BERT and a RoBERTa model as baselines (BERT, RoBERTa). We first take the representation of `[CLS]` token from pre-trained BERT/RoBERTa, on top of that, a linear layer is connected. For the two datasets, we set the top-k value to be the average number of labels in each dataset.

We can observe that our model surpasses all the selected baselines in most of the cases. Especially, both MEDA and EmoGraph applied pre-trained BERT model as our BERT-LiGCN model does, and we significantly outperform those models on all three metrics. Moreover, EmoGraph is a similar model with LiGCN but it only considers a single node type (class node) while LiGCN considers both class node and token node. This shows that, with a much complex graph structure, LiGCN is able to capture more information when doing classification. Besides, LiGCN benefits from using RoBERTa as the encoder, as RoBERTa improves upon BERT by a small margin.

4.2 Large Label Sets

We then evaluate large label sets using RCV1 and AAPD, shown in Table 6. We compare with a number of recent baselines: XML-CNN (Liu et al., 2017) applied a CNN and dynamic pooling to learn features for MLTC; Imprinting (Qi et al., 2018) is a weight imprinting method that directly set the final layer weights of deep models from new training examples; DXML (Zhang et al., 2018) focused on label co-occurrence graph to solve the multi-label long-tail issue; OLTR (Liu et al., 2019b) is a method that handles long-tail and imbalanced classification problems; BBN (Zhou et al., 2020) is a model that considers both representation learning and classifier learning; HTTN (Xiao et al., 2021) learns the meta-knowledge so as to transfer from data-rich head labels to data-poor ones. We set the top-k value to be $k = 5$ in the prediction so as to evaluate P@k and nDCG@k.

Our model can also surpass the selected baselines in general, especially with a large improvement on the F1-score for the two datasets. Surprisingly, BERT-LiGCN performs better than RoBERTa-LiGCN on P@1, P@3 and nDCG@3 in AAPD. In other words, BERT-LiGCN can predict better top-3 candidates, while RoBERTa-LiGCN can do well in predicting the 4-th and 5-th candidates. But in both BERT and RoBERTa settings, our model can perform close and better compared with these recent baselines.

5 Analysis

In this section, we first focus on ablation study of the proposed model. We then demonstrate the interpretability for labels with several case studies where we identify keywords that trigger certain la-

Method	SemEval Macro F1	SemEval Micro F1	SemEval Jaccard	RenCECps Macro F1	RenCECps Micro F1	RenCECps Jaccard
SGM (Yang et al., 2018)	0.4110	0.5750	0.4820	-	0.5560	-
Seq2Emo (Huang et al., 2019)	-	0.7089	0.5919	-	-	-
TECap (Fei et al., 2020)	0.5760	0.6820	-	0.4550	0.5310	-
MEDA (Deng and Ren, 2020)	-	-	-	0.4831	0.6076	-
EmoGraph (BERT-GCN)*(Xu et al., 2020)	0.6367	0.8108	0.6818	0.6129	0.8559	0.7481
BERT	0.5223	0.6454	0.4766	0.5344	0.6365	0.4669
RoBERTa	0.5039	0.6817	0.5171	0.5842	0.7987	0.6649
BERT-LiGCN (**ours**)	0.7368	0.8312	0.7111	0.7138	0.8615	0.7567
RoBERTa-LiGCN (**ours**)	**0.7786**	**0.8579**	**0.7512**	**0.7429**	**0.8756**	**0.7787**

Table 5: Evaluation results on SemEval-2018 and RenCECps. **BERT/RoBERTa** means the system which has a linear layer on top of the original BERT/RoBERTa. EmoGraph*:we present results of our own optimized implementation of EmoGraph. Underlined scores are the best ones among baselines.

Method	P@1	P@3	P@5	nDCG@3	nDCG@5	F1-score
RCV1						
XML-CNN (Liu et al., 2017)	95.75	78.63	54.94	89.89	90.77	75.92
Imprinting (Qi et al., 2018)	77.38	47.96	31.45	58.83	57.91	26.35
DXML (Zhang et al., 2018)	94.04	78.65	54.38	89.83	90.21	75.76
OLTR (Liu et al., 2019b)	93.79	61.36	44.78	74.37	77.05	56.44
BBN (Zhou et al., 2020)	94.61	77.98	54.25	88.97	89.68	78.65
HTTN (Xiao et al., 2021)	95.86	78.92	55.27	89.61	90.86	77.72
BERT-LiGCN (**ours**)	94.42	80.98	55.48	91.93	91.94	83.14
RoBERTa-LiGCN (**ours**)	95.61	**82.40**	**56.31**	**93.40**	**93.26**	**83.66**
AAPD						
XML-CNN (Liu et al., 2017)	74.38	53.84	37.79	71.12	75.93	65.35
Imprinting (Qi et al., 2018)	68.68	38.22	23.71	55.30	55.67	25.58
DXML (Zhang et al., 2018)	80.54	56.30	39.16	77.23	80.99	65.13
OLTR (Liu et al., 2019b)	78.96	56.28	38.60	74.66	78.58	62.48
BBN (Zhou et al., 2020)	81.56	57.81	39.10	76.92	80.06	66.73
HTTN (Xiao et al., 2021)	83.84	59.92	40.79	79.27	82.67	69.25
BERT-LiGCN (**ours**)	**84.10**	**61.33**	40.88	**80.77**	83.68	75.89
RoBERTa-LiGCN (**ours**)	82.50	61.26	**41.38**	80.39	**83.83**	**76.25**

Table 6: Results on RCV1 and AAPD: note that BERT/RoBERETa baseline have a negative result in this case.

bels. Moreover, we study and examine the meaning of label representations learned by the model.

5.1 Ablation Study

We first study the impact of graph convolutional layer numbers in Table 7. We test with 1, 2 and 3 LiGCN layers on SemEval and RenCECps using BERT-LiGCN model. In general, we see that 2-layer is the best setting. Less layers may not be enough for information exchange within nodes in the GCN models. While increasing the layer number results in training difficulties and lower performances, as some other works (Li et al., 2018) have shown.

5.2 Token-label Relations

As our proposed model provides token-label relations, we further study token-level explanations via case studies and a quantitative analysis.

Case Study We show examples by visualizing the token-label weights in Figure 2. Specifically, we take the reconstructed A_{token_label} and normalize the matrix so that all values sum up to 1. We select a sample from SemEval test set, as shown in Figure 2a: *haven't been on a holiday abroad in two years how depressing is that...* (labels: `pessimism` and `sadness`). In such a heatmap, columns are tokens while rows are the emotion labels. We can notice that our model computes a higher score to the text chunk *haven't* and *holiday abroad*, and a relatively lower score to *depressing*, by looking at the corresponding columns. Therefore, the prediction being `pessimism` and `sadness` is mostly triggered by *haven't* and *holiday abroad*. This indicates that the emotion label to be such a negative sentiment is because this person 'haven't been on a holiday abroad.'Even though there is a strong negative sentiment word

BERT-LiGCN	SemEval			RenCECps		
	Macro F1	Micro F1	Jaccard	Macro F1	Micro F1	Jaccard
1-layer	0.7131	0.8159	0.6891	0.7054	0.8091	0.6794
2-layer	**0.7368**	**0.8312**	**0.7111**	**0.7138**	**0.8615**	**0.7567**
3-layer	0.7109	0.8145	0.6871	0.7044	0.8085	0.6785

Table 7: Ablation study on number of layers: compare numbers of BERT-LiGCN layer.

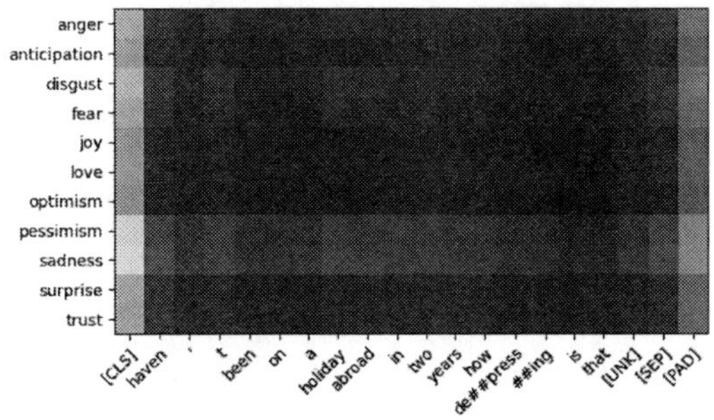

(a) An example from SemEval.

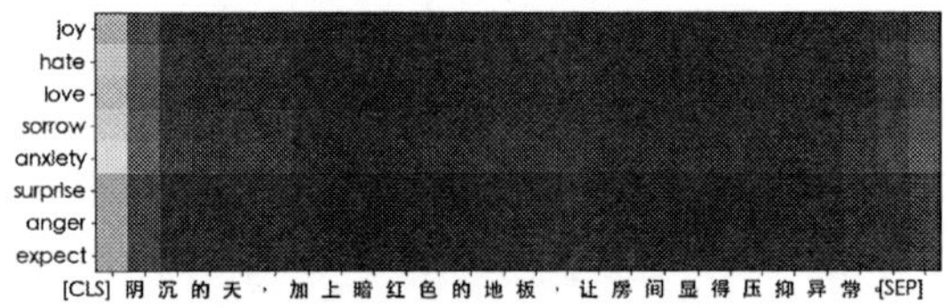

(b) An example from RenCECps.

Figure 2: Visualization of word-label weights: brighter color indicates a larger value.

depressing, LiGCN attempts to pick out implicit and deeper reasons. Besides, one can see that our model highlights other three close emotions *anger*, *disgust* and *fear*. [2]

We show another example from RenCECps test set in Figure 2b: 阴沉的天，加上暗红色的地板，让房间显得压抑异常。(*The gloomy sky, together with the dark red floor, made the room look very depressing.*) The ground truth labels are `Sorrow` and `Anxiety`. Our model successfully predicts these two class labels; moreover, the model also suggests that `Hate` is a possible label, which is reasonable in this particular example. Besides, in the annotation of the original dataset by (Quan and Ren, 2010), we find that two keywords are highlighted for this example: 阴沉 (gloomy) : Surprise=0, Sorrow=0, Love=0, Joy=0, Hate=0, Expect=0, Anxiety=0.6, Anger=0; and 压抑 (depressing): Surprise=0, Sorrow=0.5, Love=0, Joy=0, Hate=0, Expect=0, Anxiety=0.7, Anger=0. Our model also captures such a trend successfully by showing a higher score near or on these token columns.

[2]When doing classification, both special tokens of BERT `[CLS]` and `[SEP]` contain useful semantic information of the whole sequence, so the color tends to be brighter.

Quantitative Analysis So far, we have demonstrated that our model is able to identify the triggering words for each individual class from the confidence score of the token-label edges. To quantitatively show the quality of identified triggering words, we compute MSE between our best performed model and the ground truth annotations for the test set of RenCECps. Similar to previous analysis, we first normalize the constructed token-label adjacency matrix A_{token_label}, then construct a token-label matrix A_{golden} from ground truth annotations (for each sentence, there is only a few keywords, we assign zero to other non-keyword tokens). Then we are able to compute MSE score between the two aforementioned matrices: $MSE(A_{token\_label}, A_{golden})$. We also reconstruct the token-label matrix from the BERT+single model as a comparison. RoBERTa has an MSE score of 0.0901 and RoBERTa-LiGCN has 0.0020. RoBERTa-LiGCN has a significant lower MSE score compared with RoBERTa. The T-test between the two models based on the predictions is 0.016, showing a significant difference. Since other datasets do not contain token-level annotations, so we fail to conduct quantitative analysis on them.

Highlighted Tokens Additionally, in Table 8, we show a case study selected from AAPD. We keep the top tokens highlighted only. This article is correctly classified as logic in computer science(cs.lo), programming languages (cs.pl) and software engineering (cs.se), marked by different colors. One can notice that the highlighted tokens are closely related to the class fields: *object-oriented software* and *Object Programs* are associated with cs.se; *reference expressions* is associated with cs.pl; *describing program semantics* is associated with cs.lo. Note that we omit highlighting of tokens that may appear in more than two classes for simplicity.

Verifying properties of object-oriented software requires a method for handling references in a simple and intuitive way, closely related to how O-O programmers reason about their programs. The method presented here, a Calculus of Object Programs , combines four components: compositional logic , a framework for describing program semantics and proving program properties; negative variables to address the specifics of O-O programming , in particular qualified calls ;the alias calculus, which determines whether reference expressions can ever have the same value...
Classes: software engineering (cs.se) , programming languages (cs.pl) , logic in computer science (cs.lo)

Table 8: Highlighting tokens: two random paper abstracts in AAPD (Meyer, 2011). Dark color means a higher correlation between token and classes.

5.3 Label Correlations

As we model class labels as nodes in the graph, we can then investigate if and how the learned label node representations are meaningful. After training LiGCN, we take the label node representations of the last LiGCN layer and calculate cosine similarity between each label pair. We assume that the meaningful representations of a label pair should have a small angle in the latent space (i.e. their cosine similarity tends to the value of 1) if they have a positive correlation, and a large angle if they have a negative correlation. We also investigate label correlations by looking at the model predictions. We collect model predictions in the test set and each label is represented as a binary vector with the dimension equal to the size of test set, and then calculate Pearson correlation between each label pair. Similarly, if Pearson correlation value tends to be 1, then it means a positive relationship; if the value tends to be -1, then it means a negative relationship.

Selected News Topics from RCV1 In RCV1 we select 9 topics to plot heatmaps randomly: *government, financial performance, commodity market, consumer prices, domestic markets, acquisitions, funding* and *domestic politics*. Due to the limited space, we only show Pearson correlations and cosine similarities between each pair of our LiGCN model with the best performance in Figure 3. For the Pearson correlation, we could notice that the model captures strong positive relationships between the following pairs: *commodity market* and *market*, *government* and *domestic politics*, *consumer prices* and *domestic markets*. These relationships are consistent with our real life, i.e., government news and domestic political news are very similar. We see a similar trend in the heatmap of cosine similarity for the mentioned label pairs. And in this way, more positive relations are found than negative ones, for example, negative correlation between *acquisitions* and *consumer prices*.

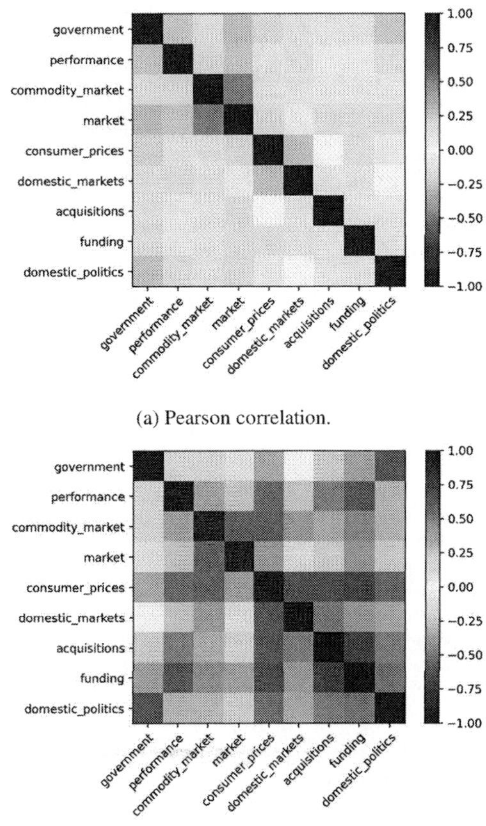

(a) Pearson correlation.

(b) Label cosine similarity.

Figure 3: Visualization of selected topics on RCV1.

6 Conclusion

In this work, we propose a label-interpretable graph model, LiGCN, to solve the MLTC problem as a link prediction task. Our model is able to provide token-level explanation for the classification and therefore enjoys better label interpretability. Experiments on four public datasets show that our model achieved competitive scores. In the future, we will experiment with more complex graph encoders, extend this idea to single-label and extreme multi-label classification tasks (Li et al., 2019b).

References

Jasmijn Bastings, Ivan Titov, Wilker Aziz, Diego Marcheggiani, and Khalil Sima'an. 2017. Graph convolutional encoders for syntax-aware neural machine translation. In *Proceedings of the 2017 Conference on Empirical Methods in Natural Language Processing*, pages 1957–1967, Copenhagen, Denmark. Association for Computational Linguistics.

Christos Baziotis, Athanasiou Nikolaos, Alexandra Chronopoulou, Athanasia Kolovou, Georgios Paraskevopoulos, Nikolaos Ellinas, Shrikanth Narayanan, and Alexandros Potamianos. 2018. NTUA-SLP at SemEval-2018 task 1: Predicting affective content in tweets with deep attentive RNNs and transfer learning. In *Proceedings of The 12th International Workshop on Semantic Evaluation*, pages 245–255, New Orleans, Louisiana. Association for Computational Linguistics.

G. Chen, D. Ye, Z. Xing, J. Chen, and E. Cambria. 2017. Ensemble application of convolutional and recurrent neural networks for multi-label text categorization. In *2017 International Joint Conference on Neural Networks (IJCNN)*, pages 2377–2383.

J. Deng and F. Ren. 2020. Multi-label emotion detection via emotion-specified feature extraction and emotion correlation learning. *IEEE Transactions on Affective Computing*, pages 1–1.

Jacob Devlin, Ming-Wei Chang, Kenton Lee, and Kristina Toutanova. 2019. Bert: Pre-training of deep bidirectional transformers for language understanding.

H. Fei, D. Ji, Y. Zhang, and Y. Ren. 2020. Topic-enhanced capsule network for multi-label emotion classification. *IEEE/ACM Transactions on Audio, Speech, and Language Processing*, 28:1839–1848.

Shi Feng, Yaqi Wang, Kaisong Song, Daling Wang, and Ge Yu. 2018. Detecting multiple coexisting emotions in microblogs with convolutional neural networks. *Cognitive Computation*, 10(1):136–155.

Mahsa Ghorbani, Mahdieh Soleymani Baghshah, and Hamid R. Rabiee. 2019. MGCN: semi-supervised classification in multi-layer graphs with graph convolutional networks. In *ASONAM '19: International Conference on Advances in Social Networks Analysis and Mining, Vancouver, British Columbia, Canada, 27-30 August, 2019*, pages 208–211. ACM.

Chenyang Huang, Amine Trabelsi, and Osmar R Zaïane. 2019. Seq2emo for multi-label emotion classification based on latent variable chains transformation. *arXiv preprint arXiv:1911.02147.*

Lianzhe Huang, Xin Sun, Sujian Li, Linhao Zhang, and Houfeng Wang. 2020. Syntax-aware graph attention network for aspect-level sentiment classification. In *Proceedings of the 28th International Conference on Computational Linguistics*, pages 799–810, Barcelona, Spain (Online). International Committee on Computational Linguistics.

Mohammed Jabreel and Antonio Moreno. 2019. A deep learning-based approach for multi-label emotion classification in tweets. *Applied Sciences*, 9(6):1123.

Yoon Kim. 2014. Convolutional neural networks for sentence classification. In *Proceedings of the 2014 Conference on Empirical Methods in Natural Language Processing (EMNLP)*, pages 1746–1751, Doha, Qatar. Association for Computational Linguistics.

Thomas N. Kipf and Max Welling. 2017. Semi-supervised classification with graph convolutional networks. In *5th International Conference on Learning Representations, ICLR 2017, Toulon, France, April 24-26, 2017, Conference Track Proceedings*. OpenReview.net.

David D Lewis, Yiming Yang, Tony G Rose, and Fan Li. 2004. Rcv1: A new benchmark collection for text categorization research. *Journal of Machine Learning Research*, 5:361–397.

Irene Li, Alexander Fabbri, Swapnil Hingmire, and Dragomir Radev. 2020a. R-VGAE: Relational-variational graph autoencoder for unsupervised prerequisite chain learning. In *Proceedings of the 28th International Conference on Computational Linguistics*, pages 1147–1157, Barcelona, Spain (Online). International Committee on Computational Linguistics.

Irene Li, Alexander R. Fabbri, Robert R. Tung, and Dragomir R. Radev. 2019a. What should I learn first: Introducing lecturebank for NLP education and prerequisite chain learning. In *The Thirty-Third AAAI Conference on Artificial Intelligence, AAAI 2019, The Thirty-First Innovative Applications of Artificial Intelligence Conference, IAAI 2019, The Ninth AAAI Symposium on Educational Advances in Artificial Intelligence, EAAI 2019, Honolulu, Hawaii, USA, January 27 - February 1, 2019*, pages 6674–6681. AAAI Press.

Irene Li, Yixin Li, Tianxiao Li, Sergio Alvarez-Napagao, Dario Garcia, and Toyotaro Suzumura. 2020b. What are we depressed about when we talk about covid19: Mental health analysis on tweets using natural language processing. *arXiv preprint arXiv:2004.10899.*

Irene Li, Michihiro Yasunaga, Muhammed Yavuz Nuzumlali, Cesar Caraballo, Shiwani Mahajan, Harlan M. Krumholz, and Dragomir R. Radev. 2019b. A neural topic-attention model for medical term abbreviation disambiguation. *CoRR*, abs/1910.14076.

Qimai Li, Zhichao Han, and Xiao-Ming Wu. 2018. Deeper insights into graph convolutional networks for semi-supervised learning. In *Proceedings of the Thirty-Second AAAI Conference on Artificial Intelligence, (AAAI-18), the 30th innovative Applications of Artificial Intelligence (IAAI-18), and the 8th AAAI Symposium on Educational Advances in Artificial Intelligence (EAAI-18), New Orleans, Louisiana, USA, February 2-7, 2018*, pages 3538–3545. AAAI Press.

Ran Li, Qingyi Si, Peng Fu, Zheng Lin, Weiping Wang, and Gang Shi. 2019c. A multi-channel neural network for imbalanced emotion recognition. In *2019 IEEE 31st International Conference on Tools with Artificial Intelligence (ICTAI)*, pages 353–360. IEEE.

Hu Linmei, Tianchi Yang, Chuan Shi, Houye Ji, and Xiaoli Li. 2019. Heterogeneous graph attention networks for semi-supervised short text classification. In *Proceedings of the 2019 Conference on Empirical Methods in Natural Language Processing and the 9th International Joint Conference on Natural Language Processing (EMNLP-IJCNLP)*, pages 4821–4830, Hong Kong, China. Association for Computational Linguistics.

Jingzhou Liu, Wei-Cheng Chang, Yuexin Wu, and Yiming Yang. 2017. Deep learning for extreme multi-label text classification. In *Proceedings of the 40th International ACM SIGIR Conference on Research and Development in Information Retrieval, Shinjuku, Tokyo, Japan, August 7-11, 2017*, pages 115–124. ACM.

Yinhan Liu, Myle Ott, Naman Goyal, Jingfei Du, Mandar Joshi, Danqi Chen, Omer Levy, Mike Lewis, Luke Zettlemoyer, and Veselin Stoyanov. 2019a. Roberta: A robustly optimized BERT pretraining approach. *CoRR*, abs/1907.11692.

Ziwei Liu, Zhongqi Miao, Xiaohang Zhan, Jiayun Wang, Boqing Gong, and Stella X. Yu. 2019b. Large-scale long-tailed recognition in an open world. In *IEEE Conference on Computer Vision and Pattern Recognition, CVPR 2019, Long Beach, CA, USA, June 16-20, 2019*, pages 2537–2546. Computer Vision Foundation / IEEE.

Bertrand Meyer. 2011. Towards a calculus of object programs. *CoRR*, abs/1107.1999.

Saif Mohammad, Felipe Bravo-Marquez, Mohammad Salameh, and Svetlana Kiritchenko. 2018. SemEval-2018 task 1: Affect in tweets. In *Proceedings of The 12th International Workshop on Semantic Evaluation*, pages 1–17, New Orleans, Louisiana. Association for Computational Linguistics.

Jinseok Nam, Eneldo Loza Mencía, Hyunwoo J. Kim, and Johannes Fürnkranz. 2017. Maximizing subset accuracy with recurrent neural networks in multi-label classification. In *Advances in Neural Information Processing Systems 30: Annual Conference on Neural Information Processing Systems 2017, December 4-9, 2017, Long Beach, CA, USA*, pages 5413–5423.

Hang Qi, Matthew Brown, and David G. Lowe. 2018. Low-shot learning with imprinted weights. In *2018 IEEE Conference on Computer Vision and Pattern Recognition, CVPR 2018, Salt Lake City, UT, USA, June 18-22, 2018*, pages 5822–5830. IEEE Computer Society.

Changqin Quan and Fuji Ren. 2010. A blog emotion corpus for emotional expression analysis in chinese. *Computer Speech & Language*, 24(4):726–749.

Rahul Ragesh, Sundararajan Sellamanickam, Arun Iyer, Ramakrishna Bairi, and Vijay Lingam. 2021. Hetegcn: heterogeneous graph convolutional networks for text classification. In *Proceedings of the 14th ACM International Conference on Web Search and Data Mining*, pages 860–868.

Duyu Tang, Bing Qin, and Ting Liu. 2015. Document modeling with gated recurrent neural network for sentiment classification. In *Proceedings of the 2015 Conference on Empirical Methods in Natural Language Processing*, pages 1422–1432, Lisbon, Portugal. Association for Computational Linguistics.

Kshitij Tayal, Rao Nikhil, Saurabh Agarwal, and Karthik Subbian. 2019. Short text classification using graph convolutional network. In *NIPS workshop on Graph Representation Learning*.

Yaqi Wang, Shi Feng, Daling Wang, Ge Yu, and Yifei Zhang. 2016. Multi-label chinese microblog emotion classification via convolutional neural network. In *Asia-Pacific Web Conference*, pages 567–580. Springer.

Lin Xiao, Xiangliang Zhang, Liping Jing, Chi Huang, and Mingyang Song. 2021. Does head label help for long-tailed multi-label text classification. *CoRR*, abs/2101.09704.

Peng Xu, Zihan Liu, Genta Indra Winata, Zhaojiang Lin, and Pascale Fung. 2020. Emograph: Capturing emotion correlations using graph networks.

Pengcheng Yang, Xu Sun, Wei Li, Shuming Ma, Wei Wu, and Houfeng Wang. 2018. SGM: Sequence generation model for multi-label classification. In *Proceedings of the 27th International Conference on Computational Linguistics*, pages 3915–3926, Santa Fe, New Mexico, USA. Association for Computational Linguistics.

Liang Yao, Chengsheng Mao, and Yuan Luo. 2019. Graph convolutional networks for text classification. In *Proceedings of the AAAI Conference on Artificial Intelligence*, volume 33, pages 7370–7377.

Chen Zhang, Qiuchi Li, and Dawei Song. 2019. Aspect-based sentiment classification with aspect-specific graph convolutional networks. In *Proceedings of the 2019 Conference on Empirical Methods in Natural Language Processing and the 9th International Joint Conference on Natural Language Processing (EMNLP-IJCNLP)*, pages 4568–4578, Hong Kong, China. Association for Computational Linguistics.

Wenjie Zhang, Junchi Yan, Xiangfeng Wang, and Hongyuan Zha. 2018. Deep extreme multi-label learning. In *Proceedings of the 2018 ACM on International Conference on Multimedia Retrieval, ICMR 2018, Yokohama, Japan, June 11-14, 2018*, pages 100–107. ACM.

Boyan Zhou, Quan Cui, Xiu-Shen Wei, and Zhao-Min Chen. 2020. BBN: bilateral-branch network with cumulative learning for long-tailed visual recognition. In *2020 IEEE/CVF Conference on Computer Vision and Pattern Recognition, CVPR 2020, Seattle, WA, USA, June 13-19, 2020*, pages 9716–9725. IEEE.

Explicit Graph Reasoning Fusing Knowledge and Contextual Information for Multi-hop Question Answering

Zhenyun Deng, Yonghua Zhu, Qianqian Qi, Michael Witbrock, Patricia Riddle
School of Computer Science, University of Auckland, New Zealand
{zden658, yzhu970, qqi518}@aucklanduni.ac.nz
{m.witbrock, p.riddle}@auckland.ac.nz

Abstract

Current graph-neural-network-based (GNN-based) approaches to multi-hop questions integrate clues from scattered paragraphs in an entity graph, achieving implicit reasoning by synchronous update of graph node representations using information from neighbours; this is poorly suited for explaining how clues are passed through the graph in hops. In this paper, we describe a structured Knowledge and contextual Information Fusion GNN (KIFGraph) whose explicit multi-hop graph reasoning mimics human step by step reasoning. Specifically, we first integrate clues at multiple levels of granularity (question, paragraph, sentence, entity) as nodes in the graph, connected by edges derived using structured semantic knowledge, then use a contextual encoder to obtain the initial node representations, followed by step-by-step two-stage graph reasoning that asynchronously updates node representations. Each node can be related to its neighbour nodes through fused structured knowledge and contextual information, reliably integrating their answer clues. Moreover, a masked attention mechanism (MAM) filters out noisy or redundant nodes and edges, to avoid ineffective clue propagation in graph reasoning. Experimental results show performance competitive with published models on the HotpotQA dataset.

1 Introduction

Question Answering (QA) is amongst the most commonly used tasks to quantify the reasoning and understanding ability of artificially intelligent systems. The performance of the most successful approaches on QA tasks such as SQuAD (Rajpurkar et al., 2016), TriviaQA (Joshi et al., 2017), SearchQA (Dunn et al., 2017), now far exceeds that of humans (Wang et al., 2018). However, most studies on these tasks have focused on single-hop reasoning, where most questions can be answered with a single document and without complex reasoning.

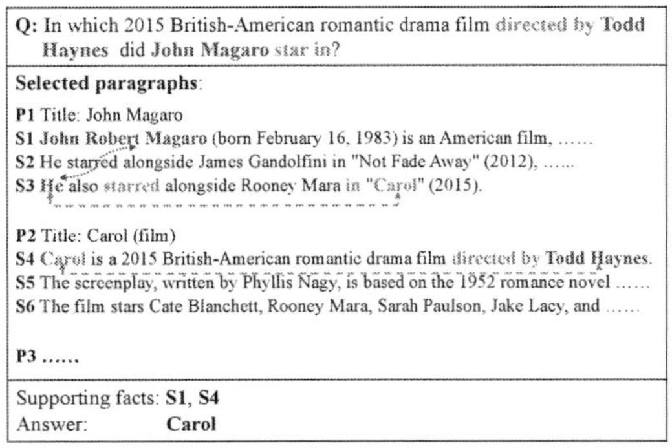

Figure 1: An example of a multi-hop question showing the utility of structured semantic knowledge for complex multi-hop reasoning. The blue dotted line denotes a coreference link between an entity *John Magaro* and a mention *He*. The green dashed lines denote semantic links between entities extracted from Open Information Extraction, *i.e., (He, star in, Carol)* and *(Carol, directed by, Todd Haynes)*.

For complex multi-hop reasoning, requiring multiple steps, these prior tasks provide a poor test. The multi-hop HotpotQA (Yang et al., 2018b) dataset, by contrast, is designed for systems that integrate information from multiple documents, reasoning to an answer explained using supporting facts.

Figure 1 is an example from HotpotQA, showing that structured knowledge, *i.e.,* co-references and RDF triples, are useful in complex multi-hop reasoning. To answer the question, the multi-hop QA model must first use the coreference in which *He* in S2 refers to *John Robert Magaro* in S1, allowing it to integrate *(He, star in, Carol)* with question-related structured knowledge *(Carol, directed by, Todd Haynes)*, thus reaching the final answer *Carol*.

Most multi-hop QA models extract entities related to the question to construct an entity graph, and then apply a GNN-based model to integrate information across nodes and predict answers (Dhingra et al., 2018; Qiu et al., 2019; Fang et al., 2020; Shao et al., 2020). However, this kind of GNN-based approach leaves challenges.

First, existing graph construction methods do

Proceedings of the 2nd Workshop on Deep Learning on Graphs for Natural Language Processing (DLG4NLP 2022), pages 71 - 80
July 15, 2022 ©2022 Association for Computational Linguistics

not precisely capture the semantic relationships between nodes, leading to unreliable integration of neighbouring nodes' information during graph reasoning. Figure 1 shows how essential such structured semantic knowledge is in multi-hop reasoning. Thus, integrating the semantics of input documents within GNN-based QA models remains a critical challenge. Moreover, graph reasoning over noisy or redundant nodes and edges may lead to ineffective information integration, of *e.g.*, the spurious *(He, star in, Not Fade Away)* in S1. This necessitates filtering out such "noise" nodes and edges unrelated to the question.

Second, most multi-hop QA models combine all clues related to the question into a graph, and then apply GNN-based inference to update all node representations synchronously without considering the order of clues in the reasoning chains. In this type of approach, it is difficult to explain how the models make decisions and how clues are passed through the graph in hops (Du et al., 2019).

In this paper, we propose a structure knowledge and contextual information fusion GNN for multi-hop QA. Our approach involves three steps: clue extraction, clue reasoning, and multi-task prediction. For clue extraction, we extract clues at multiple levels of granularity (question, paragraph, sentence, entity) as nodes, connected by semantic edges derived using structured knowledge. The motivation is that semantic edges provide more reliable information about neighbouring nodes for graph reasoning, compared to manually defined graph construction rules (Fang et al., 2020). For clue reasoning, inspired by step-by-step reasoning from CogQA (Ding et al., 2019), we first initialize all node representations using a pretrained contextual encoder, and then mimic human-like step-by-step reasoning via asynchronous update of node representations on the semantic graph. This update is a two-stage process in which nodes directly related to the question are updated first as direct clues, *e.g.*, entities *Todd Haynes* and *John Magaro* in Figure 1, followed by the remaining nodes which are updated as indirect clues, *e.g.*, *Coral*. At this point, we also apply a masked attention module to filter out noisy or spurious nodes and edges to avoid ineffective or deleterious clue propagation during GNN inference. Finally, the updated node representations are passed to a multi-task layer that predicts the final answer, the answer type, supporting facts and an interpretable reasoning chain.

We evaluated our proposed KIFGraph on HotpotQA dataset and achieved a high rank amongst published systems on the leaderboard. The main contributions of this paper are as follows:

- We construct a graph based on information fusion of structured knowledge, and contextual information, at multiple levels of granularity.
- We propose applying two-stage graph reasoning for multi-hop QA, which introduces interpretability to our reasoning model via a propagation process of information from direct to indirect clues that described by the model's outputs.
- We introduce a masked attention module to filter out noisy nodes and edges to avoid ineffective clue propagation in graph reasoning.

Hence, KIFGraph[1] provides a new perspective on how to perform global interpretable reasoning through GNN-based methods, and achieves competitive performance on the HotpotQA benchmark.

2 Related work

Knowledge-based multi-hop QA. Knowledge-based QA (KBQA) usually provide accurate answers because they use reliable inference to search structured knowledge curated by humans. CNNSM (Yih et al., 2014) decomposes questions into an entity mention and a relation pattern, then maps them to the entities and relations in a knowledge base to answer a question. HSP (Zhang et al., 2019) uses a three-stage parsing architecture to generate a logical form for complex questions, and then queries an existing database to arrive at an answer. Unfortunately, KBQA is constrained by the paucity of available external knowledge bases and limited ability to use contextual information.

Question decomposition for multi-hop QA. Recent studies have focused on decomposing multi-hop questions into single-hop sub-questions, enabling existing single-hop QA models to be applied. DecompRC (Min et al., 2019) uses a pointer model to split the question and generate sub-questions, and then answers these sub-questions using an existing single-hop QA model. QDMR (Wolfson et al., 2020) trains a seq-to-seq model to parse multi-hop questions into a sequence of query steps. These QA systems attempt to find the essential

[1] https://github.com/Tswinggg/KIFGraph

clue for each sub-question, but largely ignore any relationships between the sub-questions.

Graph Neural Networks for multi-hop QA. Motivated by work with GCNs (Kipf and Welling, 2017), recent studies have proposed that one should construct entity graphs from relevant paragraphs and apply GCNs to perform implicit reasoning by propagating contextual information along graph edges. Entity-GCN (Cao et al., 2019), MHQA-GRN (Song et al., 2018), Coref-GRN (Dhingra et al., 2018) and DFGN (Qiu et al., 2019) select entity nodes and use rules to construct edges in the entity graphs. HDE-Graph (Tu et al., 2020) and HGN (Fang et al., 2020) construct a heterogeneous graph at multiple levels of granularity to maximise direct propagation of information via graph edges.

3 Methodology

In this section, we describe in overview the KIFGraph model in Figure 2. KIFGraph involves the following three steps: $i)$ clue extraction, including use of a paragraph retrieval module and a semantic graph construction module; $ii)$ clue reasoning, including the masked attention and two-stage graph reasoning module at the centre of the figure; and $iii)$ multi-task prediction, including answer-span prediction, answer-type prediction, supporting facts prediction and reasoning chain generation.

3.1 Clue Extraction

We first utilize a paragraph retriever to select paragraphs related to the question. Then, we extract multiple-granularity clues from these paragraphs as nodes, and construct semantic edges between nodes using multiple modules, in this case Named Entity Recognition (NER), Coreference Resolution (CR) and Open Information Extraction (OpenIE) (Angeli et al., 2015). This architecture allows for later extensions of the set of knowledge sources.

Paragraph Retriever. The task of the paragraph retriever is to select relevant paragraphs that contain clues related to the question Q from given input paragraphs P, where $\mathrm{P} = \{p_0, p_1, ..., p_i, ..., p_m\}$, m is the number of paragraphs.

$$\mathrm{P_Q} = \mathrm{ParagraphRetriever(Q, P)} \tag{1}$$

The $\mathrm{P_Q}$ should contain the multiple paragraphs needed for complex multi-hop reasoning required by the question. To obtain these paragraphs, all useful clues in the question should be utilized. Similar to HGN (Fang et al., 2020), we combine a two-step hyperlink search and a paragraph ranker to retrieve relevant paragraphs from Wikipedia. The two-step hyperlink search contains two processes: $i)$ selecting paragraphs whose title appears in the question as the first-hop paragraphs; $ii)$ selecting second-hop paragraphs whose title appears in hyperlinks (provided by Wikipedia) in the first-hop paragraph. If this search also fails, we use the paragraph ranker, which is based on a pre-trained RoBERTa model (Liu et al., 2019), to select paragraphs with the highest ranking score.

Semantic Graph Construction. Existing studies construct graphs in GNN based on manually defined rules, *e.g.,* HGN and DFGN. In these methods, the semantic relationships, at multiple levels of granularity, between nodes have not adequately been considered, so nodes lack reliable neighbouring nodes for use during GNN node-representation updates. To provide them, we extract clues at multiple levels of granularity (question, paragraph, sentence, entity) as nodes $\mathcal{N}$, and then use structured knowledge extracted by multiple modules (*i.e.,* NER, CR and OpenIE) to generate semantic edges $\mathcal{E}$ and construct a semantic graph $\mathcal{G} = (\mathcal{N}, \mathcal{E})$. Specifically, we first use CR techniques to extract entity-mention pairs in retrieved paragraphs.

$$\begin{aligned} &\mathrm{coref}_{p_i}(\mathrm{pairs}) = \mathrm{CR}(\mathrm{p_i}) \\ &\mathrm{pairs} = \{(\mathbf{s_e}, \mathbf{e}), (\mathbf{s_{m_1}}, \mathbf{m_1}), ..., (\mathbf{s_{m_k}}, \mathbf{m_k})\} \end{aligned} \tag{2}$$

where $\mathrm{coref}_{p_i}(\mathrm{pairs})$ denotes the set of entity-mention pairs in paragraph p_i, $\mathbf{s}_e$ is the sentence id in which entity $\mathbf{e}$ is located, and $\mathbf{s}_{\mathbf{m}_k}$ is the sentence id of mention $\mathbf{m}_k$. Then, we iterate over the set $\mathrm{coref}_{p_i}(\mathrm{pairs})$ to build semantic edges as follows:

$$edge(\mathbf{s}_i, \mathbf{s}_j) = \begin{cases} 1, if\ \mathbf{e}\ in\ \mathbf{s}_i\ and\ \mathbf{m}_k\ in\ \mathbf{s}_j \\ 0, \qquad otherwise \end{cases} \tag{3}$$

$$edge(\mathbf{e}, \mathbf{s}_j) = \begin{cases} 1, if\ \mathbf{e}\ in\ \mathbf{s}_i\ and\ \mathbf{m}_k\ in\ \mathbf{s}_j \\ 0, \qquad otherwise \end{cases} \tag{4}$$

where if entity $\mathbf{e}$ in sentence $\mathbf{s}_i$ and mention $\mathbf{m}_k$ in sentence $\mathbf{s}_j$, it indicates that there is a semantic relationship between these two sentences. In this way, we build two types of semantic edges: $edge(\mathbf{s}_i, \mathbf{s}_j)$ between sentence nodes and $edge(\mathbf{e}, \mathbf{s}_j)$ between sentence nodes and entity nodes, *i.e.,* blue dotted lines in Figure 3.

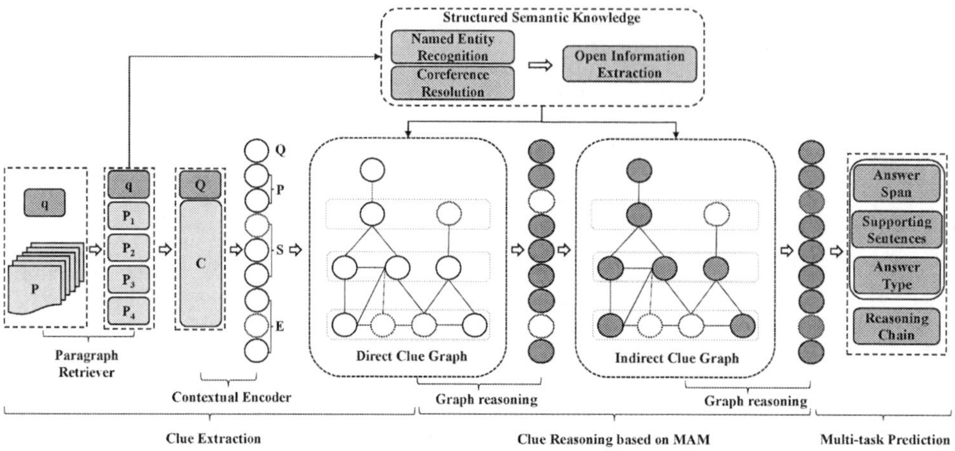

Figure 2: An overview of our proposed KIFGraph model. Specifically, it involves three key modules, $i)$ Clue extraction extracts clues related to the question into a graph; $ii)$ Graph reasoning based on MAM performs two-stage graph reasoning, from direct clue (white circle) graph to indirect clue (orange circle) graph, to asynchronous update node representations; $iii)$ Multi-task prediction conducts a multi-task layer to predict the span of answer, supporting facts, the type of question and reasoning chains.

Similarly, structured knowledge between entities is important because it can represent semantic relationships between entities accurately. To obtain this, we first use OpenIE techniques to extract this structured knowledge in the form of RDF triples.

$$\text{Triple}_{p_i}(S, O, R) = \text{RDF}(p_i) \tag{5}$$

where S, O and R represent $Subject$, $Object$ and $Relationship$ respectively, and $\text{Triple}_{p_i}(\cdot)$ is the set of RDF triples in paragraph p_i. We then build semantic edges between entity nodes based on these RDF triples. Since both S and O may be a span of text, we build edges between entities as follow:

$$\text{edge}(\mathbf{e}_i, \mathbf{e}_j) = \begin{cases} 1, if\ \mathbf{e}_i\ in\ S\ and\ \mathbf{e}_j\ in\ O \\ 0, \quad\quad otherwise \end{cases} \tag{6}$$

To sum up, the semantic graph $\mathcal{G}$ for the example in Figure 3 consists of four types of nodes (**Q**uestion, **P**aragraph, **S**entence, **E**ntity), four direct edges built by HGN (Fang et al., 2020), *i.e.,* Q-P, P-P, P-S, S-E, and three semantic edges that we construct, *i.e.,* S-S, S-E, E-E.

3.2 Clue Reasoning

Given the semantic graph, we perform two-stage reasoning over the graph, where node representations are updated asynchronously by mimicking human step-by-step reasoning from direct clues to indirect clues. Specifically, we set node representations $\mathbf{q}, \mathbf{p}_i, \mathbf{s}_i, \mathbf{e}_i \in \mathbb{R}^d$ and graph representation $\mathbf{G} = [\mathbf{q}, \mathbf{P}, \mathbf{S}, \mathbf{E}] \in \mathbb{R}^{t \times d}$, where $\mathbf{P} = \{\mathbf{p}_1, \mathbf{p}_2, ..., \mathbf{p}_{n_1}\}$, $\mathbf{S} = \{\mathbf{s}_1,\ \mathbf{s}_2, ..., \mathbf{s}_{n_2}\}$, $\mathbf{E} =$

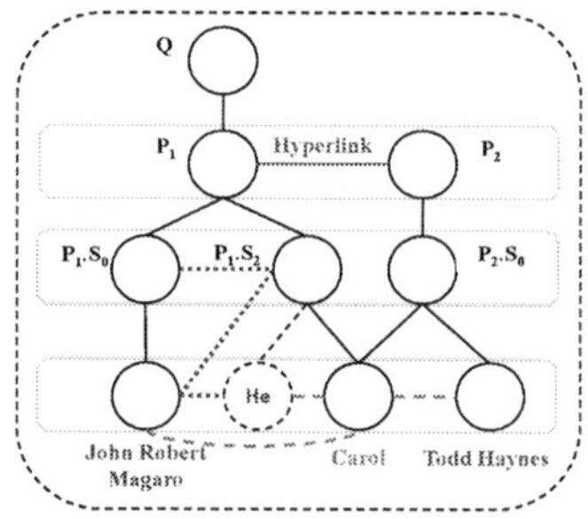

Figure 3: Semantic graph construction for the example in Figure 1. The graph consists of four types of nodes: Question Q, Paragraph P, Sentence S and Named Entity. The blue dotted lines represent semantic edges generated by coreference resolution, the green dashed lines represent semantic edges generated by OpenIE. The orange line was built using Hyperlinks as mentioned in the section Paragraph Retriever.

$\{\mathbf{e}_1, \mathbf{e}_2, ..., \mathbf{e}_{n_3}\}$, n_1, n_2, n_3 denote the numbers of paragraph/sentence/entity nodes in the graph, $t = n_1 + n_2 + n_3 + 1$ is the total number of nodes, and d is the dimension of nodes.

Contextual Encoder. We first combine all retrieved paragraphs into context C, and then initialize all representations by concatenating the question Q and the context C and feeding them into a pre-trained contextual encoder RoBERTa (Liu et al., 2019) to obtain the question representation $\mathbf{Q} = \{\mathbf{q}_0, \mathbf{q}_1, ..., \mathbf{q}_{m-1}\} \in \mathbb{R}^{m \times d}$ and the context representation $\mathbf{C} = \{\mathbf{c}_o, \mathbf{c}_1, ..., \mathbf{c}_{n-1}\} \in \mathbb{R}^{n \times d}$, where m and n are lengths of Q and C.

$$\mathbf{Q}, \mathbf{C} = \text{RoBERTa}(\text{Q}, \text{C}) \tag{7}$$

According to the previous work on Graph Attention Networks (GATs) (Velickovic et al., 2017), at least one linear transformation is required to obtain a more expressive context representation. To this end, as an initial step in obtaining a node representation, we first apply a shared linear transformation $\mathbf{W} \in \mathbb{R}^{d\times 2d}$ to generate the higher-level context representation $\mathbf{C}' \in \mathbb{R}^{n\times 2d}$. We then apply an LSTM layer to $\mathbf{C}'$, obtaining the initial representations of all nodes $\mathbf{q}, \mathbf{p}_i, \mathbf{s}_i, \mathbf{e}_i \in \mathbb{R}^d$.

$$\begin{aligned} \mathbf{p}_i &= \mathrm{LSTM}_1(\mathbf{C}', \mathbf{p}_i^{start}, \mathbf{p}_i^{end}) \\ \mathbf{s}_i &= \mathrm{LSTM}_2(\mathbf{C}', \mathbf{s}_i^{start}, \mathbf{s}_i^{end}) \\ \mathbf{e}_i &= \mathrm{LSTM}_3(\mathbf{C}', \mathbf{e}_i^{start}, \mathbf{e}_i^{end}) \\ \mathbf{q} &= \mathrm{MaxPooling}(\mathbf{Q}) \end{aligned} \quad (8)$$

where $\mathbf{p}_i^{start}$, $\mathbf{s}_i^{start}$ and $\mathbf{e}_i^{start}$ denote the start position of the i-th paragraph, sentence and entity node, and $\mathbf{p}_i^{end}$, $\mathbf{s}_i^{end}$, and $\mathbf{e}_i^{end}$ denote the corresponding end position. MaxPooling is used to calculate the question representation $\mathbf{q}$. Finally, all node representations $\mathbf{q}, \mathbf{p}_i, \mathbf{s}_i, \mathbf{e}_i$ are concatenated as the graph representation $\mathbf{G} = [\mathbf{g}_0, \mathbf{g}_1, ..., \mathbf{g}_t] \in \mathbb{R}^{t\times d}$, t is the total number of nodes.

Masked Attention Module (MAM) Since not every node and edge contains useful information, a masked attention module penalizes spurious nodes and edges before graph reasoning. For nodes unrelated to the question, we use an attention network between question representation $\mathbf{q}$ and graph node representation $\mathbf{g}_i$ to generate the mask module $\mathbf{m}$ (Qiu et al., 2019). As a result, useful nodes related to the question will be enhanced and noisy nodes will be penalized by multiplying the mask $\mathbf{m}$ and the initial node representations $\mathbf{G}$.

$$\begin{aligned} \gamma_i &= \mathbf{q}\mathbf{W}\mathbf{g}_i \\ \mathbf{m} &= \sigma([\gamma_0, \gamma_1, ..., \gamma_i, ..., \gamma_t]) \\ \mathbf{G}^\dagger &= \mathbf{m}\mathbf{G} = [m_0\mathbf{g}_0, m_1\mathbf{g}_1, ..., m_t\mathbf{g}_t] \end{aligned} \quad (9)$$

where $\mathbf{W}$ is a linear projection matrix, σ is the sigmoid function, $\mathbf{g}_i$ is the initial representation of node i and $\mathbf{G}^\dagger$ is the graph representation after masking noisy nodes.

Since GNN-based methods update node representations using information from their neighbouring nodes, noisy edges will lead to erroneous information propagation during graph reasoning. This is addressed by applying GAT to compute attention coefficients between nodes:

$$\alpha_{ij} = \frac{exp(\sigma(a^T[\mathbf{W}\mathbf{g}_i^\dagger || \mathbf{W}\mathbf{g}_j^\dagger]))}{\sum_{k\in\mathcal{G}_{i*}} exp(\sigma(a^T[\mathbf{W}\mathbf{g}_i^\dagger || \mathbf{W}\mathbf{g}_k^\dagger]))} \quad (10)$$

$$\mathbf{g}_i' = \sigma(\textstyle\sum_{j\in\mathcal{G}_{i*}} \alpha_{ij}\mathbf{W}\mathbf{g}_j^\dagger) \quad (11)$$

where α_{ij} is the attention coefficient between node i and node j, $\mathbf{g}_i^\dagger \in \mathbf{G}^\dagger$ is the masked node representation of node i, $\mathbf{W} \in \mathbb{R}^{d\times d}$ is a weight matrix, σ is an activation function and $\mathcal{G}_{i*}$ are neighbours of the node i. Since the updated node representations $\mathbf{g}_i' \in \mathbf{G}'$ is a linear combination of the representations of $\mathcal{G}_{i*}$, we can also enhance useful neighbouring nodes or penalize noisy neighbouring nodes through the attention coefficient between nodes.

In summary, MAM updates the graph representation by fusing structured knowledge and contextual information, alleviating the propagation of erroneous information from noisy nodes and edges in graph reasoning and the interference with subsequent answer prediction.

Graph Reasoning. To achieve explicit and interpretable graph reasoning, we use two-stage graph reasoning based on MAM to asynchronously update all node representations according to their order in the reasoning chain, mimicking human step-by-step reasoning. Specifically, we first divide the semantic graph $\mathcal{G}$ into the direct clue graph and the indirect clue graph. The direct/indirect graph is obtained by masking out nodes that are unrelated/related to the entities in the question, *e.g.*, orange circles in the graph are direct clue nodes directly related to the question and white circles are indirect nodes in Figure 2.

$$\mathcal{G}_1, \mathcal{G}_2 = \mathrm{Divide}(\mathcal{G}) \quad (12)$$

where $\mathcal{G}_1$ and $\mathcal{G}_2$ are the direct clue graph and direct clue graph, respectively. Then, we feed the initial graph representations $\mathbf{G}$ and question representation $\mathbf{q}$ into MAM to update the representation of the direct clues, followed by the updated graph representations $\mathbf{G}'$ and question representation $\mathbf{q}'$ are passed into MAM to update the representation of the indirect clues.

$$\begin{aligned} \mathbf{G}' &= \mathrm{MAM}(\mathbf{G}, \mathcal{G}_1, \mathbf{q}) \\ \mathbf{q}' &= \mathbf{G}'[0] \\ \mathbf{G}'' &= \mathrm{MAM}(\mathbf{G}', \mathcal{G}_2, \mathbf{q}') \end{aligned} \quad (13)$$

where $\mathbf{G}'$ is the graph representation of direct clue graph, $\mathbf{G}''$ is the graph representation of the overall graph. In this way, we achieve human-like step-by-step reasoning to update nodes asynchronously.

Finally, we use a gated attention mechanism (Fang et al., 2020) to merge the graph representation $\mathbf{G}''$ and the context representation $\mathbf{C}'$ for use in the final answer prediction step.

$$\begin{aligned}\tilde{\mathbf{C}} &= \text{Relu}(\mathbf{C}'\mathbf{W}_m) \cdot \text{Relu}(\mathbf{G}''\mathbf{W}'_m)^T \\ \tilde{\mathbf{G}} &= \text{Softmax}(\tilde{\mathbf{C}}) \cdot \mathbf{G}'' \\ \bar{\mathbf{G}} &= \sigma([\mathbf{C}'; \tilde{\mathbf{G}}]\mathbf{W}_s) \cdot \text{Tanh}([\mathbf{C}'; \tilde{\mathbf{G}}]\mathbf{W}_t)\end{aligned} \tag{14}$$

where $\mathbf{W}_m \in \mathbb{R}^{2dx2d}$, $\mathbf{W}'_m \in \mathbb{R}^{2dx2d}$, $\mathbf{W}_s \in \mathbb{R}^{4dx4d}$ and $\mathbf{W}_t \in \mathbb{R}^{4dx4d}$ are trainable weight matrices. The gated representation $\bar{\mathbf{G}} \in \mathbb{R}^{4d\times 4d}$ is used for answer span prediction.

3.3 Multi-task prediction

We follow the cascade prediction module design from (Fang et al., 2020), which contains six outputs, including paragraph selection, supporting facts prediction, entity prediction, the start and end position of the answer and answer type prediction.

$$\begin{aligned}\mathbf{O}_{para} &= \text{MLP}_1(\bar{\mathbf{P}}) \\ \mathbf{O}_{sent} &= \text{MLP}_2(\bar{\mathbf{S}}) \\ \mathbf{O}_{entity} &= \text{MLP}_3(\bar{\mathbf{E}}) \\ \mathbf{O}_{start} &= \text{MLP}_4(\bar{\mathbf{G}}) \\ \mathbf{O}_{end} &= \text{MLP}_5(\bar{\mathbf{G}}) \\ \mathbf{O}_{type} &= \text{MLP}_6(\bar{\mathbf{G}}[0])\end{aligned} \tag{15}$$

where $\bar{\mathbf{P}}$, $\bar{\mathbf{S}}$, $\bar{\mathbf{E}}$ are updated node representations which can be obtained from $\bar{\mathbf{G}}$, $\bar{\mathbf{G}}[0]$ is the first hidden representation of $\bar{\mathbf{G}}$ and each MLP_i is a multi-layer perceptron (MLP) for different outputs.

Finally, we use cross entropy loss over each output logits. The total loss function is a weighted sum of this loss.

$$\begin{aligned}L_{total} =& L_{start} + L_{end} + \lambda_1 L_{para} + \lambda_2 L_{sent} \\ &+ \lambda_3 L_{entity} + \lambda_4 L_{type}\end{aligned} \tag{16}$$

where $\lambda_1, \lambda_2, \lambda_3$, and λ_4 are hyper-parameters, and $L_{start}, L_{end}, L_{para}, L_{sent}, L_{entity}, L_{type}$ are the cross entropy loss for the corresponding logit: $\mathbf{O}_{start}, \mathbf{O}_{end}, \mathbf{O}_{para}, \mathbf{O}_{sent}, \mathbf{O}_{entity}, \mathbf{O}_{type}$.

Finally, we select nodes in the direct clue and indirect clue graph that are not masked by MAM to generate the reasoning chain:

Q→direct clues→indirect clues→Ans

4 Experiments

In this section, we compare our system KIFGraph with state-of-the-art multi-hop QA approaches on HotpotQA (Yang et al., 2018a) dataset.

4.1 Dataset and Setup

Dataset and Metrics. We evaluate our proposed KIFGraph on HotpotQA in the distractor setting. The distractor setting contains 2 golden paragraphs and 8 distractor paragraphs. In HotoptQA dataset, there are two types of questions—Bridge question and Comparison question, and two types of answer-spans of text and yes/no. Exact Match (EM) and partial match (F1) between the prediction and the golden answer are used as performance metrics. Further, a joint metric is used to evaluate both tasks simultaneously.

Setup. In semantic graph construction phase, we use the Stanford CoreNLP toolkit (Manning et al., 2014) to extract named entities, entity-mention pairs and RDF triples from the input documents, and set the number of question/paragraph/sentence/entity nodes to 1/4/40/60. In the paragraph retrieval phase, we follow HGN to select the top-K (K=4) paragraphs for a fair comparison. In context encoding phase, the maximum input sequence of RoBERTa-large is set to 1024, the hidden layer is set to 300, the batch size is 16 and the learning rate of Adam is 1e-5. In the multi-task prediction phase, the value of $\lambda_1/\lambda_2/\lambda_3/\lambda_4$ is set to 1/1/5/1.

4.2 Main Results

In Table 1, we compare KIFGraph with other published baselines on the private test set of HotpotQA. From Table 1, we observe that KIFGraph outperforms all baselines on EM/F1 metrics of the answer and achieves the second best results on the Joint EM/F1, demonstrating the progress made by KIFGraph in answer span prediction. Compared with DFGN which constructs an entity graph and applies GATs to achieve reasoning over the entity graph, KIFGraph increase performance substantially from 59.82 to 74.12 in the Joint EM/F1 metrics. We believe this is because our model performs two-stage graph reasoning based on masked attention module, which mimics the logic of human reasoning. Compared with HGN which constructs a hierarchical graph, KIFGraph improves its answer EM/F1 by constructing a semantic graph fusing structured knowledge and contextual information. In ablation studies reported below, we provide a detailed analysis to prove that the semantic graph and two-state graph reasoning contribute to its performance.

Model	Ans		Sup		Joint	
	EM	F1	EM	F1	EM	F1
Baseline Model (Yang et al., 2018a)	45.60	59.02	20.32	64.49	10.83	40.16
DecompRC (Min et al., 2019)	55.20	69.63	-	-	-	-
OUNS (Perez et al., 2020)	66.33	79.34	-	-	-	-
DFGN (Qiu et al., 2019)	56.31	69.69	51.50	81.62	33.62	59.82
IRC (Nishida et al., 2021)	58.54	72.67	36.56	79.53	23.57	59.43
TAP2 (Glass et al., 2020)	66.64	79.82	57.21	86.69	41.21	70.65
SAE-large (Tu et al., 2020)	66.92	79.62	61.53	86.86	45.36	71.45
C2F Reader (Shao et al., 2020)	67.98	81.24	60.81	87.63	44.67	72.73
Longformer (Beltagy et al., 2020)	68.00	81.25	**63.09**	88.34	45.91	73.16
FFReader-large (Alkhaldi et al., 2021)	68.89	82.16	62.10	88.42	45.61	73.78
HGN-large (Fang et al., 2020)	69.22	82.19	62.76	**88.47**	**47.11**	**74.21**
KIFGraph	**69.53**	**82.42**	61.79	87.98	46.49	74.12

Table 1: Results on the private test of HotpotQA in the distractor setting. The proposed KIFGraph model outperforms all baselines published on the leaderboard in answer prediction. "-" denotes the case where no results are available. Leaderboard: https://hotpotqa.github.io/.

4.3 Ablation studies

In this section, we verify the effectiveness of the following three aspects of the KIFGraph model on the dev set in the distractor setting: i) The semantic graph; ii) The masked attention module; iii) The two-stage graph reasoning.

Semantic graph effectiveness. As shown in Table 2, we evaluate the impact of semantic graph by adding three different types of edges we construct. As described in the section on semantic graph construction, above, we add "sentence-sentence" and "sentence-entity" edges by CR, increasing the Ans F1 by 0.12 compared to Hier.Grpah in HGN. Adding "entity-entity" edges by OpenIE, increases the Ans F1 0.22. The combination of CR and OpenIE improves the Ans F1 by 0.28. This suggests that adding semantic edges obtained by structured knowledge is effective for multi-hop QA.

Model	Ans F1	Sup F1	Joint F1
Hier.Graph	82.22	**88.58**	74.37
Hier.Graph + CR	82.34	88.21	74.36
Hier.Graph + OpenIE	82.44	88.29	74.41
Semantic Graph	**82.50**	88.30	**74.45**

Table 2: Ablation study for semantic graph (SR) on dev set. Hier.Graph denotes a hierarchical graph. CR denotes adding edges by coreference resolution. OpenIE denotes adding edges by Open information extraction. Semantic Graph denotes adding edges by combining CR and OpenIE.

Masked attention module effectiveness. To verify the effectiveness of the masked attention module, we conduct four experiments to analyse the impact of punishing noisy nodes and edges: i) w/o masked nodes and edges: noisy nodes and edges are not penalized; ii) masked nodes: only noisy nodes are penalized; iii) masked edges: only noisy edges are penalized; iv) masked nodes and edges: noisy nodes and edges are penalized. As shown in Table 3, by penalizing noisy nodes unrelated to the question and weakening noisy edges, the Ans F1 is increased by 0.04 and 0.13, respectively. The result of "masked nodes" shows that penalizing noisy nodes unrelated to the question is helpful, but all of nodes have been filtered by clue extraction, thus improvement may not be obvious. The result of "masked edges" indicates that fusing semantic graph and contextual information to penalize noisy edges can lead to significant performance improvement. This indicates the importance of masked attention mechanism for graph reasoning.

Model	Ans F1	Sup F1	Joint F1
w/o masked nodes & edges	82.50	88.30	74.45
masked nodes	82.54	88.29	74.44
masked edges	82.63	88.32	74.52
masked nodes & edges	**82.65**	**88.34**	**74.60**

Table 3: Ablation study for masked attention module (MAM) on dev set. "masked nodes" and "masked edges" denote penalizing noisy nodes and noisy edges respectively.

Two-Stage graph reasoning. To verify the effectiveness of the two-stage graph reasoning (TS). We compare two different TS schemes with graph reasoning. In Table 4, we observe that the inverse TS (Inv TS, update node representations in order from indirect clues to direct clues) yields poor results, below the original GAT. But our proposed TS (update node representations in order from direct clues to indirect clues) that aligns with the logic of human reasoning increases the Ans F1 and Joint F1 by 0.17 and 0.19 respectively. This indicates that the two-stage graph reasoning is an effective form of explicit reasoning for multi-hop questions.

Overall ablation results of KIFGraph performances on dev set in the development set of HotpotQA are shown in Table 5. We observe that our three components improve the performance of KIF-

Q: In which 2015 British-American romantic drama film directed by Todd Haynes did John Magaro star in?

Selected Paragraphs:

$\mathbf{P_1}$ Title: John Magaro

$\mathbf{S_1}$ John Robert Magaro (born February 16, 1983) is an American film.

$\mathbf{S_2}$ He also starred alongside Rooney Mara in "Carol" (2015).

$\mathbf{P_2}$ Title: Carol (film)

$\mathbf{S_4}$ Carol is a 2015 British-American romantic drama film directed by Todd Haynes.

Answer: **Carol** Supporting facts: $\mathbf{S_1, S_4}$

Direct clues: {**Q**, $\mathbf{P_1}$, $\mathbf{P_2}$, $\mathbf{S_1}$, $\mathbf{S_4}$, Todd Haynes, John Magaro}

Indirect clues: {$\mathbf{S_2}$, Carol}

Reasoning chain: **Q → Direct clues ($\mathbf{S_1, S_4}$) → Indirect clues ($\mathbf{S_2}$) → Answer**

Predicted Answer: **Carol** Predicted Supporting facts: $\mathbf{S_1, S_4}$, S_2

Figure 4: An example of KIFGraph to answering multi-hop questions. Direct/Indirect clues are unmasked nodes in the direct/indirect clue graph. Reasoning chain is generated by the intrinsic structure of KIFGraph. In this example, we only select supporting sentences $(\mathbf{S_1}, \mathbf{S_4}, \mathbf{S_2})$ as clues for the final reasoning chain.

Model	Ans F1	Sup F1	Joint F1
KIFGraph (GAT)	82.50	88.30	74.45
KIFGraph (Inv TS)	81.92	88.23	73.89
KIFGraph (TS)	**82.67**	**88.39**	**74.64**

Table 4: Ablation study for two-stage graph reasoning on dev set. "GAT" denotes that we use GAT to update the representation of all nodes, "TS" denotes that we use two-stage graph reasoning which aligns with the logic of human reasoning to update all nodes representation. "Inv TS" is an inverted two-stage graph reasoning.

Model	Ans F1	Sup F1	Joint F1
DFGN	69.38	82.23	59.89
- Semantic Graph	74.34	84.65	66.41
- TS graph reasoning	72.49	83.14	64.76
HGN	82.22	**88.58**	74.37
- Semantic Graph	82.50	88.31	74.45
- Masked attention module	82.31	88.23	74.25
- TS graph reasoning	82.34	88.27	74.39
KIFGraph (SR)	82.50	88.30	74.45
KIFGraph (SR+MAM)	82.65	88.34	74.60
KIFGraph (SR+MAM+TS)	**82.67**	88.39	**74.64**

Table 5: Ablation study for KIFGraph on dev set. We take DFGN and HGN as the baseline model. The upper part is the model ablation results by adding different modules.The lower part is our model's final ablation results.

Graph to varying degrees. Adding our three components into baseline models (DFGN, HGN and KIFGraph), demonstrates obvious performance improvements from the semantic graph and masked attention, and the utility of fusing structured knowledge and contextual information.

4.4 Case Study

The example question in Figure 4, illustrates explicit reasoning in KIFGraph. The semantic graph construction method first extracts relevant clues at multiple levels of granularity. Then, clues nodes related to the question are selected by MAM module as direct clues, *i.e.,* {Q, P1, P2, S1, S4, Todd Haynes, John Magaro}. Next, nodes connected by semantic edges to direct clue nodes become direct clues, *i.e.,* {S2, Carol}, and two-stage graph reasoning updates their representations. Finally, using all updated graph node representations, the multi-task prediction module yields the final answer and supporting facts. We also generate an explicit reasoning chain "Question→Direct clues→Indirect clue→Answer" to demonstrate interpretable reasoning for the multi-hop question. Moreover, we found that our model provides larger supporting facts, including sentences with coreferences, to make reasoning more explainable, *i.e.,* S2. Since He in S2 refers to $John\ Magaro$ in S1, explainable multi-hop reasoning requires coreference resolution; the "gold standard" supporting facts (S1 and S4) do not suffice as explanations. Unfortunately, our extended supporting facts may slightly lower performance on the HotpotQA evaluation since they are not included in the gold-standard; further analysis may show that HotpotQA dataset changes are warranted.

5 Conclusion and Future work

In this paper, we apply explicit graph reasoning to extracted knowledge and contextual information for multi-hop reasoning. We extract clues at multiple levels of granularity relating entity nodes, and construct a semantic graph from these clues. We then combine a masked attention mechanism and two-stage graph reasoning to perform interpretable inference over the semantic graph. Experimental results on HotpotQA dataset show the effectiveness of our model. In future work, we hope to extend the range and precision of the entity relations used, and we hope to extend our model to accommodate more complex multi-hop questions with unknown number of hops and non-linear reasoning.

References

Tareq Alkhaldi, Chenhui Chu, and Sadao Kurohashi. 2021. Flexibly focusing on supporting facts, using bridge links, and jointly training specialized modules for multi-hop question answering. *IEEE/ACM Transactions on Audio, Speech, and Language Processing*, 29:3216–3225.

Gabor Angeli, Melvin Jose Johnson Premkumar, and Christopher D. Manning. 2015. Leveraging linguistic structure for open domain information extraction. In *ACL*, pages 344–354, Beijing, China. Association for Computational Linguistics.

Iz Beltagy, Matthew E. Peters, and Arman Cohan. 2020. Longformer: The long-document transformer. *CoRR*, abs/2004.05150.

Nicola De Cao, Wilker Aziz, and Ivan Titov. 2019. Question answering by reasoning across documents with graph convolutional networks. In *NAACL-HLT*, pages 2306–2317.

Bhuwan Dhingra, Qiao Jin, Zhilin Yang, William W. Cohen, and Ruslan Salakhutdinov. 2018. Neural models for reasoning over multiple mentions using coreference. In *NAACL-HLT*, pages 42–48.

Ming Ding, Chang Zhou, Qibin Chen, Hongxia Yang, and Jie Tang. 2019. Cognitive graph for multi-hop reading comprehension at scale. In *ACL*, pages 2694–2703.

Mengnan Du, Ninghao Liu, and Xia Hu. 2019. Techniques for interpretable machine learning. *Communications of the ACM*, 63(1):68–77.

Matthew Dunn, Levent Sagun, Mike Higgins, V. Ugur Güney, Volkan Cirik, and Kyunghyun Cho. 2017. Searchqa: A new q&a dataset augmented with context from a search engine. *CoRR*, abs/1704.05179.

Yuwei Fang, Siqi Sun, Zhe Gan, Rohit Pillai, Shuohang Wang, and Jingjing Liu. 2020. Hierarchical graph network for multi-hop question answering. In *EMNLP*, pages 8823–8838.

Michael Glass, Alfio Gliozzo, Rishav Chakravarti, Anthony Ferritto, Lin Pan, G P Shrivatsa Bhargav, Dinesh Garg, and Avi Sil. 2020. Span selection pretraining for question answering. In *ACL*, pages 2773–2782.

Mandar Joshi, Eunsol Choi, Daniel S. Weld, and Luke Zettlemoyer. 2017. Triviaqa: A large scale distantly supervised challenge dataset for reading comprehension. In *ACL*, pages 1601–1611.

Thomas N. Kipf and Max Welling. 2017. Semi-supervised classification with graph convolutional networks. In *ICLR*.

Yinhan Liu, Myle Ott, Naman Goyal, Jingfei Du, Mandar Joshi, Danqi Chen, Omer Levy, Mike Lewis, Luke Zettlemoyer, and Veselin Stoyanov. 2019. Roberta: A robustly optimized BERT pretraining approach. *CoRR*, abs/1907.11692.

Christopher Manning, Mihai Surdeanu, John Bauer, Jenny Finkel, Steven Bethard, and David McClosky. 2014. The Stanford CoreNLP natural language processing toolkit. In *ACL*, pages 55–60.

Sewon Min, Victor Zhong, Luke Zettlemoyer, and Hannaneh Hajishirzi. 2019. Multi-hop reading comprehension through question decomposition and rescoring. In *ACL*, pages 6097–6109.

Kosuke Nishida, Kyosuke Nishida, Itsumi Saito, and Sen Yoshida. 2021. Towards interpretable and reliable reading comprehension: A pipeline model with unanswerability prediction. In *2021 International Joint Conference on Neural Networks (IJCNN)*, pages 1–8. IEEE.

Ethan Perez, Patrick S. H. Lewis, Wen-tau Yih, Kyunghyun Cho, and Douwe Kiela. 2020. Unsupervised question decomposition for question answering. In *EMNLP*, pages 8864–8880.

Lin Qiu, Yunxuan Xiao, Yanru Qu, Hao Zhou, Lei Li, Weinan Zhang, and Yong Yu. 2019. Dynamically fused graph network for multi-hop reasoning. In *ACL*, pages 6140–6150.

Pranav Rajpurkar, Jian Zhang, Konstantin Lopyrev, and Percy Liang. 2016. Squad: 100, 000+ questions for machine comprehension of text. In *EMNLP*, pages 2383–2392.

Nan Shao, Yiming Cui, Ting Liu, Shijin Wang, and Guoping Hu. 2020. Is graph structure necessary for multi-hop question answering? In *EMNLP*, pages 7187–7192.

Linfeng Song, Zhiguo Wang, Mo Yu, Yue Zhang, Radu Florian, and Daniel Gildea. 2018. Exploring graph-structured passage representation for multi-hop reading comprehension with graph neural networks. *CoRR*, abs/1809.02040.

Ming Tu, Kevin Huang, Guangtao Wang, Jing Huang, Xiaodong He, and Bowen Zhou. 2020. Select, answer and explain: Interpretable multi-hop reading comprehension over multiple documents. In *AAAI*, pages 9073–9080.

Petar Velickovic, Guillem Cucurull, Arantxa Casanova, Adriana Romero, Pietro Liò, and Yoshua Bengio. 2017. Graph attention networks. *CoRR*, abs/1710.10903.

Alex Wang, Amanpreet Singh, Julian Michael, Felix Hill, Omer Levy, and Samuel Bowman. 2018. GLUE: A multi-task benchmark and analysis platform for natural language understanding. In *EMNLP*, pages 353–355.

Tomer Wolfson, Mor Geva, Ankit Gupta, Yoav Goldberg, Matt Gardner, Daniel Deutch, and Jonathan Berant. 2020. Break it down: A question understanding benchmark. *Trans. Assoc. Comput. Linguistics*, 8:183–198.

Zhilin Yang, Peng Qi, Saizheng Zhang, Yoshua Bengio, William Cohen, Ruslan Salakhutdinov, and Christopher D. Manning. 2018a. HotpotQA: A dataset for diverse, explainable multi-hop question answering. In *ACL*, pages 2369–2380.

Zhilin Yang, Peng Qi, Saizheng Zhang, Yoshua Bengio, William W. Cohen, Ruslan Salakhutdinov, and Christopher D. Manning. 2018b. Hotpotqa: A dataset for diverse, explainable multi-hop question answering. In *EMNLP*, pages 2369–2380.

Wen-tau Yih, Xiaodong He, and Christopher Meek. 2014. Semantic parsing for single-relation question answering. In *ACL*, pages 643–648.

Haoyu Zhang, Jingjing Cai, Jianjun Xu, and Ji Wang. 2019. Complex question decomposition for semantic parsing. In *ACL*, pages 4477–4486.

Author Index

Association for Computational Linguistics
209 N. Eighth Street
Stroudsburg, Pennsylvania 18360

ISBN 978-1-7138-5630-6

CURRAN ASSOCIATES INC.
proceedings.com